CANADA'S CHANGING DEFENSE POLICY
1957–1963

CANADA'S CHANGING DEFENSE POLICY, 1957–1963,

THE PROBLEMS OF A MIDDLE POWER IN ALLIANCE

BY JON B. McLIN

THE JOHNS HOPKINS PRESS, BALTIMORE 1967
in co-operation with THE WASHINGTON CENTER
OF FOREIGN POLICY RESEARCH, SCHOOL OF
ADVANCED INTERNATIONAL STUDIES
THE JOHNS HOPKINS
UNIVERSITY

TO THE MEMORY OF
A.V.B. AND J.C.M.

PREFACE

LIKE an earthworm, this book grew from the middle toward the two ends as it progressed from conception to finished product. It began as an effort to understand and explain the curious contretemps which marked the relations between the United States and Canada during the period of development of the Arrow aircraft and the Bomarc missile. Quickly it became apparent that these were but two links in a chain of difficult military problems for Canada, stretching at least from the formation of NORAD in 1957 to the decision of the Pearson government in 1963 to acquire nuclear warheads for Canadian weapons. While the resulting six-year period is sufficiently well-defined—it will not go unnoticed that it was coterminous with the years in office of John Diefenbaker and the Progressive Conservatives—and sufficiently broad to form in itself the object of study, I have written one chapter each on the years before and after this period for two reasons. First, to give some perspective to what must otherwise appear "a tale told by an idiot, full of sound and fury, signifying nothing," it was deemed advisable to describe the context in which the events occurred. Thus, Chapter II recapitulates briefly the previous Canadian experience in post-World War II alliances; and Chapters VII and VIII describe some of the policies comprising what appeared at the time of writing to be a new role comparable in stability and satisfaction to that filled before 1957. Second—and this exemplifies the need for a perspective on those years—I wished to avoid the implication that the government of John Diefenbaker was entirely (although I do think it was mainly) to blame for Canada's defense problems of the late 1950's and early 1960's. By carrying the story back a bit, it is seen that all the problems were not created by Diefenbaker, that at least some existed in latent form when he entered office; by going forward, it is seen that what came to be at least part of the solution to the problems—in particular the Development and Production Sharing Program—was formulated under his government.

Books on recent Canadian foreign and defense policy tend to fall into two categories. First, there are the interpretative essays, which make no attempt to set forth systematically the evidence on which their interpretations are based; considering the paucity of reliable documentation for recent events, this is hardly surprising or re-proachable. Second, there are the volumes—particularly the series *Canada in World Affairs* published for the Canadian Institute of International Affairs—which draw together such evidence as exists, but which, for the most part, make little effort at interpretation. I am convinced of the need to bridge this chasm, to ground inter-pretations as fully as possible in systematic and written examinations of the evidence (to the extent that the evidence can be uncovered before official documents become available); and this book is an effort to do so. How far it succeeds is for the reader to judge.

That reader, particularly if he is Canadian, must be forewarned against one possible bias, that of the author's nationality. A national of one country writing about the affairs of another always brings to that task both advantages and disadvantages; this is more mark-edly true when an American writes about Canadian affairs, as the title and content of Mr. Acheson's recent contribution to our dialogue aptly illustrates.[1] But whatever merits or faults my American per-spective gives to this study, one characteristic should not be attrib-uted to it: the considerable attention given to the United States in the formation of Canada's defense policy is no more than propor-tional to the place it occupies in the existing state of affairs; indeed that is part of the Canadian problem.

*   *   *   *

Numerous people have contributed to this study more than they know, although of course without thereby becoming responsible for its faults. John W. Holmes, whom the Canadian Institute of Interna-tional Affairs is fortunate to have as Director-General, offered both personal and institutional help of great value. Without this help, the manuscript might have been completed; it would certainly not be what it is. Robert Osgood, Director of the Washington Center of Foreign Policy Research, supervised the preparation of the manu-script in its original form as a dissertation for the Johns Hopkins School of Advanced International Studies. His shrewd and judicious comments were invaluable, all the more so for being combined with an awareness of the importance of independent initiative and self-reliance in an author. R. J. Sutherland read the manuscript and made numerous factual corrections and other useful observations. A continuing dialogue with Harald von Riekhoff has yielded not

1. Dean Acheson, "Canada: 'Stern Daughter of the Voice of God,'" in Livingston T. Merchant, ed., *Neighbors Taken for Granted: Canada and the United States* (New York: Frederick A. Praeger, 1966).

only valuable points of information and strategic insights but great benefits of morale; the importance of good cheer in enlivening bleak Ottawa days is not to be minimized.

Perhaps my greatest debt is to those who must be thanked anonymously: the numerous present and past public servants, of the United States and Canada, who put aside time that for most of them is still a scarce commodity to answer, by letter, telephone, or personal interview, my questions about the events in which they participated. From a scholarly point of view, it is of course unfortunate that they cannot be named. Yet the continuing duties of some of them render this inexpedient; while to name some and not others would be both unfair and misleading.

I have had the good fortune to use three libraries, all of which are blessed to have librarians who belong to that minority of their profession which is more concerned to assist scholarly research than to protect its materials from use. I am therefore indebted to the staffs of the libraries of the School of Advanced International Studies, the Canadian Embassy in Washington, and the Canadian Institute of International Affairs in Toronto.

For sustenance while researching this subject, I have the benevolence of three organizations to thank. Most of the work was done under a fellowship established at the School of Advanced International Studies by the International Nickel Company. Subsequent travel and research used in converting the manuscript into book form were assisted by the Canadian Institute of International Affairs and the Research Committee of the University of Alabama.

J.B.M.

Washington, D.C.
August, 1966

CONTENTS

PART III—NEW POLICIES EMERGE

PART I

THE EARLY YEARS

CHAPTER I

INTRODUCTION

THE years 1957–1963 were a time of turmoil in Canada's defense policy. They were also a period of transition, although that was not seen clearly at the time. The troubles were caused by a disparity between the ends and means of defense policy, and the transition constituted the process whereby the two were brought into conformity once again. It was a painful process, largely because the policymakers were unclear about the ends of defense policy and about the way—rarely or never made explicit—in which the chosen means were thought to promote those ends.

The problems all concerned Canada's military contributions to its North American and North Atlantic alliances. There was considerably less controversy about Canada's diplomatic activity within the alliances; while its *extra*-alliance military activities, which were limited for the most part to occasional participation in U.N. peacekeeping operations, consistently enjoyed broad support. Thus, it is the military component of Canada's alliance policy that is the subject of examination in this book. Only peripheral attention is given to its military policy outside the alliances, or to its diplomatic activity within them.

It does not follow that political considerations have no place here. It is remarkable that a century and a quarter after Clausewitz, a reminder of the interdependence of military and political objectives needs to be given. Yet a large part of the problem in Canadian defense has been the failure to understand adequately how that principle applies to Canada.

The question may be broached by asking why or whether Canada needs a defense establishment and/or allies. The most common justification for such things is that they are vital to national security; but in the case of Canada, this argument is hardly valid. Canada's armed forces are not irrelevant to its national security, but their contribution is no more than marginal. What protects Canadian security from one potential threat—the United States—is that for reasons both selfish and benevolent, the U.S. may be relied upon not to attack. What protects Canadian security from other potential threats, including the Soviet Union, is partly its isolation, and partly the fact that for geographical reasons, Canada's security interests are so closely identified with those of the U.S. that it is assured of American protection.

Such reasoning calls into question the very basis for the maintenance of a defense establishment in Canada. A possible rejoinder might be that Canada's armed forces, while not themselves crucial to national security, must be maintained as a kind of payment of dues to secure the alliance with the U.S., since American support is crucial for security reasons. But, again, since the American commitment is grounded in geography, even a formal alliance would appear superfluous.

A third possible argument from security for the maintenance of a Canadian defense establishment and alliance with the U.S. and Western Europe is that by contributing significantly to deterrence and defense in Western Europe, Canada's security is indirectly enhanced. Such an argument would be valid so long as the likelihood of success is materially affected by Canada's contribution; while it can reasonably be argued that in the early 1950's this was the case, it is hardly true today.

Fourth, and finally, the argument from "club dues" may be used with reference not to the North American, but to the North Atlantic Alliance. That is, Canada's contribution to NATO may be thought to provide an incentive for other countries to contribute to the alliance's forces; thus, it promotes the effectiveness of European defense and, indirectly, the defense of Canada. While this argument may continue to have some validity, it is *ipso facto* very difficult to judge, and consequently difficult to use as a justification for large-scale defense expenditures.

The weakness of the foregoing arguments suggests that the maintenance of a Canadian defense establishment, and Canada's participation in a bilateral alliance with the United States and a multilateral alliance in the form of NATO must therefore be aimed at objectives other than national security. The effectiveness of Canadian defense policies must be judged accordingly. What are these non-security objectives, and how effectively can they be promoted by the kind of military contribution that Canada has been paying on the order of $1.5 billion per year to make? These objectives might be numerous in other, particularly under-developed countries.[1]

1. See James Eayrs, "Military Policy and Middle-Power: The Canadian Experience," in J. King Gordon, ed., *Canada's Role as a Middle Power* (Toronto:

In Canada there are but two, although one of them is quite broad. The narrower, more specific objective is the promotion of the interests of the Canadian defense industry. This aim will be served by policies that entail the purchase of weapons manufactured (and if possible, designed) in Canada and that maximize the possibility of export sales of Canadian-manufactured weapons. Since such sales may be measured, it is not difficult to evaluate the policies aimed at this objective, as we have done in Chapter VII.

The second non-security objective, which is both much broader and vaguer, is to support Canadian diplomacy. This has been the main purpose of Canada's military contributions to the United Nations—its participation in peacekeeping forces—as well as its alliance contributions. The latter have been by far the more important of the two, whether measured in terms of public attention or expenditure. Considering the importance of the aim, it is essential to have some way of evaluating policies designed to promote it. To do so, we must be somewhat more precise about the objective itself and somewhat more explicit about the ways in which military contributions might serve to attain it.

One particular objective of Canadian diplomacy has been to promote solidarity between the United States on the one hand, and, on the other, Western Europe in general and Britain and France in particular. While there may be argument about the degree to which Canadian policies are responsible for this solidarity (whether, e.g., Canada is a "linchpin," "bridge," or "interpreter"), there can be no doubt that by displaying "alliance-mindedness"—a willingness to bear its "fair share" and to fulfill effectively military and other commitments made to allies—Canada's military activities have made a contribution to it. This rationale of collaborating oneself, in order to increase the incentive for others to collaborate, implies nothing about the kind of military role that Canada should play, however, and very little about its size, i.e., that it should be commensurate with the capacity to contribute.

Except for this one instance, it is sensible to talk of Canada's military alliance contributions as being aimed not so much at par-

The Canadian Institute of International Affairs, 1966), pp. 67–86. In this essay, Eayrs sets forth views that are similar to those expressed here about the non-military functions of Canadian defense policy and the consequent difficulty of evaluating that policy. Elsewhere, Eayrs takes this argument further and suggests that Canada could and should reduce its defense budget by about two-thirds. The suggestion would be provocative if substantiated and explained. See *The Globe Magazine* (Toronto), October 23, 1965.

ticular objectives as at the attainment of a general influence; it is here that clarity and precision become so difficult, even while they are very important.

Influence may be sought as a means to other ends, or as an end in itself. In the former case, it may be used to promote such specific and appropriate Canadian interests as the rights of lesser powers to be consulted in the formulation of collective policy and the taking of collective decisions. Or, it may be regarded as capital, to be collected against the future day when it will be drawn on to affect specific issues, whether they involve particular Canadian interests or general policies of the alliance. In either case, influence is an appropriate tool rationally related to considered national objectives. The difficulty of identifying and measuring such a vague quantity, however, implies the possibility that it will come to be pursued not only as a means toward rational objectives, but as an end in itself.

This temptation to seek influence for its own sake has been especially strong for Canada; it is indulged in the form of a search for "some formula for its place in the sun,"[2] for a "special function in the world."[3] for a "national mission."[4] There are two particularly Canadian sources of the temptation. The first is a "great power mentality which they [the Canadian people] have inherited from the days before they emigrated and which is easily perpetuated owing to our close associations with the United States."[5] The second derives from geography, namely the fact that Canada not only shares a 4,000 mile border with the U.S., but that the bulk of its people lives in close proximity to that border. The allegiance of these people to a government in Ottawa when the attitudes, mores, values and culture of the majority of them are to such a large extent common to all of British North America is something which *prima facie* is so unnatural that it requires justification. The provision of such justification, therefore, becomes one of the goals of Canada's foreign policy. This task is difficult not only because there is no tangible measure of success, but also because it implies the necessity of having policies both broader in scope and more distinctive in content from those of the U.S. than would be expected from its relative size and its high degree of similarity. The need remains nonetheless; and

2. John W. Holmes, "Canada in Search of Its Role," *Foreign Affairs*, XLI (July, 1963), 661.

3. *Ibid.*, p. 663.   4. *Ibid.*, p. 672.

5. A. R. M. Lower, "Canada in the New, Non-British World," *International Journal*, III (Summer, 1948), 211.

the difficulty of filling it is one of the sources of frustration which will mark the episodes to be described in later chapters.

A country seeking to attain influence by means of its military contributions within an alliance may choose one of two courses. The contribution, if basically similar to that of the alliance leader, must be sufficiently great so that its withdrawal would substantially diminish the collective power of the alliance. Or, if more modest in size, the contribution must be somehow distinctive in kind, so that the importance of the role which the lesser power is uniquely equipped to perform ensures it the influence that is sought. In either case, there are obvious dangers in a small power's embracing the aspiration: deep frustrations may result when it becomes apparent that a national role is not so significant as had been imagined; or commitments may be undertaken which are beyond the capacity of the country to fulfill. For a country subject to such illusory aspirations, there is, therefore, a constant need for injunctions to "cut our coat according to our cloth."[6] But since the aspirations are also political facts, they must not only be deflated; they must also, in some way and on some occasions, be fulfilled.

This dilemma, as well as the rest of this general analysis, has characterized Canadian defense policy in recent years. Canada's relatively great influence with the U.S. and within the organs of NATO during the early 1950's owed something to the relatively large size of its military contribution—a temporary factor owing to Europe's weakness—as well as to a distinctive element, the strategic importance of Canadian geography. As these contributions waned in relative importance, influence has decreased but aspirations have remained high. Consequently, the choice between accepting a reduced role, or making the enlarged contribution that would have been needed to retain the same influential role, was a painful one. Therefore it was avoided as long as possible. Even the efforts of the Liberal government after 1963 to recast Canadian defense policy constitute an effort to avoid the choice, for they imply and aim at the possibility of gaining in distinctiveness what has been lost in relative strength.

Others might offer less theoretical explanations of the problems of the years 1957–1963, claiming that they were rather the responsibility of one man: Diefenbaker's defense *débâcle*. The present author does not take that view. It is true that many of the problems of the period were either caused or worsened immeasurably by the

6. *Ibid.*, p. 221.

ineptness of the Diefenbaker government, and there is no wish to avoid an assignment of responsibility for that fact. But that there were bound to be problems was a consequence of factors beyond even Mr. Diefenbaker's control. The acquisition by the Soviet Union of intercontinental missiles necessarily called into question the bases of Canada's defense policy by rendering defense in the old sense no longer practicable. The rising level of sophistication in armaments, even apart from missiles, inevitably reached a point at which Canada's policy of producing and/or procuring the most advanced weapons became untenable. It is precisely because dilemmas about the production and procurement of weapons reflect so faithfully these more basic dilemmas of defense policy that recent controversies about weapons systems were so important in Canada; and it is for the same reason that these "hardware" problems receive so much attention here. The fact that the arrival of these problems largely coincided with the formation of the Diefenbaker government is fortuitous; some of the hard decisions had already arisen under the St. Laurent government, and had been postponed until after the election, to be settled another day.

The need to understand correctly the term "defense policy" in relation to Canada has already been explained. Similar dangers are associated with the first two words of the title, and should be mentioned. First, to focus upon *Canada* raises the danger, which always exists in writing about lesser powers, of exaggerating the extent to which Canada's policies result from its national decisions, rather than from external factors over which it has little or no control. In most of what follows, the external factors which are direct antecedents of changes in Canadian policy are identified. But the reader would well bear in mind that other, more distant but perhaps equally important, external influences will inevitably go unmentioned. To name but one, the changing East-West confrontation, no less than developments internal to the North Atlantic area, is an important determinant of the alliance policies of individual NATO members. Second, interest in the way in which Canadian defense policy has changed should not obscure the fact that the fundamentals of that policy—alignment with the U.S. diluted in a transatlantic association, with military contributions to both—have remained constant for many years and are likely so to continue.[7]

7. See R. J. Sutherland, "Canada's Long Term Strategic Situation," *International Journal*, XVII (Summer, 1962), 199–223.

CHAPTER II

Background: The Early Years
of Canada's Peacetime Alliances

NORTH AMERICAN DEFENSE

THE signal characteristic of Canada's defense policies since World War II has been the underlying assumption that Canada would never have to fight alone, and could therefore base its plans on the likelihood of collective action. This assumption antedates any commitment to an alliance in the formal sense. It was embodied partly in Canada's early commitment to the concept of collective security, as expressed in the Charter of the United Nations. Of greater practical importance, it was reflected in the updating, soon after the end of World War II, of an older relationship usually expressed as the North Atlantic triangle.[1] The restoration, or preservation, of this geometry in military affairs began with a U.S. proposal to Canada, made shortly after the war, that the close wartime collaboration of the two countries be continued and "expanded to include exchange of information in the fields of intelligence, weapons, research and development. Joint defence plans were prepared for the approval of the Chiefs of Staff of both countries. Air defence was to be a joint effort."[2] This bilateral co-operation became tripartite in 1946 when Field-Marshal Montgomery, who had just been named Chief of the Imperial General Staff, visited North America. Somewhat exceeding his authority, he proposed that "Britain, Canada, and the U.S.A. . . .co-operate closely in all defence matters; discussions should deal not only with standardization but

1. Neither of the two legs of the triangle affecting Canada embodied a formal alliance commitment. The tie between Great Britain and Canada was the Imperial relationship, the exact obligations of which were a source of constitutional dispute in Canada during much of the inter-war period. The Canada-U.S. tie was that embodied in the Ogdensburg Declaration of August 18, 1940; while the Permanent Joint Board on Defense created by the Declaration effectively bound the countries militarily (and geography bound them even more), there was no formal treaty of alliance.

2. General Charles Foulkes, "Canadian Defence Policy in a Nuclear Age," *Behind the Headlines*, XXI (May, 1961), 2.

should cover the whole field of co-operation and combined action in the event of war."[3] His proposals were agreed to by the three governments, and, while they remained secret at the time, staff discussions which ensued yielded a large area of agreement not only about co-operation in research, development and standardization, but also about the strategy and tactics for dealing with major aggression.[4]

Notwithstanding the frequency and force of British claims of the existence of a "special relationship" with the U.S., it is rather the pattern of collaboration between the U.S. and Canada within that triangle which deserves to be so designated, (if by "special" one is referring to the degree of closeness, and perhaps even to relative importance). This entirely natural consequence of North American geography appeared in the bilateral forms of U.S.-Canadian co-operation which were undertaken as early as the winter of 1946–47.[5] At that time the two countries, with the U.S. forcing the lead, undertook programs for the construction of weather and long range navigation (LORAN) stations in the Canadian North.[6] Canada's relative lack of initiative in these areas did not stem from a failure to grasp the increasing strategic significance of the region. The need to maintain in these areas a sufficient presence to preserve Canada's claim to sovereignty over them gave Canada an even greater interest, although dependence upon the U.S. for ships and aircraft to reach them made this a difficult task. Rather, it stemmed from apprehension lest, little by little, it would become responsible for the expensive task of defending both countries against attack from the north. In the case of the weather and LORAN stations, costs were shared. Most of the equipment was supplied by the U.S. and the buildings by Canada; the stations were jointly supplied and manned, but a Canadian was always in charge.[7] In the event, this apprehension was largely overcome. As early as 1948, the Canadian government was seriously considering constructing a radar screen, in spite of the large cost involved.[8] For their part, the U.S. authorities never

3. Bernard Law, 1st Viscount Montgomery, *The Memoirs of Field-Marshal the Viscount Montgomery of Alamein* (London: Collins, 1958), pp. 438–41.

4. Foulkes, "Canadian Defense Policy in a Nuclear Age," p. 3.

5. There was agreement even earlier in the area of defense production. See Chapter VII.

6. Lester B. Pearson, "Canada's Northern Horizon," *Foreign Affairs*, XXXI (July, 1953), 581–91; and Robert A. Spencer, *Canada in World Affairs: From UN to NATO, 1946–1949* (Toronto: Oxford University Press, 1959), p. 315.

7. *Ibid.*

8. James Forrestal, *The Forrestal Diaries*, ed. Walter Millis with the collaboration of E. S. Duffield (New York: Viking Press, 1951), p. 474.

suggested that Canada alone should bear the cost of building a system to defend the two countries against attack from the north.[9]

Gradually, and as needed, other forms of co-operation were undertaken. The two navies held joint exercises. The Royal Canadian
Air Force assisted U.S. aircraft in transit to Alaska.[10] A winter ex-
perimental station was opened at Churchill, on Hudson Bay, which
led to Soviet charges that a U.S. base was being constructed at
Churchill. In response, the Canadian government invited all military
attachés posted to Ottawa—including those from Soviet-bloc countries—to visit the site to see for themselves that the charge was
untrue. This they did.[11]

As the number of measures of bilateral co-operation increased,
the need to define some principles of collaboration became apparent.
On February 12, 1947, agreement was announced on a program
comprising five elements: (1) there should be an interchange of
personnel between the two countries to promote mutual familiarity
with the two defense establishments; (2) there should be general
co-operation and exchange of observers for military exercises and
for weapon tests and development; (3) standardization of arms,
equipment, organization and methods of training should be promoted; (4) there should be "mutual and reciprocal availability of
military and naval and air facilities in each country"; (5) in all
co-operative projects, the sovereign control of each country over
activities within its boundaries was affirmed. Mackenzie King, in
announcing the agreement, pointed out that there was no formal
instrument such as a treaty or executive agreement governing this
collaboration, and that it could be curtailed or discontinued by either
country at any time. The informality of the arrangements was
likened to that which marked co-operation within the British Commonwealth. At the same time that these principles were laid down,
the first word in the title of the Permanent Joint Board on Defense,
which had been created in 1940, was affirmed; this in itself assured
that the defense collaboration of the two countries would continue
to be somewhat intimate.[12]

The announcement of these principles of bilateral co-operation,
with their emphasis upon Canada's determination to exercise ultimate control over U.S. installations in Canada, did not succeed in
forestalling criticism from elements that were sensitive to any U.S.
presence in Canada. This became surprisingly apparent in June,

9. Spencer, p. 308. 10. *Ibid.*, p. 316. 11. *Ibid.*, pp. 311–12.
12. Canada, House of Commons, *Debates* (1947), I, 346. (Hereafter referred
to as *Debates*.)

1947, during the parliamentary debate on the *Visiting Forces Act,* which was to regulate the juridical status of American servicemen in Canada. The acuteness of this sensitivity seemed somewhat surprising in view of the small number of U.S. servicemen who were then in Canada, or likely to come soon thereafter. The secrecy with which operations in the Arctic were treated brought to the surface suspicions about the U.S. which were never far out of the Canadian mind. These suspicions had already been apparent in the eagerness with which Canada repurchased the installations built in Canada during World War II from the U.S., even at prices which some Canadians regarded as excessive.[13] This sensitivity towards U.S. incursions into Canada explains why Canadians are not prone to speak of their "special relationship" with the U.S., although they might do so with equal, if not more, justice than the United Kingdom.

THE EARLY YEARS OF NATO

This sensitivity also explains the ardor with which Canadians received the idea of an Atlantic alliance. Never before had Canada been a party to a formal alliance in peacetime. But in the late 1940's, apprehension concerning Soviet power and objectives in Europe caused all Western countries to reconsider their security policy. Canadians, self-conscious of their role as a "bridge" between the U.S. and Europe, and aware of the importance of American support to Europe at that time, saw the course of promoting North American-Western European collaboration as a natural one. Moreover, circumstances led to increased Canadian-U.S. co-operation, until the two countries were allied in effect if not in name. Therefore, distaste for alliances in general became less relevant for Canada than a calculation of what kind of alliance would be most favorable, or least unfavorable, for it. In particular, Canada needed a counterweight to the U.S., if an alliance were not to mean unacceptable degrees of U.S. control. In the past, this counterweight had been Britain; the early postwar military collaboration among these three countries corresponded to this old pattern. But the diminished power of Britain relative to the U.S. in the postwar period, as well as the increased involvement with the U.S. as a result of the new strategic importance of North America, made it increasingly clear

13. D. W. Jones, "Canada's Search for a Role in Continental Defence since 1945." (Unpublished M.A. thesis, Carleton University, Ottawa, March, 1964), p. 6.

that a more effective counter was needed. The impression grew in Canada that the associated Brussels Pact powers potentially constituted such a counter; the more people in bed—so ran the metaphor used to illustrate this—the less likely one was to get raped. There was no need for the advocates of this argument to explain why there should be such safety in numbers, given the instinctive consensus in favor of such a course.

On the basis of this consensus, the Canadian government was able to play a role in the negotiation of the North Atlantic Treaty that was unusually significant for a country of Canada's size. Circumstances contrived to provide "one of those instances, rare for a Middle Power, in which Canada was able to take a significant initiative in the development of high policy."[14] This initiative took the form of a series of official speeches, delivered in 1947–48, which broached ideas being considered at that time in many Western capitals. Most of these ideas were somewhat ahead of the thinking, at least as publicly expressed, elsewhere. Various speeches were made by the Prime Minister, W. L. Mackenzie King, the Secretary of State for External Affairs, Louis St. Laurent, and two top civil servants in the Department of External Affairs, Lester Pearson and Escott Reid. Between June 16, 1947, when Pearson spoke at Rochester, New York, and July 6, 1948, when negotiations among representatives of the U.S., Canada and the Brussels Treaty Powers began in Washington, the ideas suggested provided substance for debate among the statesmen concerned, as well as preparation of the North American populace for events to come. These addresses took the character of a debate, for when they began, different conceptions of a new security organization were presented. In particular, the speakers took different sides on the question of whether the new organization should, or should not, be an agency of the United Nations. These conceptions became progressively more well-defined until June 19, 1948, when St. Laurent advocated a regional pact with geographical limits and a functional character almost identical with what was to become the North Atlantic Treaty Organization.[15] This process of debate and definition of ideas was useful to the statesmen of the countries involved, both because the substance of

14. Robert Spencer, "Triangle into Treaty: Canada and the Origins of NATO," *International Journal*, XIV (Spring, 1959), 88.

15. An exposition in detail of the changing ideas in these speeches has been well-done elsewhere and would be tedious to repeat here. See *ibid.*; Spencer, *Canada in World Affairs: From UN to NATO, 1946–1949*, pp. 245–262; and Arthur C. Turner, *Bulwark of the West* (Toronto: Ryerson, 1953), pp. 7–13.

the discussion was relevant, and because it helped them to gauge the public response to ideas which they were considering themselves but were not yet free to discuss publicly. It was also useful in preparing North American opinion for the idea of a peacetime alliance. This was especially true in the United States, where Canadian officials made several speeches during the period in which the Vandenberg Resolution was under consideration.[16]

In the actual negotiation of the North Atlantic Treaty, Canadian diplomats continued to play an active role. They were "concerned with, and made some contribution to, three significant areas: the degree of commitment, the status of individual states, and the non-military aspect of the alliance."[17] On the subject of commitments, the Canadians shared a common interest with the Americans; they both wanted to guard the right of their legislatures to declare war, against the European desire for assurance of automatic response to aggression. The formula reached in Article V was a satisfactory compromise: a member would take "forthwith, individually and in concert with the other parties, such action as it deems necessary, including the use of armed force."[18]

On the second question, that of status, Canada's concern was partially an old and general one. In the immediate post-war years, not to mention earlier instances, both in the U.N. and at the Paris Peace Conference, it had been concerned with insuring the status of the small and middle powers. The so-called "functional theory" had been one instrument devised to serve this purpose. To this perennial concern was now added a more specific one. From 1946–49, Canada had enjoyed a privileged status in western defense planning by virtue of its membership in the secret tripartite planning group. Some Canadian ministers briefly toyed with the idea that this position could be continued even after the establishment of NATO, but it was dismissed for fear of antagonizing France. Having made this concession, Canadians were even less disposed than normal to accept hierarchical arrangements in the alliance. Mr. Pearson made this clear in his first speech as a minister:

> If obligations and resources are to be shared, it is obvious that some sort of constitutional machinery must be established under

16. Spencer, "Triangle into Treaty: Canada and the Origins of NATO," p. 93.
17. *Ibid.*, p. 94.
18. The text of the North Atlantic Treaty may be found, among other places, in *NATO: Facts about the North Atlantic Treaty Organization* (Paris, 1962), pp. 198ff.

which each participating country will have a fair share in determining policies of all which affect all. Otherwise, without their consent, the policy of one or two or three may increase the risk and therefore the obligations of all.[19]

"On no other basis," he added on a later occasion, "could Canada—or indeed any other self-respecting nation—sign the Pact."[20] These principles were not held to require that every alliance member be represented in all organs of the alliance, but that every organ must "derive its powers from a constitutional grant of those powers to it by all the members of the organization."[21] This proviso cleared the way for Canadian acceptance of the Standing Group; but otherwise the principle was pursued vigorously by Canadian diplomats during the negotiations. The desire not to compromise its position on this issue has even been cited as one explanation for the otherwise curiously detached position which Canada took towards the Berlin Blockade, which was under way at the same time as the negotiations (Canada did not participate in the airlift, even though it had a military mission in Berlin, while Australia and South Africa did.) While it is not easy to measure or evaluate the effect of this campaign, Mr. Pearson cited as the satisfactory result Article IX, which provided for the Council, a body which he called a "genuine agency for collective consultation and collective decisions."[22] It is against this background that one must consider his later attempts to invest the Council with more authority and its consultative process with more importance. These factors also render more comprehensible Canada's opposition, several years later, to General de Gaulle's proposal for a three-power *directoire* to concert western policies on a worldwide basis.[23] While the most basic explanation for this position is the usual antagonism of a lesser power to hierarchical arrangements which reduce its status, there was perhaps an added element of dissatisfaction that another power should enjoy a privileged position similar to that which Canada had held and surrendered.

Perhaps the most ardent effort of Canadian participants in the

19. Canada, Department of External Affairs, *Statements and Speeches,* 48/48 (September 21, 1948), pp. 5, 6.
20. Lester Pearson, "Canada and the North Atlantic Alliance," *Foreign Affairs,* XXVII (April, 1949), 377.
21. Canada, Department of External Affairs, *Statements and Speeches,* 48/48 (September 21, 1948), pp, 5, 6.
22. Spencer, "Triangle into Treaty: Canada and the Origins of NATO," p. 95.
23. *New York Times,* November 6, 1958, p. 11.

negotiation of the North Atlantic Treaty was directed at the inclusion in the text of provisions for non-military co-operation. It is easier to understand the motives for this effort than it is to comprehend why it produced the particular formulation that became Article II of the Treaty. One motive was a distaste for military solutions to international problems, and a consequent desire to insure that NATO would be, as two Canadian Prime Ministers called the Brussels Pact, "no mere military alliance."[24] An appreciation that economic weakness could weaken the NATO countries quite as mortally as inadequate military preparedness suggested that the extra-military element should be economic. The other important motive was a desire to seize the occasion when U.S. and Western European interests coincided to establish their co-operation—a high-priority goal of Canadian foreign policy—on such a firm basis that it would continue even when the current threat should pass. This was the wish which was later to flower into advocacy of the Atlantic Community. A considerable amount of Canada's diplomatic capital appears to have been expended to secure the inclusion of an article to cover these urges. The Canadian view "was disliked by the United Kingdom, regarded as unimportant by the American Secretary of State, and opposed as likely to interfere with the Marshall Plan."[25] Yet, after a "bitter and contentious"[26] debate, Canada prevailed; included in the text as Article II was an undertaking by the parties to "contribute toward the further development of peaceful and friendly international relations by strengthening their free institutions," to "seek to eliminate conflict in their international economic policies," and to "encourage economic collaboration between any or all of them."[27] The formulation even became known as the "Canadian article." This victory of Canadian diplomacy in the short run was to become, however, a long-run failure. As we shall see, the pious words which had been so hard-won were to prove unsusceptible of conversion into tangible results. This was indeed predictable, for the admonition to strengthen free institutions was redundant, and something that all original signatories except Portugal would have done anyway. If they would not have done so, it is unlikely that NATO was the proper agency for affecting their policy.

24. Mackenzie King, in *Debates* (1948), III, 2303; and St. Laurent, in Canada, Department of External Affairs, *Statements and Speeches*, 48/15 (March 24, 1948), p. 7.
25. Spencer, *Canada in World Affairs: From UN to NATO, 1946–1949*, p. 274.
26. *Ibid.*
27. *NATO: Facts about the North Atlantic Treaty Organization*, p. 198.

The economic clauses, on the other hand, were of real importance; although agencies other than NATO existed, or were being created to implement them. Subsequent attempts were to be made to give effect to Article II without much success, as we shall see.

It is too early to assess, and perhaps never will be possible to measure, the difference, if any, which this active Canadian role made in the negotiations leading to NATO's establishment. Lord Ismay singled out St. Laurent as the first man who "turned a general reflection into a practical possibility."[28] Winston Churchill acknowledged that the treaty owed much to "Canadian inspiration and the personal initiative of Mr. St. Laurent."[29] These tributes suggest that Canada's diplomatic efforts filled a need and were not without effect. Yet equally as important for future Canadian alliance policies as the reality of this contribution was the general belief that it had been a "significant initiative in the development of high policy." The inference drawn from this conclusion was that such contributions from Canada would be feasible on a continuing basis. This assumption was to mark Canada's military and diplomatic efforts within the alliance in coming years, without adverse effect at first, but with increasing inconvenience as Canada's relative power later became disproportionate to its aspirations.

The divergence of views held in the United States at the time of NATO's founding about the nature of the alliance[30]—whether it was to be a guaranty pact, or the basis for the construction of an integrated military force—did not exist to any significant degree in Canada. As early as August 13, 1947, Canadian officials had spoken of the need for each member of a regional security organization to accept "the binding obligation to pool the whole of its military and economic resources with those of other members."[31] Subsequent speeches in Canada and the U.S. by Canadian officials and ministers confirm this commitment to "effective co-operation" and "pooling of resources."[32] The Canadian military was united in viewing NATO as a framework within which the available forces of member nations

28. Lord Ismay, "Atlantic Alliance," *International Journal*, IX (Spring, 1954), 80.

29. Spencer, "Triangle into Treaty: Canada and the Origins of NATO," p. 97.

30. See Robert Endicott Osgood, *NATO: The Entangling Alliance* (Chicago: University of Chicago Press, 1962), pp. 28–40.

31. Canada, Department of External Affairs, *Statements and Speeches*, 47/12 (August 13, 1947), pp. 12, 13.

32. Spencer, *Canada in World Affairs: From UN to NATO, 1946–1949*, pp. 260, 61.

could be welded effectively into an organization capable of offering some defense to Western Europe. After NATO had been established and had adopted the doctrine of "balanced collective forces," the Canadian government represented this as meaning no less than an international division of labor in the area of collective defense, and wholeheartedly supported it.[33]

Acceptance of this view, however, was not at first held to entail a commitment to send Canadian forces to Europe. During most of 1950, Canadian spokesmen made emphatic that no military commitment had been undertaken and that for the time being it was in the interest of the European allies, as well as Canada, that the Canadian contribution to "balanced collective forces" be in the form of equipment, not men. This was the rationale for Canada's program of mutual aid, under which equipment worth one billion dollars was transferred to the European allies by 1956.[34] The effective cost of this contribution to Canada was somewhat less than that figure, however, since old stocks of equipment worth about $280 million constituted roughly 30 per cent of that amount.[35] This equipment consisted mainly of U.K.-type equipment which was given away as mutual aid, since Canada was at the time converting extensively from U.K. to U.S. types; it served to equip one division each for Belgium, Italy and the Netherlands.[36] Nonetheless, a significant amount of the total aid came from current production; this included, by 1956, almost 600 modern aircraft and 1000 aircraft engines.[37] Even this element of foreign aid was turned to Canada's advantage, however, for some of the items included in it, such as Sabre aircraft, were not needed by Canadian forces in sufficient numbers to permit an economical production run. The additional numbers needed for mutual assistance increased the required production run to the point that it was economical to produce the items in Canada, and therefore served to increase the capacity of the Canadian defense industry.[38] In addition to these material components, the Canadian aid program included the training of about 5800 allied aircrewmen in Canada.[39] By 1962, the total value of these various forms of aid exceeded one-and-three-quarters billion dollars.[40] The one category of aid which might appropriately have been supplied (and was not) was raw materials. Reportedly, the Temporary Council Committee sug-

33. The spokesman was Pearson. *Debates* (1950), III, 3189.
34. *Ibid.* (1956), V, 5214.   35. *Ibid.* (1956), VI, 6214.
36. Ronald S. Ritchie, *NATO: The Economics of an Alliance* (Toronto: Ryerson, 1956), p. 92.
37. *Debates* (1956), V, 5214.   38. Ritchie, pp. 90, 91.
39. *NATO Letter*, XI (May, 1963), 12.   40. *Ibid.*

gested in 1951 that Canadian aid should be at least partly in the
form of wheat and aluminum; but the suggestion was rejected, on
the grounds that the government could not afford to give away items
upon which it depended mainly for its foreign exchange earnings.[41]
This unwillingness produced, in some quarters, a concern that Canada might not be contributing its "fair share" to the alliance.[42] But
the total volume of its aid compared favorably, in relative terms,
to that of the U.S.[43] Some pride was taken in the fact that Canada
was a producer, and not a consumer, of aid (as, during the 1930's,
it had been a producer and not a consumer of security, in the language of that day). This would be seen later when Canada's acquisition of Bomarc was disparaged on the (inaccurate) grounds that
it marked the first time that Canada had accepted U.S. aid.[44]

The government's preference for substituting military assistance
for military forces was not permitted to go unquestioned for long.
The outbreak of war in Korea and the announcement by the U.S.
on September 9, 1950, of its intention to increase its forces in Europe
set the stage for a change in Canadian policy. When General Eisenhower visited Ottawa shortly after his appointment as Supreme Allied Commander in Europe, he asked for a contingent of Canadian
forces; and his request was favorably received by the Canadian
government. After the December meeting of the NATO Council,
the Minister of National Defense, Brooke Claxton, announced that
the government was considering the dispatch of troops to Europe.[45]
In the Speech from the Throne on January 30, the government
announced its decision to send these forces. The commitments entered into were to provide one infantry brigade group of 5,000 men
(later increased to 6,500), for the central front in Germany; and
eleven (later increased to twelve), squadrons of interceptor aircraft
performing an air defense role.[46] The two additional brigades needed
to complete one division were to be kept in reserve in Canada. The
commitment was made, like the dispatch of U.S. troops, on the
understanding that North American forces would be brought home
as and when Europe recovered its military strength.[47] This commitment has remained unchanged, although for most of the period

41. *Financial Post*, December 22, 1951.   42. *Ibid.*, April 3, 1954.
43. B. S. Keirstead, *Canada in World Affairs: September 1951 to October 1953*
(Toronto: Oxford University Press, 1956), p. 153.
44. See below, Chapter IV.
45. *Globe and Mail* (Toronto), December 20, 1950.
46. Keirstead, pp. 151, 52.
47. Canada, House of Commons, Special Committee on Defense, *Minutes
of Proceedings and Evidence* (October 22, 1963), p. 496.

in question the ability to provide these reserves and transport them quickly in an emergency has been in serious doubt. An additional commitment was made to provide a certain number of Canadian ships, eventually fixed at thirty, which were to be earmarked for the Atlantic Command of NATO. The brigade group was sent to Europe during the winter of 1951–52, and the squadrons which were to form the Number One Air Division were in place by April, 1953.[48] Both units were significant additions to the meager defenses of a Europe which was just beginning to rearm. Such criticism as there was of the scope of these commitments came from the Conservative opposition, and from foreign sources such as American newspapers and British parliamentarians.[49] Domestic critics, for the most part, suggested that the commitments were less than Canada's due. Most of the foreign criticism, on the other hand, derived from the fact that Canada shared with Iceland the characteristic of being the only countries in the alliance without conscription. The government exercised caution in this area, rightly or wrongly, for fear of a repetition of the 1944 conscription crisis or something like it. In fact, the supposition that French Canadians were less ready to meet the call of military service than their Anglo-Saxon compatriots was not unquestionable: of the 10,587 Canadians who served in Korea, 3,134 came from Québec. This represented a proportion slightly higher than that of the population of Québec in that of the country, while the percentage of French Canadians in the force was almost exactly that of French Canadians in the country.[50] None of these criticisms ever had a significant impact, however; the greater danger lay perhaps not so much in lack of support as in the constant temptation to be complacent about a contribution which was, for a non-European country and a non-Great Power, rather sizable.

Diplomatically, as well as militarily, Canada was active during the early years of NATO. This diplomatic activity was greatly strengthened by the presence in the government as Secretary of State for External Affairs of Mr. Lester Pearson, whose personal stature lent a special strength to Canada's diplomatic position. It

48. Keirstead, p. 152.

49. The newspapers were *Newsweek* and the Chicago *Tribune;* the MP's were George Wigg and Immanuel Shinwell. See Keirstead, p. 156.

50. Figures taken from James Eayrs, "Canadian Defence Policies since 1867," in Canada, House of Commons, *Special Studies Prepared for the Special Committee of the House of Commons on Matters Relating to Defence* (Ottawa: Queen's Printer, 1965), p. 17.

was also marked by a definite ideology, which has on occasion been called Canada's "Article II complex." This phrase is appropriate in a double sense: it connotes the fixation which characterized Canadian diplomacy on the goals of Article II; it suggests the equally valid point that not one but a complex of goals are covered by the language of that article. These include (1) a broad extension of the functions with which the alliance is concerned; (2) an increased frequency and importance of political consultation among members of the alliance; and (3) the development of an organizational structure within which to consolidate these practices and activities. All involve the promotion of multilateralism and integration. This is an ironic characteristic of Canada's diplomacy, because for a generation Canada was the foremost opponent of similar schemes of integration within the British Commonwealth.[51] (This commitment to integration also makes curious the mediatory stance taken by Canada in the 1965–66 dispute with France over integration.) These general goals were effectively furthered by many specific Canadian actions which were not undertaken explicitly with reference to Article II. One of these was the Canadian proposal of September, 1950, to simplify the organization and enhance the importance of the NATO Council by investing it with responsibilities which were shared until then with two other bodies—the Defense Committee and the Defense Financial and Economic Committee.[52] This proposal was approved and carried out in 1951. Another measure was the decision to leave to SACEUR and the international secretariat the responsibility for deciding to what countries Canadian mutual aid should be allocated. This course, no doubt undertaken largely to avoid the embarrassments which bilateral arrangements would have involved, contributed to the strengthening of those elements within the alliance which took a collective, rather than a national, approach to the solution of problems.[53] A third Canadian initiative of this sort was the formation in 1954, under the leadership of Senator Wishart Robertson, of a Canadian-NATO Parliamentary Association to foster contacts with members of the legislatures of

51. W. E. C. Harrison, *Canada in World Affairs: 1949 to 1950* (Toronto: Oxford University Press, 1957), pp. 51, 52. The difference, of course, was that in the Commonwealth there was no counterweight to Britain, so unification was expected to promote the dominance of British influence; integration in NATO was not expected to lead to similarly dominant U.S. influence because of the presence in the coalition of strong European countries.

52. Lord Ismay, *NATO: The First Five Years, 1949–1954* (Paris, 1954), p. 41.

53. *Debates* (1956), VI, 6274; and *Montreal Daily Star*, August 21, 1952.

other NATO countries.[54] This act was followed by the creation of similar organizations elsewhere, and by the series of NATO Parliamentarians' Conferences which have been held annually since 1955. These conferences are independent of NATO itself, but they have served, in however intangible a way, to galvanize support for the broader goals of an Atlantic Community among those responsible for supporting national contributions to the alliance.[55]

Productive of more rhetoric but less significant results than the foregoing was another, more systematic effort to implement the goals of Article II. This effort was represented by the work of the five-nation committee appointed under the chairmanship of Lester Pearson in 1951, and of the so-called Three Wise Men, one of whom was again Mr. Pearson, in 1956. The first of these groups (which included in addition to the Canadian foreign minister representatives of Belgium, Italy, the Netherlands, and Norway), was commissioned by the ministerial council which met in Ottawa in September, 1951, to investigate the meaning of the "Atlantic Community." Its creation and composition were largely in response to pressures to implement Article II. The willingness of the U.S., in particular, to have this subject investigated further was explained as a concession made to the countries which had opposed the geographic extension of the alliance to Greece and Turkey, a decision which was also reached at Ottawa.[56] The result of the Pearson Committee's labors was a report which was "accepted by the Council, but with very small results in practice." The significance of its conclusions lay "in their modesty and in the limits they set to what is possible with NATO as it is."[57] The one kind of economic collaboration which might have been undertaken by NATO without infringing on the prerogatives of other organizations was co-operation in defense production. The Canadian Defense Minister had proposed in 1950 that NATO agree to adopt common standards on such military items as personal weapons, light motor vehicles and anti-tank weapons; reportedly, Canada even went so far as to submit schedules of weapon characteristics.[58] But the Pearson Committee Report produced nothing so specific as this. The conclusion seemed inescapable that those who

54. Ritchie, p. 115.
55. *NATO: Facts about the North Atlantic Treaty Organization*, p. 74.
56. *Globe and Mail* (Toronto), September 18, 1951.
57. *Atlantic Alliance: NATO's Role in the Free World*, a Report by a Chatham House Study Group (London, New York, 1952), pp. 99, 100.
58. *Globe and Mail* (Toronto), April 20, 1950.

were most vocal about increasing collaboration under Article II were unable to specify how this might be done.

The strong supporters of "doing something about" Article II became less vocal in the following years as a result of this exercise, and also because of the fact that NATO was concerned primarily, during the early 1950's, with constructing "positions of strength." By 1955, however, there were good reasons for taking another look at NATO's non-military co-operation.[59] (1) the recognition that the Soviet threat could be economic as well as military raised the question of NATO's suitability as an agency of economic collaboration; (2) NATO unity seemed to be endangered increasingly by particular intra-alliance disputes (e.g., frictions between Iceland and Britain over fisheries, and between Britain, Greece and Turkey over Cyprus) requiring new instruments and procedures for solution; (3) those who saw in NATO an incipient Atlantic Community were concerned that as the Soviet threat receded in a period of *détente*, a substitute cement for the alliance should be found in place of fear.[60] For these reasons, advocacy of improving consultation and other types of non-military collaboration was resumed by Mr. Pearson as early as the NATO ministerial meeting in May, 1955.[61] By the meeting held in May, 1956, there was sufficient support for this view for the Council to appoint a committee of "Three Wise Men," composed of Pearson, Halvard Lange of Norway and Gaetano Martino of Italy, "to advise the Council on ways and means to improve and extend NATO co-operation in non-military fields and to develop greater unity within the Atlantic Community."[62] The report, like its predecessor in 1952, considered institutional or functional changes in the organization less important than increasing use of the channels of collaboration that already existed. It gave special attention to the importance of more regular and more effective political consultations among the members. Indeed, it derived much of its importance from the fact that it was prepared shortly before, and released shortly after, the most notable failure of consultation within the alliance: the Suez crisis of November, 1956. (Canadian diplomacy during that crisis constitutes the single most consequential instance of the

59. James Eayrs, *Canada in World Affairs: October 1955 to June 1957* (Toronto: Oxford University Press, 1959), pp. 64, 65.

60. Lester B. Pearson, "After Geneva: A Greater Task for NATO," *Foreign Affairs*, XXXIV (October, 1955), pp. 663–78.

61. *Montreal Daily Star*, May 10, 1955.

62. "Non-military Co-operation in NATO: Text of the Report of the Committee of Three," *NATO Letter*, V (Special Supplement to No. 1, January 1, 1957), 3.

kind of mediation of inter-member disputes that the Report sought
to promote.)[63] Some improvement in regular consultation followed
the Council's adoption of the Report, though it is a moot question
whether this resulted more from the Report itself or from the desire
to correct the disastrous lack of communication so evident at the
time of Suez. There have not been any long-term changes in NATO
practice that can be attributed directly to the effect of the Report.

On the specific political and military issues which dominated the
debates within NATO during the early 1950's, Canada was inclined
to take positions on issues of general importance as well as on those
affecting its particular interests, although the vigor with which it
did so varied according to the instance. Two episodes will illustrate
the degree of Canadian concern with issues which were at the center
of alliance attention at that time: the strategic debate associated
with the phrase "massive retaliation"; and the question of forming
a European Defense Community or otherwise associating Germany
with the western allies. The former debate was joined by Canada
at an early stage. It was on January 12, 1954, in a speech to the
Council of Foreign Relations, that Secretary Dulles referred to
"the basic decision . . . to depend primarily upon a great capacity
to retaliate, instantly, by means and at places of our own choosing."[64] He explained that in the future collective defense would
have to be based less on local defense and more on the "community" deterrent. He implied that the U.S. would, or might,
respond with attacks upon the centers of communist power to
aggression occurring anywhere on the periphery of the Sino-
Soviet bloc. There was a vigorous reaction, both domestic and
foreign, to this speech, but none was more blunt than Canada's
view as presented by Mr. Pearson in a speech to the National Press
Club in Washington, March 15. Pearson asked for clarification of
the terms "instantly," "means," and "our" in the above formulation.
He was disturbed that the first term might imply an excessively
automatic response to aggression, that the second suggested the possible use of inappropriately powerful means of retaliation for some
local conflicts, and that the third did not make clear whether the
U.S. contemplated such retaliation without first consulting its allies.

63. Of the various available accounts of the Suez episode, the one which most
fully covers the Canadian role is Terence Robertson, *Crisis: the Inside Story of
the Suez Conspiracy* (New York: Atheneum, 1965). The relevant documentary
material is contained in James Eayrs, *The Commonwealth and Suez: A Documentary Survey*, (New York: Oxford University Press, 1964).

64. *New York Times*, January 13, 1954, p. 2.

He felt it necessary to caution against the dangers of "entrenched continentalism," and explained the Canadians' anxious "feeling that our destiny may be decided, not by ourselves, but across the border 'by means and at places not of our choosing'; to adopt a famous phrase."[65] Coincidentally, on the day after Mr. Pearson's speech, an article by Dulles was released in which he made some of the desired clarifications; Dulles emphasized, for example, that the free world "must not put itself in the position where the only response open to it is general war." He explicitly denied that the new policy entailed a move away from collective defense or a U.S. troop withdrawal from Europe.[66] He added an additional oral clarification that the U.S. "in most cases" would consult its allies before retaliating.[67] These clarifications of, or amendments to, the doctrine of massive retaliation were welcomed in Canada, but they did not go far enough to remove all of the anxiety which the doctrine had created. In subsequent debates in Parliament, and in the Stafford Little Lectures at Princeton in early 1955, Mr. Pearson continued to explain the shortcomings of that doctrine. In the latter, he offered as a substitute an early version of the theory of graduated deterrence.[68] It is impossible to measure the effect which these Canadian representations had on the subsequent evolution of U.S. strategic doctrine, but it is reasonable to suppose that it was positive, and that the whole issue was a proper and feasible one for Canadians to try to influence.

Canada, like other members of the alliance, received the prospect of German rearmament with something less than complete enthusiasm, but it supported the proposal for the establishment of a European Defense Community from its inception, not as "the only means to this end but . . . as a satisfactory arrangement and indeed as the only one which has been put forward officially."[69] It was not too committed to this proposal to consider alternative courses. As early as January, 1954, German membership in NATO, or a series of bilateral pacts with Germany, were publicly mentioned by Mr. Pearson as other possibilities.[70] But the government was sufficiently

65. *Ibid.*, March 16, 1954, p. 1, Text in Canada, Department of External Affairs, *Statements and Speeches*, 54/16 (March 15, 1954).
66. John Foster Dulles, "Policy for Security and Peace," *Foreign Affairs*, XXXII (April, 1954), pp. 358, 363.
67. Donald C. Masters, *Canada in World Affairs: 1953 to 1955* (Toronto: Oxford University Press, 1959), p. 31.
68. See the published version of the lectures, Lester B. Pearson, *Democracy in World Politics* (Princeton: Princeton University Press, 1955), pp. 9–39.
69. The spokesman was Pearson. *Debates* (1954), IV, 3326.
70. *Ibid.* (1953–54), II, 1586–87.

concerned about the outcome of the French vote that the Canadian foreign minister resorted to the extraordinary measure of sending a telegram to Premier Mendès-France, expressing the hope that the Assembly would ratify the treaty. A Canadian journalist aptly observed at the time: "It is perhaps the measure of the Canadian government's concern for the possible effects of French failure to ratify the pact that the minister was ready to make such a departure from Canadian practice."[71] Although the French rejection of EDC was reportedly received in Ottawa with "deep concern and disappointment,"[72] Canadian diplomacy did not lose its equilibrium. On the same day, Mr. Pearson suggested that the alternative lay in considering the German question "in an Atlantic context";[73] a week later he made explicit that by this phrase he meant the admission of Germany to NATO.[74] Thus, he seemed as ready to take initiatives on behalf of Canada in working out alternatives as Sir Anthony Eden was on behalf of Britain. But he was not equally charged with responsibility for the task. In fact, Canada was not originally included in plans for the London Conference where the alternative German solution was worked out; it was only invited after protesting its exclusion on the grounds that Canadian troops were stationed in Germany, and that Canada was therefore properly concerned with the outcome.[75] In the event, Canada was one of the nine powers represented at London. To the extent that it played an active role in these deliberations, it appeared to stress the desirability of preserving NATO as the main organ of collective defense even after the creation of Western European Union. In characteristic Canadian tradition, it thereby sought to avoid an organizational split between North America and Western Europe.[76]

RENEWED EMPHASIS ON NORTH AMERICA

The apprehension implied in that role, that pressures were increasing toward continentalism in defense collaboration, was well-justified. By 1955, the diminishing tension in Europe rendered less

71. George Bain in the *Globe and Mail* (Toronto), August 28, 1954.
72. *Ibid.*, August 30, 1954.
73. Canada, Department of External Affairs, *Statements and Speeches*, 54/38 (August 30, 1954).
74. *Ibid.*, 54/39 (September 7, 1954).
75. *Globe and Mail* (Toronto), September 6, 1954.
76. Lester B. Pearson, "Western European Union: Implications for Canada and NATO," *International Journal*, X (Winter, 1954–55), pp. 1–11.

acute NATO's need to maintain and strengthen its forces there, while the prospect of German rearmament held out the possibility that German troops might eventually comprise part of those forces and thereby replace North Americans on the central front. In North America, on the other hand, the effort to insure the protection of the strategic deterrent was demanding increasing attention and resources, from Canada as well as the U.S. It was not surprising therefore that in 1955, proposals were made in Parliament and in the press to bring the Canadian troops home from Europe.[77] The government seemed to be sharing these thoughts, although it was less free to spell them out. Pearson had emphasized in the debate on the Paris accords that neither there nor in London had he undertaken any new commitments regarding the size or duration of stay of Canadian forces in Europe.[78] In his parliamentary discussion of defense policy in the fall of 1955, he made a decided shift in emphasis from European to North American defense, and left the impression that a withdrawal or reduction in the forces in Europe was being contemplated.[79]

No decision on this question was to be made before the resignation of the St. Laurent government in 1957, but this did not delay the increased effort that was being made to strengthen continental defenses. The most noteworthy part of this effort, of course, was the construction of three electronic networks to give warning of Soviet attack via the polar route, and to co-ordinate the North American defense against such an attack. These three were: the Pinetree Line, undertaken originally as a purely U.S. venture, but extended into Canada by an August, 1951 agreement under which two-thirds of the costs of the Canadian stations were borne by the U.S.; the McGill Fence, or Mid-Canada Line, which was not a radar line, but an electronic screen which could detect but not track penetration by an aircraft (it was designed, built, financed and operated by Canada); and the Distant Early Warning (DEW) Line, which was undertaken in 1954 by the U.S., and became operational by the summer of 1957. In addition, Canada contributed nine squadrons to continental air defense; interestingly, this number was less by a quarter than the number maintained in Europe. This fact did not go unnoticed: "The anomaly of maintaining Canadian forces, and particularly air forces, on the continent of Europe while at the same time admitting American units into the defence of Cana-

77. *Debates* (1955), III, 3044; and *Saturday Night*, October 29, 1955.
78. Masters, p. 140.   79. *Globe and Mail* (Toronto), September 30, 1955.

dian air space has occasionally been galling to Canadian national sentiment."[80] An attempt was made to remove or abate this gall not by decreasing Canadian dependence upon U.S. interceptors for air defense, but by making very clear the terms upon which Canadian-U.S. co-operation was to take place. Canadian permission was granted for U.S. facilities on Canadian soil only when the following conditions were met: (1) the U.S. requested the facilities; (2) the need was justified, according to the judgment of the Canadian government; (3) Canada did not need, or could not provide such facilities itself.[81] In the event that these conditions were met, the facility was allowed on the further understanding that Canada's ultimate control, or sovereignty, be recognized. This general recognition was then supplemented with a more detailed agreement working out the specific problems involved in the project in question. For example, the 1955 exchange of notes governing co-operation on the DEW Line makes provisions for such things as: Canadian ownership of the sites; arrangements for liaison between the DEW project office and the Canadian government; Canada's right to inspect sites in construction and plans; the right of Canadian contractors and electronic firms to bid on an equal basis with U.S. firms for construction and electronic contracts; Canada's right to assume the operation and manning of the stations in the future, if it should so desire; preferential treatment to be given to Canadian labor and transport firms in work associated with the sites; the NATO Status of Forces Agreement to be in force; and other matters affecting Canadian Eskimos.[82] Such detailed provisions did not prevent the occurrence of some untoward incidents, or remove the more generalized fear of becoming "the world's most northerly banana republic."[83] This general sensitivity perhaps would have been even more acute if it had been more widely appreciated that, as the Canadian government acknowledged as early as 1956,[84] the purpose of the radar networks and interceptor squadrons was not so much the defense of Canada's populace as of the SAC force upon which the policy of deterrence depended. Nevertheless, such measures, coupled with U.S. efforts to brief servicemen going to Canada about the national sensitivities, served to keep adverse reactions to a minimum.[85]

80. Edgar McInnis, *The Atlantic Triangle and the Cold War* (Toronto: University of Toronto Press, 1959), p. 143.

81. According to a later explanation by Pearson. *Debates* (1960), VII, 7607.

82. *U.S. Department of State Bulletin*, XXXIII (July 4, 1955), 22–25.

83. *Maclean's Magazine* (June 23, 1956).

84. *Debates* (1956), V, 5211.   85. Masters, p. 65.

CRITICISMS AND CONSENSUS

There is such a naturalness about Canada's adoption and execution of the policies described above for co-operation with the U.S. and NATO that it may be wondered whether serious criticism implying alternative policies, as distinct from mere carping about inevitable trends such as the increasing interdependence of the U.S. and Canada, was ever heard. The fact is that basic alternatives were offered to Canada's defense policies in both the North American and NATO areas; these alternatives however, never commanded widespread support. Whatever appeal they possessed was reduced further by the tendency of some of those who advanced them to become overly polemical and dogmatic in their advocacy. Opposition spokesmen offered two alternatives to the government's policy regarding Canada's forces for NATO. General George Pearkes, the defense spokesman of the Progressive Conservatives who was later to become Defense Minister, suggested that Canada could not make the "large contribution of trained manpower at the strategic spot at the strategic time."[86] He suggested that an infantry brigade was the wrong kind of force for Canada to provide, and that an armored force with a high fire-power/manpower ratio would more accurately reflect Canada's special strength, namely its large productive capacity. The government's reply to this suggestion, significantly, was that it undertook to provide what NATO considered would be most useful, and this was a brigade of infantry.[87] The current Leader of the Opposition, George Drew, suggested a more basic change: the conversion of the entire Canadian Army into an air mobile strike force which could be used either in NATO or Canada's North; this would have possessed the advantage that the transport capacity thus created would have relieved Canada of its dependence on U.S. transport for contact with the Canadian North, and therefore reinforced its claim to sovereignty over these areas, while serving at the same time to fill a NATO role.[88] Minister of National Defense Ralph Campney's reply to this proposal was that neither in North America nor in NATO was the need for mobility so great as to justify spending the $350 million, which was his estimate of the cost of sufficient airlift capacity for one division.[89]

The most vocal critics of the government's contribution to North American defense were all retired military officers. Three former

86. Keirstead, pp. 149, 50.   87. *Ibid.*
88. *Montreal Daily Star*, June 18, 1955.   89. *Ibid.*

Army generals—Guy Simonds, H. D. G. Crerar, and W. S. Macklin—differed about details but offered similar criticisms of existing defense policy and proposals for change. What united them was the view that the sizable expenditures being made for North American defense were unjustified and could be more profitably spent in creating more well-balanced conventional forces, useful for peace-keeping operations in the under-developed parts of the world. Undertakings such as the development of the CF–105 interceptor and the construction of the McGill Fence were criticized as having been based more on a desire to demonstrate Canadian technological prowess than to create effective defenses, since both were regarded as obsolescent at the time of their completion. On the specific question of the McGill Fence they were joined by a retired RCAF officer, Group Captain Charles Limbrick, who had been head of radar in the Royal Canadian Mounted Police, and whose criticisms therefore carried some weight. While the alternative policies suggested by these men were not always clear or compelling, their general criticism that Canadian defense policies were determined to too large an extent by considerations of national prestige and by an exaggerated affinity between the RCAF and the USAF were indeed prophetic.[90]

The existence of these criticisms and suggested alternatives should not obscure the fact that Canada's defense policies from 1949 (and even before) to 1957 were supported by a remarkable consensus. Issues of defense policy were not politically important during this period, and played only minor parts in the national elections of 1953 and 1957. This is somewhat surprising, in view of the importance of defense policy and the size of the defense budget. It also presents a striking contrast to the years after 1957, when such issues became increasingly controversial and culminated in the second instance in Canadian history when a government fell for the loss of a parliamentary vote.[91] What is the explanation for this sharp change? What were the characteristics of these policies, or of the circumstances in which they operated that engendered such general support and made them, by this token, so satisfactory? How was this consensus dissipated after 1957?

90. Although their articles are legion, representative are the views contained in General W. H. S. Macklin, "The Costly Folly of Our Defence Policy," *Maclean's Magazine* (February 18, 1956); and General Guy Simonds, "Canada"s Defence Blunders," *Maclean's Magazine* (June 23, 1956).

91. The first was Arthur Meighen's Conservative government, which fell on July 2, 1926.

Partial answers to these questions are readily apparent and have frequently been given: NATO was a satisfying instrument for Canadian foreign policy because it institutionalized the fundamental requirement of that policy, namely the alignment of U.S. and U.K. policies in the North Atlantic area; Canadian influence with the U.S., exercised both directly and through NATO, was disproportionately great for a temporary period after World War II because of the debilitated condition of Western Europe and the consequent relative increase in Canadian power, but was bound to diminish when European strength had revived.[92] These statements are correct as far as they go, but a fuller explanation is needed in order to show how the policies which were suitable for the early 1950's led to serious problems and controversies by 1957–58.

Canada's alliance policies, prior to 1957, may be divided into two categories. On the one hand, many of its policies within NATO, especially those of a diplomatic rather than military character, were quite characteristic of lesser powers, especially given the added, special Canadian interest in preventing a European-North American split. These were the policies designed to promote multilateral collaboration within the alliance, to consolidate in institutional form the measures of integration that were achieved, to broaden consultation to include as many countries and as many subjects as possible, and to extend cooperation to spheres other than the military. Here belongs the emphasis on Article II, on consultation within the NATO Council, on integration within SHAPE. It was thought, by other small allies as well as by Canada, that such policies would maximize the influence of lesser powers within the alliance, and would also serve to promote the continuation of an association that they hoped would be permanent. In Canada, it was thought that such policies would help also to make NATO into the kind of organization that would serve effectively as a counter to the U.S. From these views follows, as a military corollary, the judgment that Canada should promote the strengthening of NATO's integrated forces by making a contribution to them. Nothing is implied about the kind of forces this contribution should be composed of.

On the other hand, certain of these policies resemble more closely the policies of the members of the NATO Standing Group (i.e., Great Powers), than those of other small countries in the alliance. This point has often been expressed in the utterances of Canadian

92. Masters, p. 184; Holmes, "Canada in Search of its Role"; and Coral Bell, *The Debatable Alliance*. (London: Oxford University Press, 1964), p. 9.

leaders, as well as in diplomatic and military policies. Although "Canada is neither a great nor an overseas Power," as Mr. Pearson wrote in 1951, "it has accepted heavy international responsibilities," which, by implication, *were* given to resemble those of Great Powers.[93] A few years later, his ministerial colleague, Ralph Campney, made the point even more clearly: "Canada is building and maintaining a defense effort that is really out of' all proportion to our status as a middle power."[94] This might be regarded as the characteristic exaggeration of a politician, but Mr. Campney was well-supported by the facts. Canada alone of the alliance members who were not in the Standing Group had undertaken commitments going beyond that of local defense (in spite of the immensity of the problem of local defense in the case of Canada). That commitment, moreover, was for the provision not merely of reserve forces or intervention forces but for forces on the central front. While the question of whether these troops would have nuclear weapons was not answered before 1957, the absence of any attempt to find for them roles different in kind—as opposed to size—from those of their Great Power associates, made it increasingly likely that such weapons would be acquired. It was assumed[95] that while not every type of weapon would be produced in Canada, the kinds of armament especially needed by Canadian forces could be produced within the country, regardless of the level of sophistication demanded. Not until 1959 was this assumption, after a very painful experience, explicitly rejected. The only military role deliberately eschewed by Canada on the grounds that it exceeded the country's requirements and ability was that of strategic bombing. Even this continence was practiced reluctantly: the Vice-Chief of the Air Staff reportedly said that "We were sorry to have to do it [forego the strategic role], because we had done rather well in the bomber field."[96] In 1959, the RCAF again accepted a role involving nuclear, if not strategic, bombing. One of the government's critics, General Simonds, noted a curious feature of these ambitious policies: "What seems wholly inconsistent and anomalous is that the same Canadians who argue that Canadian military considerations are of negligible importance seem perfectly willing and happy to maintain an expensive and disproportionately weighty overhead control, paralleling

93. Lester B. Pearson, "The Development of Canadian Foreign Policy," *Foreign Affairs*, XXX (October, 1951), 17.

94. *Debates* (1956), V, 5209.   95. See Chapter IV.

96. *Financial Post*, May 14, 1955.

that of the Great Powers."[97] Not at all anomalous (a government spokesman might have replied), if one was interested in military contributions not for security reasons but as means of purchasing influence.

Why were these policies so widely supported in Canada and, by that measure, so successful? No doubt, partly because they were thought to be more effective than they were in fact. The consequences of some of these policies were more illusory than real. It is doubtful, for example, if Canada's emphasis upon Article II has made much practical difference in the collaboration among NATO countries. It is also difficult to regard NATO as having been an effective counter to the U.S. from the Canadian point of view. However much the existence of NATO might have influenced American policy in other parts of the world in directions desired by Canadian governments, all attempts to involve NATO in North American affairs—and thereby curtail U.S. influence in Canada—have failed.[98] Moreover, it is less than apparent that it would be in Canada's interest to do this if it could. As has been noted, one is not necessarily safer from rape with fifteen people in the bed.[99]

This point should not be overworked, however. More important is the fact that for the most part, Canada's alliance contributions have been effectual to some degree. The increment added to allied power by Canada's military contributions is manifest, although there may be argument as to whether these were the right kind of contributions as well as about the utility of certain particular undertakings, such as the Mid-Canada Line. We have also seen that there is considerable evidence of the utility to the alliance of Canadian diplomacy, especially when it is applied to particular problems rather than generalized ideals.

The goals of Canadian alliance policy described in the introduction are, with one exception, not of a type the attainment of which is readily measurable. The exception is the aim of promoting the Canadian armaments industry; this was demonstrably achieved in the years before 1957.[100] For policies designed to achieve the other goals—promoting trans-Atlantic ties, insuring the rights of small powers within the coalition, and gaining influence in the formulation of "high policy"—to be considered successful, it is not necessary to

97. Simonds, "The Costly Folly of Our Defence Policy."
98. See Chapter III.
99. Sutherland, "Canada's Long Term Strategic Situation."
100. See Chapters IV and VII.

measure their contribution to the attainment of those goals. If the goals have been satisfactorily realized, it is necessary to show only that the policies have served to promote them at a cost that is not excessive. This has been the case. The U.S. has been tied to Western Europe in an integrated alliance; certain procedural safeguards exist within that alliance for the status of lesser powers; and opportunities exist for Canada's voice to be heard in the formulation of policy both in the U.S. and NATO. The net effect of Canadian policies in the attainment of these results cannot be determined. But the policies did serve to promote them. They appeared (and appearance can be, especially where public support is concerned, as important as reality) to make some impact upon important issues. And the cost was not excessive.

This last point merits some elaboration, because it suggests the key to the difference between the success of these policies prior to 1957, and their failure after that date. In the early years of the alliance, influence came cheap. Contributions of military forces and equipment that were only modest in absolute terms represented a substantial proportion of allied power. There was no necessity to pay the political and psychological cost involved in a decision to acquire nuclear weapons. And even the most sophisticated weapons were not beyond the capacity of Canadian industry to produce. All of these conditions were changing constantly as the years passed. As the European countries recovered their economic, political and military strength, it would require more sizable military contributions to purchase the same amount of influence that had been more cheaply acquired. As nuclear weapons came into tactical deployment, a decision to acquire them would have to be faced. And, as technology advanced, armaments would attain degrees of sophistication and cost which fewer and fewer countries could bear. If there is meaning in the term "middle power," which is often used in Canada to describe its status, it is perhaps that Canada was of just such a size that all these decisions were difficult ones. Part II describes the issues in which, however imperfectly and unclearly, they were reached.

PART II

MILITARY PROBLEMS OF ALLIANCE IN THE DIEFENBAKER YEARS

CHAPTER III

The North American
Air Defense Command

T HE issue which started the disintegration of the remarkable
degree of unity which had theretofore marked Canadian thinking
about defense policy was the establishment in 1957 of a joint international command for North American air defense. Although it
could not have seemed likely at the time, this was to be the first
of a series of increasingly controversial issues which would dominate
Canadian politics for the next six years. That the question did become controversial, despite the absence of significant disagreement
on the substantive issue between the two major parties or between
the Canadian and American governments, is important to observe;
the reasons which made it so will help to explain the fervor of
subsequent defense debates in which significant substantive differences *were* at issue. Moreover, the dispute itself rendered those later
issues less soluble, for the rancor it aroused contributed to the difficulty of taking what were already hard decisions.[1]

FORMATION OF THE JOINT COMMAND

The merging of air defense commands had a history of controversy before it erupted as an issue in Canadian politics and Canadian-American relations: it had been, for years, a sensitive issue
with the U.S. armed forces.[2] Interservice rivalry, involving chiefly
the Army and Air Force, prevented the formation of a unified U.S.
command for air defense until 1954; voluntary co-operation rather
than integration was the basis of the relationship between the Army
Antiaircraft Command and the Air Force Air Defense Command
until in September, 1954, the Continental Air Defense Command

1. See the testimony of General Charles Foulkes in Canada, House of Commons, Special Committee on Defence, *Minutes of Proceedings and Evidence*
(October 22, 1963), p. 510. (Hereafter referred to as Foulkes testimony).
2. Samuel P. Huntington, *The Common Defense: Strategic Programs in
National Politics* (New York: Columbia University Press, 1961), p. 340.

(CONAD) was established under General Benjamin Chidlaw.[3] However the Army component of that command continued to be dissatisfied with what it regarded as its subordinate position; its protests led to the separation, in September, 1956, of the Air Defense Command—the USAF component of CONAD—from CONAD head-quarters.[4] Even as late as May, 1959—long after the command, in the form of NORAD, had become international—these purely American interservice rivalries continued; they were reported to have played a part in the resignation of General Earle Partridge and his replacement on August 1, 1959, by General Laurence Kuter.[5] The problem, in this instance, was the ambiguous nature of the commander's authority over his forces. While he disposed of them operationally, he did not feel that he had a sufficiently large voice in the allocation of forces to his command by the three component services, whose prerogative such assignments remained. This situa-tion was later pointed out in criticism of the NORAD agreement during the Canadian debate.

The logical extension of this joint command to include Alaska and Canada as well as the continental United States was publicly advocated even before the U.S. joint air defense command became a fact. As early as 1953, General Omar Bradley suggested that such a continental command be created.[6] One year later, Congressman Sterling Cole who as Chairman of the House Armed Services Com-mittee had long advocated an increased air defense effort, proposed the signature of a continental defense pact with Canada, which would be a North American equivalent of NATO.[7] Encouraged, perhaps, by the establishment of CONAD the following month, Cole repeated his suggestion to Secretary of Defense Wilson and Admiral Radford, Chairman of the Joint Chiefs of Staff, when they appeared before the House Armed Services Committee in January, 1955. How-ever, Wilson and Radford both felt it unnecessary and politically inexpedient to raise the subject with the Canadians at that time.[8]

Within the services, if not on the political level, the idea was

---

3. U.S., Congress, Senate, Subcommittee on the Air Force of the Committee on Armed Services, *Study of Airpower Hearings*, 84th Cong., 2d Session, 1956, pp. 234ff.

4. Huntington, p. 341.   5. *New York Times*, May 3, 1959, p. 1.

6. *Halifax Chronicle Herald*, August 28, 1953.

7. *New York Times*, August 21, 1954, p. 5.

8. U.S. Congress, House, Committee on Armed Services, *Hearings on Sundry Legislation affecting the Naval and Military Establishments*, 84th Cong., 1st Sess., 1955, Book I, pp. 223, 224.

already being discussed.[9] The strategic logic of North American geography, the changing technology of air defense, and the closeness of the Canadian and American air forces—a phenomenon that we shall have cause to remark more than once in this work[10]—were making it increasingly likely that some kind of joint command would be formed by the time the air defense system was completed. (This may effectively be dated from the summer of 1957, when the DEW Line was finished.) Such a command appeared "inevitable," Air Marshal Roy Slemon told the Aviation Writers' Association in Montreal, in early June, 1955. But Secretary of Defense Wilson surmised that in so speaking, Slemon was "on his own";[11] and the Canadian Minister of National Defense, Ralph Campney, said that Slemon had not been stating government policy or making a prediction but merely expressing the trend in military thinking. Slemon recognized, according to Campney, that the problem was purely a political one.[12] Reportedly, Slemon had merely expressed what had been taken for granted for some time among many of his RCAF subordinates.[13]

On May 11, 1956, a joint U.S.-Canadian military study group was established and given the task of exploring the operational and technical problems which would result from a joint command.[14] The terms of reference set for this study group by the Canadian Chiefs of Staff Committee included support for "the principle of a single commander";[15] the study group found the principle compatible with the operational problems and, when it returned its report in December, recommended the "establishment of a joint headquarters to provide for the operational control of the air defense of Canada and the United States."[16] The recommendations of the study group were approved by the chiefs of staff of both countries and by Secretary Wilson in early 1957.[17] The American Joint Chiefs, for their part, were eager to put the joint command into effect by

9. According to Sidney Smith, Canadian Secretary of State for External Affairs, a joint command was envisaged and preparations made for it as early as 1954. See *Debates* (1958), I, 190.

10. This point was made repeatedly by persons interviewed by the author. It was well-illustrated by an incident recounted in one of the interviews: the U.S. Navy, which wanted information about the USAF that it could not, because of the politics of the situation, ask for directly, asked members of the Royal Canadian Navy to have the RCAF find out from the USAF and pass the information back along this circuitous route.

11. *Montreal Daily Star*, June 7, 1955.

12. *Debates* (1955), IV, 4346, 4347.

13. *Montreal Daily Star*, June 7, 1955.

14. *Debates* (1957–58), II, 1060–61.   15. *Ibid.*, p. 1061.

16. *Ibid.*, p. 1060.   17. *Ibid.*

mid-year, when the last of the radar networks would become operational. Delay was thought to be dangerous at a time when the Soviet long-range bomber force had become substantial.

During the same period, when this matter would normally have been considered and acted on in Canada, the Canadian government was preoccupied with thoughts of a coming election. The process of gaining governmental and parliamentary approval was begun, but was not completed before electoral considerations intervened. On February 18, Ralph Campney recommended to the cabinet defense committee the establishment of an integrated command "with a re minder that the United States should recognize 'the need for adequate consultation with the Canadian authorities on matters which might lead to the alerting of the air defence system.' "[18] On February 28, he communicated to U.S. authorities the proposal that the Deputy Commander of the joint command should be a Canadian; at the same time, he indicated that he expected Canadian government approval of the agreement by March 15, the date of the next cabinet defense committee meeting.[19] The item was placed on the agenda of that committee, and on March 11, copies of a submission by Campney on the subject were sent to the secretary of the committee in preparation for its consideration on March 15.[20] In fact, the item was removed from the agenda and was not considered by the committee. To explain this to the Americans, a mission was sent to Washington on March 24 to convey to the Joint Chiefs of Staff this account: while there was no disagreement about the substance of the agreement, the question at the moment was potentially a political one, and formal approval would be withheld until such time as it ceased to be so.[21] Finally, on April 26, Campney notified the U.S. Joint Chiefs that the Canadian government's decision— which was not likely to be negative—would not be taken before June 15.[22]

The significance of this date lay in the government's announcement on April 6 that the national election would be held on June 10. The Liberals had been in office in Ottawa continuously since 1935; they enjoyed a parliamentary advantage of 168 to 53 over the Progressive Conservatives; and, according to the pundits' predictions, there was little doubt that the election would return them to office for another four years.[23] There is, therefore, every reason

18. *Ibid.*, p. 1061.   19. *Ibid.*   20. *Ibid.* (1958), I, 992.
21. *Ibid.* (1957–58), II, 1061.   22. *Ibid.*
23. See John Meisel, *The Canadian General Election of 1957* (Toronto: Univer-

to suppose that the Liberal government chose to postpone briefly the NORAD issue so as to deal with it in the less politically-charged atmosphere immediately after the election, confident that they would still have the responsibility for doing so.

Prime Minister Diefenbaker later attempted to establish that the Liberal government had, before the June 10 election, all but formally given its approval to the NORAD agreement; much of the above information was disclosed by him during the parliamentary debates as part of this attempt. He alleged, not without ambiguity, that Minister of National Defense Campney, in the February 18 communication described above, "spoke for the cabinet on that occasion."[24] It is true that by allowing negotiations to take place, the government had become partly committed. But Lester Pearson, now Leader of the Opposition, repeatedly and explicitly denied that the cabinet defense committee, or the cabinet, had approved or even formally considered the agreement;[25] Diefenbaker's charges then became less encompassing and more accurate: "The diplomatic steps to cover the military arrangements were not taken. Everything else had been done."[26] He might have added, and later did,[27] that the political effects of the proposed joint command had not been weighed by the Liberal government. In fact, of the various aspects of the proposed agreement, only the political effects were in the exclusive domain of the cabinet. The military arrangements had been worked out by the chiefs of staff; the Department of External Affairs, in spite of the above quotation of Diefenbaker's, for two years had been seized of the diplomatic aspects of the agreement, as both Diefenbaker and Sidney Smith later admitted, and had been involved in more recent developments by its representative on the Chiefs of Staff Committee.[28] Only the political effects of the agreement could be considered by the cabinet alone; and therefore it was apparently for political reasons that the cabinet refused to deal with it before the election. According to Mr. Pearson, the cabinet had postponed it because, with an election approaching, ministers were scattered across the country campaigning, and a quorum was seldom

---

sity of Toronto Press, 1962), p. 237. It is interesting that in his review of points at issue in this election Meisel does not mention defense policy. The consensus of the mid-1950's had not yet been dissipated.

24. *Debates* (1957–58), II, 1061.   25. *Ibid.*, pp. 1061, 1062; (1958), I, 244.
26. *Ibid.* (1958), I, 995.   27. *Ibid.* (1958), II, 1424, 25.
28. *Ibid.*, p. 1424; also, Canada, House of Commons, Standing Committee on External Affairs, *Minutes of Proceedings and Evidence* (December 5, 1957), p. 34.

42

CANADA'S CHANGING DEFENSE POLICY

present in Ottawa.[29] But as was pointed out by Mr. Diefenbaker, whose political perceptions were usually sharper than his logical acumen, the postponement occurred on March 15, three weeks before the election campaign began on April 6.[30] It is apparent that "even in the serene world in which the St. Laurent government lived, the political implications of military integration seemed ominous."[31]

The June 10 election was one of the biggest upsets in Canadian political history.[32] Three indicators of the confident expectation of a Liberal victory may be cited: (1) the government did not bother to exercise, before the election, its prerogative of filling by appointment sixteen vacant Senate seats; (2) nine constituencies were lost by default because the Liberal headquarters failed to approve the nominated candidates; (3) the final sample taken by the Canadian Institute of Public Opinion prior to the vote showed a 43 to 37 per cent margin for the Liberals.[33] The result was the first election since 1925 in which no party obtained a parliamentary majority. In such circumstances, constitutional practice dictated that the first attempt to form a government be made by the party with a plurality; and it was the Progressive Conservative Party which had won a plurality of six.

The narrowness of this margin made it likely that the government would plan to call another election at the earliest opportunity at which the margin might be increased. This factor ensured that any issues that would arise in the next few months would be handled with a view to their political consequences. It also reinforced the uncertainty and confusion that necessarily marked the actions of a government as new and inexperienced as was Mr. Diefenbaker's. The Opposition, for its part, was also characterized by a kind of inexperience—Louis St. Laurent was replaced by Lester Pearson as the Liberal Leader—and by a heightened proneness to making political calculations, for purposes of the impending election. The country would have benefitted if controversial issues had awaited the holding of a new election and the consolidation of its position by the government. But circumstances were not so kind: in the area of defense alone, according to the chairman of the Chiefs of Staff

29. *Debates* (1958), II, 1000.   30. *Ibid.*, pp. 1424, 25.
31. E. James Arnett, "The Canadian Debate on Continental Defence, 1957–1960." (Unpublished paper, Harvard Law School, April 1, 1964), p. 10.
32. For a general account of this election, see Meisel. A lively, if somewhat journalistic, version may be found in Peter Newman, *Renegade in Power: The Diefenbaker Years* (Indianapolis, New York: Bobbs-Merrill, 1963).
33. Newman, pp. 53–56.

Committee, the government was "faced with three of the most awkward . . . problems any minister had ever faced."[34] Two of these involved prospective purchases of aircraft: the Canadian-produced-and-designed CF–105 Arrow and the American F–104. The third was NORAD.

The Chiefs of Staff Committee were eager to have the NORAD agreement put into effect at an early date; one reason, as later revealed by General Charles Foulkes who was chairman of that committee at the time, was to avoid the embarrassment which would result if the news should leak out that it had been approved by the U.S. and not by Canada.[35] The chiefs of staff regarded this issue as so pressing that they raised it again with the lame-duck Liberal government on June 12, two days after the election. General Sparling, of the Canadian joint staff in Washington, was sent to explain to Admiral Radford, Chairman of the Joint Chiefs, that the issue had been placed before the St. Laurent government on June 14. However, it had not felt that it was in a position to take final action on an international agreement at that time.[36]

When the Conservatives came into office, General Foulkes approached the new Minister of National Defense, George Pearkes, with arguments for the early activation of the joint command. Personal factors were perhaps more significant than usual at this point. General Pearkes was a military man, a holder of the Victoria Cross. He had also shown something less than the proper regard for the principle of civilian control on an earlier occasion. This incident occurred during World War II when the use of Canadian troops in the Aleutian campaign was contemplated; Pearkes, who was the Canadian commander involved, incurred the disapproval of Prime Minister Mackenzie King for failing to clear the project with the government before entering into discussions with the Americans.[37] Such characteristics as these illustrate how General Pearkes was probably disposed to give greater weight to the purely military than to the diplomatic or procedural aspects of the issue. Another relevant consideration was Pearkes's long personal and political friendship with Diefenbaker, whom he had nominated for the Con-

34. Foulkes testimony, p. 510.

35. *Ibid.* This concern for the effects of information leaks in Washington is a justifiable one, as the Bomarc episode shows, although its seriousness may, in this case, have been exaggerated. See below, Chapter IV.

36. *Debates* (1958), II, 1424.

37. James Eayrs, *The Art of the Possible: Government and Foreign Policy in Canada* (Toronto: University of Toronto Press, 1961), p. 82.

servative party leadership in an early and unsuccessful attempt in 1948.[38] Whether or not such factors determined the tactics of General Foulkes in obtaining a government decision, they undoubtedly contributed to his success.

The procedure followed by Foulkes was, first, to convince Pearkes of the desirability of an early approval of the agreement previously accepted by both the Canadian and American joint chiefs and by Secretary Wilson. Once this was done, the Prime Minister was approached, persuaded, and his promise obtained to convey the decision to Secretary of State Dulles, who was to visit Ottawa on July 28. Whether or not it was in order to meet this deadline that the decision was rushed, it appears highly probable that Diefenbaker took the decision after, at most, informal consultation with other ministers but without its formal consideration by either the full cabinet or the cabinet defense committee. Neither the cabinet nor the Department of External Affairs was consulted about the matter at this stage, although the Department had been involved earlier in the question of a joint command. Diefenbaker was serving as his own Secretary of State for External Affairs, at that time. Sidney Smith, who was appointed to that position on September 13, told the Standing Committee on External Affairs of the House as the question was becoming controversial the following December:

> So far as this department is concerned—and I say this very emphatically—so far as this department is concerned, we have not been brought into this picture whatever. This has been a discussion on a military basis. This department deals with the political aspect of it.[39]

In his later testimony, he qualified this comment somewhat, noting that the Department had been concerned with this question for the two previous years under the St. Laurent government, and that the Department's head, Mr. Diefenbaker, had of course been involved in the July decision.[40] But he did not refute the important point, which is that Diefenbaker at this stage acted without consulting the permanent officials of the Department.

Some, at least, of those officials would have counselled delay, not out of opposition to NORAD but on the grounds that it was not

38. Newman, p. 28.

39. Canada, House of Commons, Standing Committee on External Affairs, *Minutes of Proceedings and Evidence* (December 3, 1957), p. 20.

40. *Ibid.* (December 5, 1957), p. 34.

an unimportant agreement and that political ambiguities ought therefore to be cleared up in advance. But the advice upon which Diefenbaker was acting held that it was a relatively unimportant agreement. General Foulkes has since made his viewpoint clear:

> There were no boundaries upstairs, and the most direct air routes to the U.S. major targets were through Canada. Therefore, air defence was to be a joint effort from the start. It is important to keep this point in mind: that the decision for joint air defence was taken in 1946 not 1958, as some of the critics claim when discussing NORAD.[41]

From the military standpoint, the establishment of a joint command could be regarded as no more than the latest in a series of improvements in the implementation of a policy which had long been agreed upon. What it did was to bring under centralized control all U.S. and Canadian air defense forces. The continent was subdivided into a number of regions (the original eleven declined to six by 1966) some of which included both American and Canadian territory and all of which were subordinated to NORAD headquarters in Colorado Springs. The staff at that headquarters was to be integrated between the two nationalities, with the commander an American and his deputy a Canadian. The entire complex would function in an emergency as one system with one common battle plan, the local forces in some areas being commanded by Canadians, in others by Americans. Militarily, the step was a logical improvement over the more limited and *ad hoc* co-ordination that had been practiced previously; it was not a radical departure.

The political importance of the agreement, however, was not negligible, and Diefenbaker, more than most, ought to have perceived this. When the issue did emerge into controversy, it strained the relations between Diefenbaker and the advisers upon whose counsel he had relied, a strain which made more difficult the solution of other military problems still facing the government. This aspect of the NORAD decision, as well as the way it was reached, was illuminated by General Foulkes in later testimony before the Commons' Special Committee on Defense, in a statement remarkable for its candor:

> Unfortunately—I am afraid—we [the military] stampeded the incoming government with the NORAD agreement, and as it had a rather rough passage in the House, the administration was very

41. Foulkes, "Canadian Defence Policy in a Nuclear Age," p. 5.

chary at taking on some of the other tough military problems without a great deal of investigation.[42]

THE NEGOTIATION OF A FORMAL AGREEMENT

The agreement reached on Dulles's Ottawa visit was revealed
a few days later in the form of a joint announcement by Pearkes
and Wilson:

> The Secretary of Defense of the United States, the Honorable
> Charles E. Wilson, and the Minister of National Defence of Canada,
> the Honorable George R. Pearkes, announced today that a further
> step has been taken in the integration of the air defense forces
> of Canada and the United States. (The two governments have
> agreed to the setting up of a system of integrated operational control
> of the air defense forces in the Continental United States, Alaska
> and Canada under an integrated command responsible to the Chiefs
> of Staff of both countries). An integrated headquarters will be set
> up in Colorado Springs and joint plans and procedures will be
> worked out in peacetime, ready for immediate use in case of emer-
> gency. Other aspects of command and administration will remain
> the national responsibility. This system of integrated operational
> control and the setting up of a joint headquarters will become
> effective at an early date. This bilateral arrangement extends the
> mutual security objectives of the North Atlantic Treaty Organiza-
> tion to the air defense of the Canada-U.S. region.[43]

As this statement was not supplemented in the weeks after its
release by any further information from the government, the Opposition became more and more restless to know what the joint command
entailed. The first question on the subject was asked about a week
after the new session of Parliament opened on October 14; Mr.
Pearson asked if the system was in operation, and if the relevant
documents would be tabled. Mr. Pearkes, in reply, evaded the first
part of the question and in addition, seemed to be withholding perti-
nent documents when all he tabled was one order-in-council appoint-
ing Air Marshal Slemon as the Deputy Commander of the joint
command and setting his salary.[44] That there were no other orders-

---

42. Foulkes testimony, p. 510. The account contained in the preceding three
paragraphs is based largely upon the following, the accuracy of which was
confirmed by interviews: *Globe and Mail* (Toronto) (January 14, 1959); Harold
Greer, "Canada Shelves the Arrow," *The Nation* (February 7, 1959); Newman,
p. 347; *Economist*, CLXXXIX (December 27, 1958), 1165, 66; *Financial Post*,
September 6, 1958.
43. *U.S. Department of State Bulletin*, XXXVII (August 19, 1957), 306.
44. *Debates* (1957–58), I, 242.

in-council (which embody formal government decisions and their
approval by the Governor-General) on the subject was later con-
fessed by Mr. Diefenbaker.[45] This, in the eyes of the Opposition,
constituted an even more serious breach of proper procedure than
did the concealment of information; moreover, it fed their suspicions
that the matter had not been considered at all by the cabinet. Questioning on the subject resumed on November 4. In spite of the reti-
cence of the government spokesmen, replies to these questions revealed that the joint command was operative on the basis of an
interim and purely verbal arrangement with the United States.[46]
The plan was to embody the experience gained under this interim
operation in a formal exchange of notes to be worked out later.
Questions were asked also about the degree of authority of the
NORAD commander over Canadian forces and the circumstances
in which he must, and those in which he might not, be required
to consult with the Canadian and American governments before
ordering those forces into action. To these queries, contradictory
and confused answers were given.[47]

In these early questions may be seen the main lines of the debate
that was later to be conducted formally. Information was sought
about and criticism directed at (1) the procedure whereby the government's decision had been taken to enter the joint command; (2)
the procedure followed with the United States in putting that decision into effect; (3) the arrangements for U.S. control of Canadian
forces and, even more so, what was regarded as the inadequate guar-
antees of civilian control of the military. At this stage, the criticisms
were still latent, since the government's failure to provide information prevented the emergence of anything that could be called a
debate. The only substantial statement made on the subject during
the 1957–58 parliamentary session, which was prorogued on February 1, was Mr. Diefenbaker's discourse of November 13, which
consisted mainly of an attempt to implicate the former government
in the decision and thereby disarm its criticisms. This attempt was
beside the point, even if successful—which it was not—because the
criticisms being directed at NORAD at that time were not substantial, but procedural. This was an early example of a Diefenbaker
trait which was to show itself on later occasions: he found it easier

45. *Ibid.* (1957–58), I, 813.
46. *Ibid.*, p. 758; it had become operational on September 12. See the *Globe
and Mail* (Toronto), January 4, 1959.
47. See, e.g., the statements of Pearkes on November 7, 1957, and January
4, 1958; *Debates* (1957–58), I, 849, 50; and III, 2872, 73.

and/or more congenial to attack the former government or the Opposition than to explain what his own government was doing. Because of this dearth of information, discussion of NORAD during the remainder of the 1957–58 session was restricted to opposition questions as to the course of negotiations with the U.S. of a formal note. From government spokesmen came the replies that progress was being made but that it was, of course, a slow and tedious process.[48] The House was repeatedly assured that when a note was ready, it would be submitted to Parliament for its consideration.[49]

The long-delayed exchange of notes embodying the principles upon which NORAD was to operate took place on May 12, 1958, the same date as the opening of the 1958 session of Parliament. The texts of the notes were released one week later.[50] When these were tabled in Parliament, another procedural dispute immediately arose to postpone once more the overdue debate on the substance of the agreement. The issue on this occasion was whether Parliament should be offered the opportunity, in the form of a resolution on the question, to debate and register its approval or disapproval of the agreement. On more than one occasion in January,[51] Pearkes had assured the House it would have such an opportunity; but Sidney Smith, who tabled the notes, said that a resolution would not be submitted, since "the government regards this as an amplification of and extension under the North Atlantic Treaty."[52] After this was criticized by opposition party spokesmen as inconsistent with constitutional practice, the government reversed itself again. The Prime Minister—without, however, conceding the constitutional point—agreed on May 20 to the submission of a resolution.[53]

The Debate

On June 10, 1958, some ten months after the decision to establish a joint North American command and nine months after it began operations, the House of Commons began its debate of the NORAD agreement. In reviewing this debate, it is useful to distinguish between procedural and substantive issues, even though the line between them is not always a sharp one. The procedural criticisms, most of which have already been noted, were most graphically pre-

48. *Ibid.*, III, 2860 ff; IV, 3597, 4020, 4158.
49. *Ibid.*, III, 2868. (Pearkes was the spokesman).   50. See Appendix I.
51. *Debates* (1957–58), III, 2868.   52. *Ibid.* (1958), I, 192.
53. *Ibid.*, p. 244.

sented by Mr. Pearson in his address, which opened for the Opposition. He outlined what he considered normal procedure for the conclusion of important international agreements such as NORAD, the
procedure which was actually followed in the case of the North
Atlantic Treaty. The agreement should be considered in turn, he
said, by the cabinet Defense Committee and the full cabinet; this
should be followed by the signature of an agreement by the governments concerned; the question should then be formally considered
by Parliament, the sense of the House being expressed in a resolution; only then should the agreement be put into effect.[54] He hardly
needed to add, in the case of NORAD, that this procedure appeared
to have been violated on every count. It seemed highly probable
then, and appears even more likely today, that neither the cabinet
Defense Committee nor the full cabinet was the agency of decision;
the implementation of the agreement preceded not only its discussion
by Parliament but antedated by some eight months the signature
of a formal agreement between governments. The government
tended in the course of the debate to undermine its own arguments
for these deviations from normal procedure. The decision to put
the joint command into effect before signing a formal agreement
was defended largely by the assertion that experience in operating
the command would be the best guide in the selection of the principles which ought to be embodied in the agreement.[55] But this argument was dealt a severe blow by the Prime Minister himself, when
he admitted that the agreement tabled was almost identical with
that drawn up under the St. Laurent government without such experience in operating the command.[56] Again, the government argued
that by putting the command into force without waiting for intergovernmental agreement, it had gained ten months' time during
the crucial period following the Russians' launching of Sputnik I.[57]
Critics failed to see how NORAD, at this time a joint command
of anti-bomber defenses (although later it was charged with the
operation of the Ballistic Missile Early Warning System), offered
protection against missile attack. They were even inclined to draw
the opposite conclusion: that the launching of Sputnik I—which did
not have in any case the same kind of psychological impact in Canada
as in the U.S.—made anti-bomber defenses less important, and
therefore that the politically distasteful act of joining NORAD could

54. *Ibid.*, p. 1000.
55. See, e.g., Pearkes on November 4, 1957: *Ibid.* (1957–58), I, 702.
56. *Ibid.* (1958), I, 994.   57. *Ibid.*, II, 1043.

be averted.[58] Moreover, the government's own argument for hurrying was destroyed by the revelation that no RCAF squadrons had been assigned to NORAD during this period; such allocation did not take place until June 26, 1958.[59] Such arguments were not convincing. The impression was left, as General Foulkes revealed later, that it was the wish not to be embarrassed by a possible leak (disclosing that the U.S. and not Canada had approved the agreement), and not military logic, which dictated the course followed.

Two further procedural criticisms should be noted briefly. First, what already has been seen as the reluctance of the government to provide information in Parliament about the NORAD agreement was sometimes alleged to involve an element of active suppression of information. It was suggested, for example, that the government conspired to keep General Partridge away from the press, when he visited Ottawa during the period in which NORAD was under fire.[60] It is difficult to evaluate the veracity of such an allegation, and it is noted here merely for its relevance to future incidents. Its importance is lessened, moreover, by the fact that General Partridge had access at any time to the Canadian public by way of the American press, as was shown by the wide notice given his September 6, 1957, interview with *U.S. News and World Report*. The second criticism to be noted here concerns the principle of civilian control of the military. While one part of this question—the problem of insuring political control of military commanders in emergency situations—is regarded as a substantive one and treated below, there is also a purely procedural aspect: the role of the military in the reaching of the Canadian decision to join NORAD. Whatever breach of proper procedure there was in General Foulkes's "stampeding," if there was any at all, its importance probably has been exaggerated, since the whole process of the government's decision—of which this was only one aspect—was, as we have seen, at variance with constitutional practice. In a country as strongly anti-militarist as Canada, its chief significance was not that it represented a dangerous trend, but that the civilian leaders overreacted, became highly suspect of their military advice, and thereby put a strain on the relations between their military advisers and themselves, a strain which rendered more difficult the solution of many military questions which would soon have to be faced.[61]

58. *New York Times*, November 10, 1957, p. 84.
59. *Debates* (1958), II, 1029; *Globe and Mail* (Toronto), June 26, 1958.
60. Canada, Senate, *Debates* (1958), p. 219.
61. See Greer; also Foulkes testimony, p. 510.

Discussion of the substance of the NORAD agreement revolved around three questions: (1) command arrangements governing the relations of American and Canadian forces and of civilian and military authorities within each country, especially in times of emergency; (2) increased political consultation between Canada and the United States which was regarded as a corollary of greater military integration; (3) and the relationship of NORAD to NATO. Some attention, although less than they deserved, was also given to the strategic significance of the agreement and to its economic implications. These five areas will be discussed in turn.

Of the many confused parts of this entire debate, none was more confused than the question of what command arrangements NORAD involved. The source of the confusion, in this case as elsewhere, lay in the tendency of the Diefenbaker government to set forth its policies not in the clearest terms possible but in what (it thought) were the most politically palatable terms. In the case of NORAD, this tendency may be seen as early as the August 1, 1957, announcement, which revealed the agreement to set up a system of "operational control," not of "command," even though the joint headquarters was referred to in the same document as an integrated command. The inspiration for this linguistic hairsplitting was indicated by General Partridge, the first Commander in Chief of NORAD:

> I am in operational control of the system rather than in command of it. Insofar as Canada is concerned, this is a very important difference. The Canadians—like ourselves—prefer to have their troops commanded by one of their own officers. By command I mean administration, logistics, supply, training, indoctrination.[62]

This terminological distinction was insisted upon by the government spokesmen throughout the debate; it was regrettable, not because it did not correspond to a real distinction (for it did), but because emphasis on it obscured the significance of the joint command. That command, if it was militarily justifiable, had to involve giving to a commander in Colorado Springs effective authority to use Canadian forces to engage an attacking force; if NORAD was less than this, then the government was not justified in representing it as a military advance.

The main question involved was what, if any, consultation had to take place with the Canadian government before CINCNORAD could order into action the RCAF squadrons under his "operational control." In his September 6 interview, General Partridge, asked if

62. *U.S. News and World Report* (September 6, 1957), p. 72.

he had to get the President's permission before using a nuclear-tipped
air-to-air missile under his command, replied:

> Yes. However, the President has given his approval to use, without
> reference to anybody, any weapon at our disposal if there is a
> hostile aircraft in the system. . . . We probably would be on the
> phone talking to people when the thing went off.[63]

The following November, however, General Pearkes said that Partridge would be able to commit Canadian and American forces "after
consultation with the governments concerned."[64] It did not escape
notice that, taken together, these two statements led to the conclusion
that Canadian Air Marshal Roy Slemon, the deputy commander
of NORAD, had more authority over American than Canadian forces
during the periods when he assumed command in General
Partridge's absence. Such a conclusion must be rejected, however,
since General Pearkes's statement, which was none too certain at
the time it was made, was modified by him later on more than
one occasion. In January, he acknowledged that the Canadian air
defense commander at St. Hubert through whom, at that stage,
the NORAD commander was to control Canadian forces[65] could
order Canadian forces into action, in accordance with the rules of
engagement which had been in force for many years, without consultation with the Canadian government.[66] (Later, with the introduction of SAGE, the chain of command became no longer national
but directed from CINCNORAD to subordinate binational headquarters.) Although he did not go so far as this in the June debate, he
gave an explanation which was still consistent with Partridge's interview (and relevant to the later controversy during the 1962 Cuban
missile crisis): "As I have emphasized frequently, consultation must
take place beforehand, and there would be little more than clearance
given during an emergency."[67]

The reader who finds these comments less than clarifying has
a good deal of company in current editorial comment. The entire
NORAD affair (editorialized the Toronto *Globe and Mail*), "was
hardly a credit to our Parliamentary system."[68] The *Montreal Daily
Star*, which judged as disappointing the performances of Diefenbaker, Sidney Smith and Pearkes alike, summarized: "The government does not come out too well from all this."[69] While the government's inability, for security reasons, to reveal the detailed terms

63. *Ibid.*, p. 78.   64. *Debates* (1957–58), I, 758.
65. *Ibid.* (1958), II, 1041.   66. *Ibid.* (1957–58), III, 2872, 3.
67. *Ibid.* (1958), II, 1029.   68. June 13, 1958.   69. June 12, 1958.

of reference which would have answered many of these questions undoubtedly made its task more difficult, it could not escape responsibility for a sloppy parliamentary effort.

The hubbub over command arrangments served to obscure another part of the agreement which represented, from the Canadian viewpoint, a considerable achievement. This concerned the consultation which the two governments would undertake in normal times, prior to emergency situations. The relevant paragraph is forthright:

> The two Governments consider that the establishment of integrated air defence arrangements of the nature described increases the importance of the fullest possible consultation between the two Governments on all matters affecting the joint defence of North America, and that defence cooperation between them can be worked out on a mutually satisfactory basis only if such consultation is regularly and consistently undertaken.[70]

Such a commitment was a highly desirable, if not indeed a politically necessary, part of the agreement for the Canadian government. It was needed to meet the criticism, which was often made despite this paragraph's inclusion,[71] that NORAD would involve Canada, more automatically than before, in any war in which the U.S. engaged. The importance of the commitment might be disparaged, since without the will to consult it would be worthless. But Sidney Smith's expression of the determination, in Washington as well as Ottawa, to fulfill the undertaking had a convincing ring; the military negotiators, who successfully insisted on behalf of Canada on the inclusion of this undertaking in the agreement, did so against substantial U.S. resistance, which presumably would not have existed if the Americans had not regarded the assurance as meaningful. Channels of consultation were agreed upon, and arrangements were made to consult on three levels: heads of government, chiefs of staff, and diplomatic.[72] It was acknowledged that consultation could not be equally full in all circumstances; and in view of the controversy surrounding this question in the 1962 Cuban missile crisis, it is well to record here Mr. Diefenbaker's recognition of this:

> These consultations naturally will be intensified in times of emergency. It cannot be overlooked that the advantages of surprise lie with the aggressor and that therefore the time available for consultation in an emergency may be very short. To that end we believe that every precaution must be taken to ensure that the Canadian

70. See Appendix I.   71. Minifie, p. 78, e.g.
72. Interviews. Cf. General Charles Foulkes, "The Complications of Continental Defence," in Merchant, ed., pp. 121, 22.

government is consulted concerning circumstances which could conceivably lead to this country being committed to war, and also
to ensure the maintenance and preservation of our joint
co-operation.[73]

One of the most far-fetched, if understandable, aspects of the government's presentation of the case for NORAD was its attempt to
associate that agreement as closely as possible with NATO. At the
time he tabled the agreement, Sidney Smith not only used the supposed NATO connection as a pretext for not submitting a resolution
on NORAD to Parliament. He also referred to NORAD as "the
practical application of the principle of interdependence within
NATO," and not only as an integral but as an "integrated" part
of NATO.[74] The gesture responded to a long-felt Canadian preference—partly instinctive, partly intellectualized—for multilateral
rather than bilateral commitments. At the time of NATO's formation, Canada had suggested the possibility of making North America
a NATO command, with its own supreme commander responsible
to the NATO Council; the suggestion was not, however, acceptable
to the United States.[75] In the case of Korea, Canadian reluctance
to send troops which would form part of American units was overcome when the alternative arose of contributing to a multinational
Commonwealth brigade.[76] In 1955, the influential *Winnipeg Free
Press* suggested that a NATO Northern Command, consisting of
Iceland, Denmark, Norway and perhaps Britain, as well as Canada
and the U.S., be created to operate the DEW Line and other warning
networks.[77] Why the European countries, which were having trouble
enough reaching agreement on a unified air defense system for
Europe,[78] should be interested in taking on additional responsibilities
for North America was not clear; it was not necessary to find out
if they would, since by this date not even the Canadian military
was in favor, and the proposal died an early death.[79] In the case
of NORAD, the Canadians who negotiated the agreement must have
sought the inclusion of the greatest possible number of references
to NATO in order to meet these foreseeable objections.

73. *Debates* (1958), I, 999.   74. *Ibid.*, pp. 190, 91.
75. Interviews. Cf. Foulkes, "The Complications of Continental Defence,"
pp. 117–19.
76. Interviews; also Keirstead, p. 310.
77. December 10, 1955; cited by James Eayrs, *Canada in World Affairs;
October 1955 to June 1957*, p. 152.
78. F. W. Mulley, *The Politics of Western Defence* (London: Thames and
Hudson, 1962), pp. 180 ff.
79. Interviews.

If they did, indeed, base their strategy on the expectation of such comments, they were not disappointed. Both sectional and partisan opinion lamented the purely bilateral character of the agreement, and advocated bringing it somehow under NATO. The former, sectional objections were expressed, for example, in a series of editorials in *Le Devoir* which continued long after the parliamentary debate had ended.[80] The partisan proponents of incorporating NORAD into NATO were the Liberals and the CCF. The former, under Mr. Pearson, endorsed this course with a vigor that is explicable only by the fact that they were out of office, and therefore free of the responsibility of having to try to convert it into fact. At a later date, he carried the argument further by suggesting that Canada seek to have the U.S. Strategic Air Command put under collective NATO control.[81] There was also an anomaly in the CCF's support of this idea, as Mr. Diefenbaker did not fail to note.[82] All CCF members who advocated bringing NORAD under NATO (and the only eight votes cast against the resolution were cast by these members) were from British Columbia. On June 2, only eight days before the parliamentary debate began, the BC wing of the party had gone on record as favoring Canadian withdrawal from NATO. These factors, and the important additional one that no one seriously suggested that the United States would agree to such a multilateralization of North American defense, combine to leave the impression that those who suggested this course were seeking to score debating points and were offering an illusory, not a real, alternative.

Not only the opposition parties were playing this political game, however; the government was busily engaged in the more impossible attempt to demonstrate that NORAD was, in some meaningful sense, already a part of NATO. It is true that the Canada–U.S. Regional Planning Group is recognized by NATO to have responsibility for preparing plans for the defense of North America. But it has no assigned forces nor command functions, as have the other geographical divisions of the NATO area. As if the text of the agreement—which explains the joint responsibility of CINCNORAD to the U.S. and Canadian chiefs of staff, and does not mention NATO except in very general terms—did not make this clear, the Secretary-General of NATO, Paul-Henri Spaak, obliged with a clarification in an interview:

80. See, e.g., May 21, 1958. 81. *Debates* (1959), V, 5369.
82. *Ibid.* (1958), II, 1060.

Q. Do you consider NORAD part of NATO? A. (Mr. Spaak) No,
it is not under the command of NATO. Q. Do you think of it
as an extension of NATO? A. Well, we are very interested in it
but NORAD is not under the command of NATO. I think it is
a very good experiment.[83]

While government spokesmen continued to extract from this admittedly ambiguous interview interpretations compatible with theirs,
they gradually moderated their claims for the connection between
the two organizations. On June 10, the most that Mr. Diefenbaker
seemed disposed to claim was that NORAD "is part of the NATO
concept; . . . it is in Canada's interest within the alliance to regard
it as such."[84] A few days later, he seemed to be as tired as everyone
else of trying to establish the connection: "Without discussing the
connection between NORAD and NATO I wish to say that I believe,
whether it is a part of NATO or not, it does strengthen NATO,
which is all that matters."[85] This whimper, which was entirely compatible with the positions of the opposition parties, provided a fitting
end to a dispute which had been very largely semantic.

The strategic implications of NORAD were almost completely
ignored during the debate, no doubt because largely there was general agreement with the main strategic premise: that the active air
defense of North America would continue to be the most feasible
and appropriate military role for Canada to play and that, given
that judgment, effectiveness required a joint command. To evaluate
this premise would have involved answering the question: Is that
contribution to air defense, which it is within Canada's means to
make, the most effective way to counter the Soviet threat? All
of the variables in this question—the degree to which the Soviet
threat was military, the technological level of that military threat,
and the amount of air defense hardware which it was within Canada's means to buy and operate—were changing in 1957. The decision to join NORAD meant that Canada had opted to stay in the
air defense business in a big way, if only because the pride and
sense of decency of the Canadian air force officers at Colorado
Springs meant that they would insist on making a contribution of
forces commensurate with the responsibility which they had been
given. Their insistence on this level of air defense forces would
constitute a very great pressure on Canadian policy-makers in Ottawa. But the implications of this decision, which the debate ought

83. *Ibid.*, I, 1004. (Cited by Pearson).
84. *Ibid.*, p. 998.   85. *Ibid.*, II, 1423.

to have brought out, were not made clear. These issues were largely economic, and some observers did, at least, ask the right questions on this subject. Two days after the announcement to form a joint command, the Toronto *Globe and Mail* asked what more military integration would mean for the Canadian aircraft industry, although the main theme of the editorial was what it regarded as the regrettably small RCAF contribution to NORAD. During the parliamentary debate a CCF member, Mr. Herridge, asked the same worried questions and waxed prophetic when he wondered if NORAD entailed a commitment to acquire SAGE and Bomarc, which Canadian industry could not produce. "It is precisely because of the seemingly inevitable tie-up with the United States at the economic level that it is all the more important to avoid putting ourselves in a politically subordinate position to the United States," he reasoned.[86] But these voices were out of tune with the chorus, which continued to sing military irrelevancies; this was illustrated by press reports to the effect that the Canadian military people were quite uninterested in the NORAD debate, being exercised with such questions as the introduction of SAGE into Canada and the problem of balancing military trade with the United States.[87] It is also shown by the fact that the development and production sharing program—something of an achievement for Canada—is generally assumed to have received its original impetus from the cancellation of the Arrow aircraft, instead of from the military integration involved in NORAD, as is in fact the case.[88]

THE MEANING OF THE DEBATE

At the outset of this chapter it was noted that NORAD became a controversial issue, despite the absence of fundamental partisan disagreement on it. By now, it should be clear that there was not much disagreement of this sort. It is true that eight members of the CCF voted against the NORAD resolution, and that some continuity exists between the 1957–58 NORAD controversy (which was a domestic and political one), and the later controversy over nuclear weapons (which was genuinely military and international), with which NORAD was politically associated. This continuity exists by virtue of the vote of NDP, the successor party to CCF, calling for withdrawal from NORAD in 1962 because of its connection with

86. *Ibid.*, I, 1018–21.   87. *Financial Post*, June 14, 1958.
88. Interviews; see below, Chapter VII.

nuclear weapons. The major opposition party, the Liberals, also differed with the government, at least on the question of tactics. It
suggested that agreement to join NORAD be withheld until the
U.S. made concessions on trade[89] and on ties to NATO,[90] a proposal
which was described by others as meaning "NORAD if necessary
but not necessarily NORAD,"[91] in the spirit of Mackenzie King. But
it never questioned the basic validity of the NORAD concept; indeed,
the *Globe and Mail* reported that Pearson's speech in the debate
sounded more like a defense of NORAD than did Diefenbaker's.[92]

It should also be clear by now that the pact became controversial
in spite of this fundamental agreement, because of certain procedural
mistakes of the Conservative government and of its tendency to
act furtively and conceal information, a course which was politically
unprofitable even though it was probably politically inspired. Explanation should not stop here, for there are factors—other than
such contingent ones as inexperience—which must predispose a government to act in such a way on issues of this sort. These factors,
which are closely interrelated, are identified here and later may
be taken consciously into account. First, there is the fact that
almost any significant issue of defense policy in Canada will involve
the U.S. also. This stems not only from the obvious factors such
as geography and joint participation in NATO, but also from the
extraordinarily close co-operation between the Canadian and U.S.
military. Political problems arise when the viewpoint of a branch
of the Canadian military is closer to that of its U.S. counterpart
than to that of other Canadians, military or political; and this situation has often recurred. Secondly, any issue between Canada and
the United States is potentially controversial, because of Canadian
sensitivity about its sovereignty, stemming from the disparity in
size. There is no dearth of evidence of such sensitivity; it occurs
in even striking ways. An example of this is the testimony of General Pearkes before the Standing Committee on External Affairs
of the Senate, in which he suggested that if Canada did not agree
to join NORAD, the U.S. would just "move in."[93] The conclusion

89. *Debates*, II, 1426. Some of the Liberal proposals, including the one referred
to here, were made from platforms outside the House, since the party was
without a defense spokesman in Parliament. Paul Hellyer had been defeated
in the 1957 election. See Jones, p. 77.

90. *Debates* (1959), II, 1491.

91. James Eayrs, *Northern Approaches: Canada and the Search for Peace*
(Toronto: Macmillan, 1961), p. 175.

92. June 11, 1958.   93. *Globe and Mail* (Toronto), June 26, 1958.

which follows is that any issue of defense policy, even if the controversy stems from purely domestic factors, may become an issue of Canadian-American collaboration in defense and rub off on other questions. This provides the explanation for the facts that the NORAD issue, though its controversy did not involve partisan or international differences of substance, contributed to sensitivity on later issues which did involve international differences, and that the bitterness and frustration of these issues, which will now be discussed, date back to the "serene" days of the St. Laurent government and to the proposals for joint defense of North America.

CHAPTER IV

Hardware for North American Defense

THE second issue, after NORAD, with which the Diefenbaker government had to grapple—in immediacy if not necessarily second in importance—was the question of giving new equipment to the Canadian air defense forces which had just received a new command structure. The two issues were related, primarily because the establishment of a joint command reaffirmed a belief in the feasibility and importance of mounting active air defenses against manned bombers. It points up the importance of the later issue, however, to stress its difference from the NORAD controversy. In the latter instance, there was basic agreement among the principal parties to the dispute about the strategic desirability of a joint command. Given the decision to have active defenses against the manned bomber, the controversy arose from political and constitutional factors which could largely have been avoided. The purchase of expensive aircraft and missilery, on the other hand, raises problems which are inescapable; therefore consideration of such purchases directed attention, in however confused a fashion, to the basic questions of defense policy: What should be the scope of the total defense effort, and what is the most appropriate way to allocate the sum of these limited resources? Although controversy and crisis do not necessarily have to occur before these questions are considered systematically by policy-makers, such has been the case in Canada in recent years. This fact provides the justification for the tendency of this study to focus on the controversial policy questions, rather than on the equally important and more permanent factors which are not controversial because they are generally accepted. The form which these questions began to assume in Canada in 1957–59 was something like this: (1) Could Canada continue to produce the most advanced equipment needed by its armed forces? Could it even afford to purchase such equipment from the United States? (2) Should its major defense effort continue to be the provision of active defense against manned bombers?

THE AVRO CF–105 ARROW

All these questions were involved in the decision, which faced the Diefenbaker government already when it assumed office in June, 1957, to produce or discontinue the development of the CF–105 Arrow jet aircraft. The Arrow was a Mach Two all-weather interceptor, designed and developed by A. V. Roe of Canada, Ltd., a subsidiary of the Hawker-Siddeley group. It was planned as the successor aircraft to the CF–100, which was also designed and built by Avro; the CF–100 was the standard aircraft of the RCAF air defense forces during the 1950's, but its subsonic speed had rendered it obsolescent by the end of that decade. By 1957–58, the costs and stage of development of the Arrow had reached a point where the decision of whether or not to put it into production could not be postponed much longer. To appreciate the factors weighing on that decision, it is necessary to review the history of the aircraft's development.

Although specifications for the CF–100's successor were laid down as early as 1949,[1] it was knowledge gained during the Korean war about Soviet aircraft developments that turned these into a hard "requirement."

> During the Korean war the introduction of the MIG–17 fighter revealed that the Soviet Union was well advanced in jet production, and there were indications that the Russians had the capability of producing turbo-jet bombers. It was therefore considered at that time that by 1958 the Soviets might have the capability of attacking North America with turbo-jet bombers carrying atomic bombs. This appreciation generated a requirement for a supersonic jet fighter to replace the CF–100 after 1958.
>
> Canada was, at this time, primarily responsible for the air defence of Canada. The only arrangement for United States support dealt with reinforcing after the battle had begun.[2]

Following the 1952 recommendation by the chiefs of staff that an airframe be developed, funds for design studies were authorized by the government in May, 1953; in December, of the same year, a program for the development of two prototype airframes was approved.[3] According to early estimates, the aircraft was expected to be ready for operational use in 1958, and some 500–600 would be ordered, at a cost of between $1.5 and $2 million apiece.[4]

---

1. Foulkes testimony, p. 509.
2. Canada, House of Commons, Special Committee on Defense Expenditures, *Minutes of Proceedings and Evidence* (May 17, 1960), p. 88. (Hereafter referred to as Halpenny Committee *Proceedings*.)
3. *Ibid.*, p. 89.   4. *Ibid.*

Such were the meager beginnings of the Arrow program. In retrospect, one is struck by the comparative lightheartedness with which some of these heavy commitments were entered into. "Never again would there be any doubt that Canada can manufacture anything that can be manufactured elsewhere," C. D. Howe, the first man in charge of the Department of Defense Production, had said at the end of World War II.[5] Since that time, the Canadian defense industry in general, and the aircraft industry in particular, had grown substantially and provided an important supplementary source of supply for the overstretched American defense industry during the Korean war. Canadian manufacturers had produced one of the more advanced versions of the U.S.-designed F–86 Sabre, and had designed and produced the CF–100 long-range interceptor— within the short period of three-and-one-quarter years—and the Argus maritime reconnaissance aircraft.[6] Both of these were highly regarded in the industry, and some were purchased by the U.S. Air Force.[7] It was not surprising therefore that when the government of the day made its first cryptic allusion to the program for the development of the CF–105, little dissent was heard.

Some criticisms made by the Socialist CCF did suggest that the program might be beyond Canada's means, or at least that the same result might be more cheaply and expeditiously arrived at through closer co-operation with either Britain or the U.S. in aircraft development.[8] But such apprehension was not widespread and was, anyway, readily answered. First, such co-operation with Britain and the U.S. as was deemed fruitful was allegedly already being carried out.[9] Secondly, that such co-operation could not be carried to the point of jointly establishing requirements was said to be determined by the peculiarities of Canadian geography. Canadian requirements differed from those of Britain because the greater expanse of territory involved dictated the use of a long-range aircraft. The American requirements, on the other hand, equalled or exceeded those of Canada with respect to range, but differed in other respects: (1) with more airfields and a warmer climate, the Americans did not share the Canadians' concern at the possibility of crashes in isolated country; the RCAF requirement for the more reliable, two-

5. Cited by James Eayrs, "Sharing a Continent: The Hard Issues," *The United States and Canada,* ed. John Sloan Dickey (Englewood Cliffs, New Jersey: Prentice-Hall, Inc., 1964), p. 65.
6. *Debates* (1952), III, 2743.   7. Interviews.
8. *Debates* (1953–54), V, pp. 4903–4920; and (1955), V, 5636.
9. *Ibid.* (1954), VI, 6438.

engine plane was therefore, for the Americans, expendable; (2) the more sophisticated American ground environment relieved American fliers of some of the navigational duties which in Canada made advisable the use of two-man interceptors, with one man serving as navigator; (3) "Canadian air bases were relatively close to the mid-Canada line; therefore, it was necessary for an aircraft to be able to rise quickly from the base, in order to engage a bomber between the time that it came over the mid-Canada line and air stations. Therefore, it had to have supersonic speed from, really, the start out."[10] U.S. squadrons, being located further south, would have more time between warning of attack and engagement with the attacking force; they could, therefore, use a plane that gained speed more slowly.[11] For these reasons, the Canadian government of the day rejected, as unsuitable for Canada, the interceptors then under development in other countries which had been investigated before the decision was made to design and develop in Canada a successor for the CF–100.[12] That the peculiarities of the Canadian situation may have been exaggerated was later shown when the RCAF proved quite happy in 1961 to get the F–101's which it had looked at and rejected in an earlier day.[13] That there were peculiarities and that they were real and valid contributing factors to the decision to develop the Arrow remains, however, a fact.

Most important for understanding the equanimity with which the Canadian aircraft industry, air force, and government undertook this development program is the relatively small scope of the program envisaged at that time. Of the four aircraft components—airframe, engine, fire control system, and weapon—only the first was originally planned to be developed in Canada. By 1957, three of these were being developed in Canada and the fourth, the fire control system, with Canadian funds. The story of the gradual expansion of this program is a classic case of the difficulties which all but the greatest Powers have in the missile age in keeping up with armaments technology.[14]

The first element to be added to the program was the engine. Original plans envisaged the use of the Rolls-Royce RB–106 or the Wright J–67, and eventually settled on the latter.[15] Then,

10. Halpenny Committee *Proceedings* (May 20, 1960), p. 127.   11. *Ibid.*
12. *Debates* (1954), VI, 6438.   13. Interviews.
14. For a concise summary of this whole story, see Foulkes testimony, pp. 509, 510.
15. "The Avro CF–105 Arrow Rolls Out," *Interavia*, XII (*December*, 1957), 1261–63.

as the programme went along, the A. V. Roe Company on their own, through their subsidiary Orenda Engine Co., started to develop an engine. About eighteen months after this engine was developed out of their own funds, it showed considerable progress. At the same time the development of the American engine, which the Air Force had planned to buy, was slipping. So, after a great deal of discussion and heart searching, it was agreed to develop not only the airframe but the engine.[16]

Development of this engine remained behind that of the airframe, and arrangements were eventually made for the use in the first five pre-production models of the Pratt and Whitney J–75. Both of the Arrows which were test-flown used this engine, and at the time of the aircraft's cancellation it had never been mated with its intended, the Orenda PS–13 Iroquois.[17]

The fire control system was the next developmental project for which Canada assumed financial responsibility, although in this case the physical work was done by RCA in Camden, New Jersey. The contract was awarded to RCA because—according to the scant evidence available—the Hughes Aircraft Company, which enjoyed a considerable lead in the development of fire control systems, would not produce the forty-inch radar disc which the RCAF considered necessary for the sophisticated performance which they sought in the Arrow; it was too large for the U.S. interceptors then in development, and Hughes refused to develop it, presumably because of the shortness of the Canadian production run. The contract was then awarded to RCA, despite the reported opposition of Avro, which presumably preferred the inferior performance of a system using a smaller radar disc to the vagaries of development by a firm with much less experience in the field. If this was its position, it was to be vindicated, for developmental changes in this ASTRA fire control system were major causes of delay and rising costs of the aircraft as a whole; reportedly, between fifty and sixty changes in airframe design had to be made because of modifications in ASTRA. General Pearkes later admitted that by the end of 1958, ASTRA was still in an early stage of development, and that it had never been put into an Arrow.[18] Hughes, despite its early reluctance, eventually developed a comparable fire control system—after a U.S. requirement was created for it in the later models of the F–106— which was cheaper and more reliable than ASTRA. As will be seen,

16. Foulkes testimony, p. 509.
17. Halpenny Committee *Proceedings* (May 25, 1960), p. 144.
18. *Ibid.* (May 18, 1960), p. 97.

this system was considered for use in the Arrow in a last-minute attempt to save the aircraft by lowering its cost. According to one estimate, the $400 million spent on the development of the Arrow would have been reduced by some $100 million if this venture into the development of a fire control system had been forgone.[19]

Somewhat more complicated were the steps which led to Canada's undertaking the development of an air-to-air missile for use on the Arrow. Canadian money had already been expended on missile development before it was decided to acquire an American weapon instead. When responsibility was later assumed for the development of this weapon, it was more a question of a return to more ambitious parts of a familiar territory than, as in the case of the fire control system, of charting unknown parts. The Velvet Glove was the Canadian-designed air-to-air missile that originally was planned for use with the later models of the CF–100 and, presumably, the CF–105. It was undertaken in 1951 in response to a specific military requirement, but also with the objective of giving Canadian scientists, engineers and military planners some experience in what was rightly felt to be the increasingly important field of missilery.[20] But by the mid-1950's,

> it was discovered that, although "Velvet Glove" had developed satisfactorily toward meeting the original objective, the armament requirement for Canadian fighter aircraft had changed so much that the missile as originally envisaged would not have been satisfactory by the time of its final development. . . . As a result, the existing requirement for "Velvet Glove" was inadequate and it became necessary either to up-grade the requirement or to obtain a completely new weapon. Which of these two courses should be followed was not an easy choice to make, and there was by no means unanimous approval of the decision to abandon the "Velvet Glove" programme in favour of purchasing the licence rights to an American air-to-air missile, the "Sparrow." This, however, was the course which was finally adopted.[21]

But not for long. The Sparrow II, which was the model chosen, was the responsibility of the United States Navy at the time the RCAF settled on it; but, as it was not a high-priority item for the USN, budget constraints soon forced its abandonment, although its development was reportedly near completion.[22] The Canadians were

19. This paragraph is largely based on an article by Harold Greer in the *Globe and Mail* (Toronto), January 13, 1959.
20. Captain D. J. Goodspeed, *A History of the Defence Research Board of Canada* (Ottawa: Queen's Printer), pp. 127–33.
21. *Ibid.*, p. 132.
22. Halpenny Committee *Proceedings* (May 17, 1960), p. 87.

offered the choices of buying instead the Sparrow I or III, neither of which fully met RCAF specifications, of financing the development to completion in the U.S., or of completing themselves the development of Sparrow II. Since it was the view of the Minister of Defense Production, C. D. Howe, that as a result of Velvet Glove "a fully developed missile production complex has . . . been added to the defense production base,"[23] and since the second alternative was politically unacceptable, it was not surprising that the third course was adopted. This entailed setting up the facilities at Hamilton, Ontario, to carry on this development. The combination of these factors contributed to a critical delay in the plane's expected date of operational readiness at a time when strategic requirements were rapidly changing.[24]

This is the process by which Canada within two or three years had become responsible for the development not only of an airframe but also of an engine, fire control system and air-to-air missile. The cost increases which this entailed, and even the accompanying delays might have been bearable if there had been no change in the number of aircraft required. But other factors were operating here:

> Originally the Air Force had planned nine regular squadrons and eleven auxiliaries which were to get this type of aircraft. However, with the complexities and complications of operating jet aircraft, it was found that the auxiliary pilots could not reach a standard of training which could handle something like the 105, so the flying efforts of the reserve had to be curtailed and the requirements for the additional eleven squadrons worth of aircraft were cut out of the programme. Therefore, the programme shrank from the original 400 aircraft to something a little more than 100.[25]

These developments had a chastening effect on the ministers responsible for the Arrow's progress. "I can say that now we have started on a program of development that gives me the shudders,"

23. *Montreal Daily Star*, March 28, 1956.
24. According to one report, there was some confusion about whether the USN had actually dropped the Sparrow II development. Rumors to the effect that it had been dropped led Ottawa to make inquiries in Washington, where it was told that it had not been dropped. When plans then proceeded to manufacture the missile under license in Montreal, final word was received that it had in fact been dropped, thus making those plans irrelevant. The same sequence was later enacted in the case of the Lacrosse missile, though Canada did not decide to carry its development to completion. See Blair Fraser, "Next Question on Defense. Will the U.S.A. drop the Bomarc?," *Maclean's Magazine* (January 3, 1959).
25. Foulkes testimony, p. 509.

said C. D. Howe in June, 1955.[26] The Minister of National Defense, Ralph Campney, speaking shortly thereafter, went to some length to demonstrate his awareness of the risks involved:

> Once you are committed to one particular phase it is difficult to detach yourself even if you find that you have made a mistake. I think it is better to be careful and try to get the answer as far as you can before launching upon production, because these are extremely costly projects to develop.[27]

At about the same time, the program began to be attacked by critics outside the government, both on the grounds that it was too expensive and that it would be obsolescent by the time it would be completed.[28] The Minister, however, retained his basic confidence: "From what I have seen so far we have every reason to expect—and that is all I can say at the moment—that the CF–105 project will be a success."[29] It may be thought that such statements, being formal statements of policy, did not necessarily reflect the government's true judgment of the Arrow's prospects. It is true that during the last part of its life, the St. Laurent government adopted the policy of reviewing the program every six months to see whether it should be continued.[30] But there is better evidence that before 1957 it was hardly questioned that the Arrow would eventually be put into production. First, tooling-up for production was carried on at the Avro plant in Malton concurrently with the development; this practice was to avoid the one- to two-year delay which would have been caused if development were completed before tooling-up began, as well as to reduce overall unit costs. Such a policy assumed the eventual production of the aircraft; otherwise, far from reducing costs, it would merely increase development costs without producing compensating savings elsewhere.[31] Secondly, far from keeping a close watch on development costs of the Arrow complex, before the latter part of 1957 no one knew—though one might have made a shrewd guess—what those costs were. The accounting system then in use reflected the piecemeal way in which the program had grown, and did not provide figures on the total cost of all four components. The implied assumption was that there was little danger that the total costs would exceed Canada's means. Only in 1957–58 was a

26. *Debates* (1955), V, 5380.   27. *Ibid.*, VI, 6090.
28. Simonds, "Canada's Defense Blunders." Other critics called for the establishment of a parliamentary defense committee to investigate Simond's charges, but the government declined. See *Debates* (1957–58), II, 1205.
29. *Debates* (1956), VI, 6124.   30. *Ibid.* (1959), II, 1499.
31. *Christian Science Monitor* (May 2, 1958).

system devised to determine accurately the total cost of the Arrow's development.[32] This factor helps to explain the discrepancies in estimates of the Arrow's cost which were made. In 1955, the expected cost was $2.6 million each.[33] On March 30, 1957, the Minister of National Defense estimated that the aircraft would cost $2 million each.[34] Later in the same year, the Government was asked about rumors that the plane would cost $8 million each.[35] In early 1958, an official spokesman estimated that the first thirty-seven preproduction models would cost $6.1 million each, although if the plane were put into production, subsequent units would cost less.[36] In July, 1958, General Pearkes set the estimate at $4.5 million per aircraft.[37] Part of this vagueness was undoubtedly attributable to the tendency—which lived on far into the period of the Arrow's post-mortem—to confuse "fly-away" costs, which disregarded development expenses, with average unit costs, which did include such expenses. This technique, though sometimes it was doubtlessly genuine confusion, could be used to support a pro-production or pro-cancellation position by exaggerating or underestimating the airplane's cost. But the confusion also had a real basis, since, until the new accounting system was instituted, all estimates involved a certain amount of guesswork.

This obscurity about costs, which allowed ministers to evade the hard fact of cost escalation, provides a major explanation for one of the most curious features of the whole Arrow episode: the delay between the cost increases of 1955–56 and the government's early awareness of them, and the first attempt to reduce them late in 1958. There was also another, political reason for the delay. The St. Laurent government did not want to grasp this nettle so soon before the general election of June, 1957. Along with NORAD, it was postponed in the expectation that it would be dealt with shortly after the election.[38] After the election resulted in the unexpected change of government, there was another reason for postponement: the Diefenbaker government did not have a majority in the House, and planned from the beginning to hold an early election. In order to avoid dealing with so sensitive a matter during this period, it therefore took early action to continue the Arrow's development for one year beyond October, 1957; it was during this year that costs would increase even more rapidly than before.[39]

32. Jones, p. 86; Interviews.
34. *Ibid.* (1957), III, 2914.
36. *Ibid.* (1958), I, 820.
38. Foulkes testimony, p. 509.

33. *Debates* (1959), II, 1279.
35. *Ibid.* (1957–58), II, 1911.
37. *Ibid.* (1959), II, 1292.
39. *Debates* (1957–58), I, 511; interviews.

The decision could not, however, be postponed indefinitely, as both cost and strategic factors were militating for change. The latter, represented by Soviet ICBM launchings as early as August, 1957, and by the launching of Sputnik I on October 4 (ominously the same day that the Arrow was first shown to the public) were publicly recognized by both the Prime Minister and the Minister of National Defense in November, only a month after the announcement had been made of the postponement of a decision on the Arrow. Mr. Diefenbaker stressed the intensification of the general review of defense policy which would occur as a result of the Sputnik launching; and General Pearkes emphasized the pointlessness of remaining committed to the acquisition of obsolete weapons.[40] The question, of course, was whether the introduction of intercontinental rockets into the Soviet forces rendered obsolete such anti-bomber weapons as the Arrow. Whatever the answer to this question, the preponderant majority which Mr. Diefenbaker enjoyed in the House of Commons after the election of March 31, 1958, removed any basis for further delaying the decision.

The fact that the costs of the Arrow were rising sharply during 1957 and 1958 was known to the public in only an obscure way.[41] When Mr. Diefenbaker revealed in his statement of September 23, 1958, that it would cost $12.5 million each to produce 100 Arrows, it was a sobering revelation.[42] Even in an expanding budget, such costs would have been a strain. According to one estimate, the defense budget would have had to be increased by 30 per cent to acquire both the Arrow and the SAGE–Bomarc system.[43] But the Diefenbaker government had come into office pledging reduced expenditures and more nearly balanced budgets, not the reverse; the pressure to hold the line, if not reduce, defense spending thus bore

40. *Globe and Mail* (Toronto), November 5, 1957.
41. See James Eayrs, *Northern Approaches: Canada and the Search for Peace*, pp. 21, 22. The article originally appeared in the September, 1958 issue of the *Canadian Forum* under the title, "I Shot an Arrow Into the Air . . . ."
42. See Appendix II. Since this figure was often used in the polemics which followed, it is well to be clear about what it, and the other commonly mentioned figure of $7.8 million per plane, represented. It represented neither the "fly-away" cost, including production but not development costs, nor the average total cost, including both development and production costs, but rather the cost per plane of carrying the program forward from September 1, 1958, until 100 aircraft had been produced. It thus included the cost of completing development, producing 100 aircraft, and buying the necessary ground handling equipment, parts and weapons. The $7.8 million figure covered the same items for the case in which the Falcon missile and MA–1 fire control system would be substituted for ASTRA and Sparrow II. See Halpenny Committee *Proceedings* (May 20, 1960), pp. 136, 37.
43. *Financial Post*, October 4, 1958.

directly on the Arrow program. There were two ways to reduce the burden of these costs to Canada. The first was to increase the number of aircraft produced, and therefore achieve cheaper unit costs.[44] The second was to try to lower the cost by lowering the specifications that had been demanded, or by substituting less costly components than those being developed in Canada.

The former method was tried first. One way to increase the production run would have been to use the Arrow not only for the RCAF's NORAD squadrons but also for the Canadian Number One Air Division in Europe which, anyway, would soon be due for re-equipment.[45] The requirements of such a possibility had not been explicitly considered in setting specifications for the Arrow, but within the Canadian military the option of using the Arrow Mark II (the version with the Iroquois engine) in Europe was never excluded.[46] Apparently, the possibility was never seriously considered on the ministerial level.[47] One reason was the uncertainty then surrounding the future of Canadian airmen in Europe.[48] Another was the absence in Europe of the semi-automatic ground environment which was needed to bring the Arrow to its full effectiveness, whether or not there was a necessity for it. Another was that such dual use of the aircraft would still not have made its production economical, in the absence of sales to other countries.

Therefore it was towards the conclusion of such sales that the Diefenbaker government, strengthened by its March, 1958, electoral victory, turned. An attempt was made to interest Britain in the Arrow, but no progress was made in this direction.[49] Far from being interested in buying a Canadian plane, the British were interested, even at that date, in having Canada settle on the TSR–2 which they were developing.[50] Therefore, the Arrow's future depended on sales to the U.S. Air Force.

In reviewing the history of this sales effort, it is well to be mindful of certain questions which underlay the polemics that followed the Arrow's cancellation; the answers to them will appear in the

44. Halpenny Committee *Proceedings* (May 20, 1960), pp. 136, 137. In the case of the CF–100, the first seventy aircraft off the production line cost $1.089 million each, the last 208 only $535,000 each; thus a reduction of about 50% in unit costs was achieved.
45. See below, Chapter V.   46. Interviews.
47. *Debates* (1959), V, 5401; and *Globe and Mail* (Toronto), December 16, 1958.
48. See below, Chapter V.
49. Halpenny Committee *Proceedings* (May 18, 1960), pp. 98, 99.
50. Interviews.

following account. Was there ever a serious possibility that the USAF might buy the Arrow for its own use? If so, why did it not do so? If not, why did Canadians continue for so long seriously to entertain this prospect? Were the Americans responsible in any other way for the predicament in which the Canadian government, Air Force, and aircraft industry now found themselves?

This problem of selling aircraft to the U.S. did not arise in 1957, nor even with the Arrow. At a time when the Diefenbaker government was still trying to interest the U.S. in the Arrow, Mr. Pearson recalled his experiences of an earlier day:

> I know also from my own experience in the past that when we tried to get the United States interested in the CF–100 some years ago, at a time when the CF–100 was admitted in Washington to be certainly the best all-weather fighter on this continent, we made no progress at all. The aircraft industry down there was not going to allow any interference with its own right to produce its own aircraft for its own government. I believe the minister will be having the same trouble with the CF–105.[51]

Mr. Pearson's experiences were not limited to the CF–100, for the St. Laurent government, of which he was a member, had considered involving the U.S. in the development of the Arrow as early as November, 1955:

> Ministers deferred consideration of a proposal to proceed with the CF–105 development program pending inquiries to be made by the Minister of National Defence of the United States, secretary of war, as to the possibility of United States sharing in or taking over the whole program. . . . The Minister of National Defence proceeded to Washington and had discussions with the U.S. secretary of air [at that time Donald Quarles]. While no record is available of these discussions, it is understood that the United States secretary of air expressed some concern as to the possibility of the Canadian government not proceeding with this aircraft, as they did not expect anything to appear in the U.S. development field to take the place of the CF–105 to meet requirements in Canada. However, it is believed that no commitment was received from the United States secretary of air that the United States would purchase any of these aircraft for their own use.[52]

51. *Debates* (1958), III, 3230.
52. Halpenny Committee *Proceedings* (May 18, 1960), pp. 98, 99. The quotation was read from a government memorandum and Gen. Pearkes was later criticized for the indiscretion of making public what was constitutionally and traditionally confidential information. That he went to such lengths—although the error was perhaps partly one of ignorance—suggests the importance that was attached to demonstrating that the government had been encouraged by the U.S. to develop the Arrow.

This reaction was interpreted by Campney as "encouragement to go ahead."[53] However enthusiastic might have been the comments of American airmen to their Canadian *confrères* about what was admittedly an exciting, sophisticated aircraft, this "encouragement" meant little in terms of material help. No U.S. money went into the development of the Arrow,[54] although there were instances both before and after the Arrow in which such assistance was rendered when the USAF was interested in a particular project. In 1955, it took over the costs for development by Avro of a VTOL aircraft, after the Canadian government had abandoned it.[55] In the later case of the Bomarc, part of the purchase and installation costs were borne by the U.S. in its eagerness to get these weapons into operation. After it became apparent that the costs of the Arrow's development were becoming excessive, the Canadians proposed to the USAF that it take over the Arrow project in its entirety; this proposal was declined.[56] Nor was there a U.S. undertaking to assist in the development of a fire control system, or to continue to completion the development of Sparrow II in response to the Canadian interest; and there is no evidence that such an undertaking was sought.[57] U.S. participation in the development of Arrow was limited to the provision on commercial terms of such parts as had to be bought in the U.S., and the loan of a B-47 in which to test the Orenda Iroquois engine.[58]

There were even some suggestions that the U.S. not only had not assisted the Canadian development effort but had contributed to its difficulties by withholding information. In particular, it was alleged that Canadians had learned only in 1955 or 1956, "perhaps for the first time,"[59] that the U.S. was developing, in the form of the F-106, an aircraft competitive with the Arrow. The qualification "perhaps" is important in this case. In view of the close liaison between the two air forces and the absence of a plausible American motive for withholding the information, the conclusion seems inescapable that Canadian officials who were ignorant of U.S. aircraft

53. *Debates* (1959), II, 1279.
54. Halpenny Committee *Proceedings* (May 18, 1960), p. 99.
55. *Globe and Mail* (Toronto), August 23, 1955.   56. Interviews.
57. There was a report that the USAF offered to provide without charge the Hughes fire control system adopted by the Canadians after the abandonment of ASTRA, and that the Canadian government declined. Whether or not the report is true, the Arrow was practically dead at this point anyway; and the minor cost reduction which this would have permitted would not have been enough to save it. See the *Globe and Mail* (Toronto), January 13, 1957.
58. *Ibid.*, February 9, 1956.   59. *Debates* (1959), II, 1279.

development programs did not want to know or were not willing to make the effort to find out. Nevertheless the statement assumed some political import: a CCF spokesman, accepting as a fact that there had been such a denial of information, criticized such "callous disregard for Canada" by the U.S.[60]

These factors are mentioned in explanation of the rather curious misunderstanding which arose when Canada intensified its efforts to sell the Arrow to the U.S. in 1958. These efforts had awaited the Arrow's first flight test, which had been postponed several times; when it finally took place successfully on March 25, 1958, the sales effort proceeded.[61] The performance of the Arrow in these tests was one of the strong points of the Canadian negotiators. It had, on one flight, reached a speed of 1000 miles per hour in a climb at 50,000 feet.[62] In its Mark II model, it was expected to have no difficulty in breaking the world speed record, then set at 1404 miles per hour.[63] It was thus expected to be the best interceptor available for North American defense between its expected appearance in late 1961 and that of the American F-108 some years later.[64] It was argued that integration of defense production went with integration of operational forces, and therefore that in return for consenting in NORAD to the latter, Canada had the right to expect that the U.S. would not hesitate to order superior Canadian military goods, when they were performing needed roles.[65] The Arrow, it was felt, demonstrated such superiority. Finally, it was felt that the expressions of interest in the plane by American airmen had carried the strong implication that a purchase for the USAF would be seriously considered.[66]

Misunderstanding arose, because there is no evidence that any such serious intention among high-level personnel on the American side had ever existed. It was true that there had been much interest in the Arrow's development in the USAF, but this had largely been a "state-of-the-art" interest, rather than a desire to purchase the aircraft for USAF use.[67] This misunderstanding became apparent at a meeting in Washington between delegations led by the two ministers of defense, McElroy and Pearkes, in August, 1958. The Americans were interested at this time in their own projects, namely in gaining Canadian support for a new air defense package to include

60. *Ibid.*, p. 1562.   61. *Ibid.*, p. 1279.
62. *Times* (London), October 10, 1958.
63. *Globe and Mail* (Toronto), November 12, 1958.
64. *Debates* (1959), V, 5387.   65. *Ibid.*, II, 1294.
66. Interviews.   67. Interviews.

Bomarc squadrons, SAGE centers and gap-filler radars. In terms of development, they were interested in pressing ahead with work on the F–108. Since the Canadians came to the meeting largely to get help or an order for the Arrow, there was some talking at cross-purposes. The Canadians were told that no such help would be forthcoming, and some members of the American delegation, puzzled at the ardor of the Canadian sales pitch, even questioned the desirability of the Canadians' acquiring a new interceptor; the important thing was the early introduction of Bomarc squadrons into the air defenses. The sting of these remarks did not affect the immediate decisions, but it eventually made it politically more difficult for a Canadian government to buy, as its new interceptor, an American aircraft.[68]

The one year lease on life given to Arrow by the Conservative government expired in October, and after this meeting it began to seem clear that the impending decision could only be negative. The decision was finally announced by Mr. Diefenbaker on September 23 in a statement to the press as Parliament had been prorogued some two weeks before.

This September 23 statement is one of the most important, if one of the most confused and disingenuous, that was made on the subject of defense during the tenure of the Diefenbaker government. It was not limited to the subject of the Arrow's future, but was rather a more general statement on air defense policy. The decisions announced were as follows: (1) The Arrow was not put into production, but its development was to be continued for another six months, after which there would be another review; (2) the ASTRA and Sparrow systems were to be immediately discontinued, and modifications to be made in the Arrow to permit the use of a Hughes fire control system and Falcon missile; (3) new air defense equipment, consisting of Bomarcs, SAGE, and gap-filler radars were to be introduced into Canada; (4) production-sharing arrangements were to be negotiated with the U.S. to guarantee to Canadian industry an equitable share of the increasingly integrated programs of development and production of equipment for North American defense.[69]

The confusion and disingenuousness applied not to these decisions but to the justifications given for them. Confusion stemmed from the government's attempt to represent the changes as the results of "the rapid development that has taken place during the past year

68. Interviews; and *Debates* (1959), II, 1280, 1281.
69. See Appendix II.

in missiles for both defence and attack."[70] Talk of this development, or of the "rapid strides being made in missiles by both the USA and the USSR,"[71] could have referred to ICBM development or to improvements in air defense missiles. The fact that the statement was made in 1958, and the reference to "revolutionary changes," make it clear that the former was meant. But this was not spelled out in the statement; it would have undermined the logic of the decision to place Bomarc squadrons in Canada, since the Bomarc is exclusively an anti-bomber (more correctly, anti-air-breathing projectile) weapon, and the Arrow was not being produced on the grounds that the bomber threat was being replaced by that of ICBM's. The result was a masterpiece of vagueness. The impression was left that Canada's air defenses were being modernized, since they were to get missiles instead of manned interceptors; moreover, a difficult decision—to hold-up on the Arrow—was justified in terms of strategic necessity. But by refraining from spelling out that strategic argument—the emergence of ICBM's and consequent obsolescence of anti-bomber defenses—the government concealed the fact that the same argument undermined the basis for its Bomarc decision. There was, in fact, a perfectly legitimate way to reconcile the two decisions. The introduction of ICBM's did not eliminate, but only reduced in relative importance, the threat from manned bombers. Some defense against the latter would continue to be needed, if only to complicate the task of Soviet military planners. But being relatively less important, such defenses could not claim justifiably the resources involved in such sophisticated hardware as the Arrow. The considerably cheaper Bomarc might still be worth the money to Canada, which did not have to bear the cost for its development. It is remarkable that this argument was not made by government supporters of the decision. The failure to do so may be explained in part by the comparative unfamiliarity of the Canadian attentive public with such "cost-effectiveness" arguments. The curious reluctance of government spokesmen throughout this episode to admit that the Arrow was too costly for Canada cannot be explained in this way only. A more basic explanation will be offered below.

The disingenuousness of the government's statement consisted partly in its attempt to associate its military advisers with its attempt to represent the policy changes as dictated by strategic factors. References to "detailed advice from its military experts," "the prepon-

70 *Ibid.*   71. *Ibid.*

derance of expert opinion," and "opinions of military and other experts" tended to conceal the fact that the statement—as one can discern from reading it—was prepared by ministers without the presence of military advisers. Indeed, the Chiefs of Staff Committee had explicitly opposed the coupling of the Bomarc and Arrow announcements, as well as the emphasis on strategic, rather than economic, determinants of the decisions.[72] In discussing and evaluating these determinants, it is advisable to distinguish between the judgment given to the government by its military advisers, and the political use to which this advice was put. The relevance of this distinction will be discussed later; it is sufficient now to note its existence.

More excusable, or at least understandable, was the disingenuous reason given for continuing development of the Arrow for an additional six months. The desire to ease the problem of adjustment for the industry, to find a way to keep in Canadian employment some of the technical personnel whose jobs would be affected, and the wish to avoid worsening the problem of winter unemployment were legitimate motives for such a continuation; undoubtedly there was also a remote hope that the cost reductions made possible by the introduction of new fire control and weapon systems might save the aircraft after all. It was perhaps easier to justify the continuation, however, on the added ground that the international outlook was "uncertain and tense." No explanation was offered of how this was related to the development of the Arrow, which could not, in the short run, be brought to bear on any international situation. Presumably the argument, which, it was said later explicitly referred to the Far East situation, had reference to the Korean experience, when Canadian aircraft production had been sorely needed. The implication ran that these production facilities should not be dismantled lest a similar occurrence might arise again.[73] That such an occasion should occur in 1958 seemed remote, however; and the government never justified its reasoning by arguing that this was not the case.

As might be expected from the foregoing, the interpretations placed upon the Prime Minister's statement varied considerably. The *New York Times* dispatch portrayed the decision as one to "scrap" the Arrow.[74] General Guy Simonds, a former Chief of the

72. Interviews.
73. Halpenny Committee *Proceedings* (May 20, 1960), p. 137.
74. September 28, 1958, p. 29.

General Staff who had long opposed Canadian development of the Arrow[75] was quoted as saying "the government seemed to leave little doubt that it has merely delayed until next March final cancellation of the supersonic Arrow interceptor program."[76] On the other hand, a strong case could be made that cancellation was not inevitable. The Conservative *Globe and Mail*, in giving its approval to the September decision, held that production might be undertaken in the spring,[77] and added, for good measure, "we may be sure the Canadian government has not the slightest intention of letting the first-rate Avro team of scientists and technicians be dissipated."[78] The A. V. Roe Company spokesmen expressed confidence, as they had every tactical reason to do, that the aircraft would eventually be put into production.[79] More authoritative than statements of Avro personnel were those of the Defense Minister. On January 23, 1958, General Pearkes said that the Arrow's future depended "entirely" on the nature of the threat, not on its cost.[80] On November 25, he had said that manned interceptors would continue to be needed in the foreseeable future[81]—thereby adding his voice to a chorus which included the commander of NORAD, his deputy, and at least three members of the U.S. Joint Chiefs of Staff.[82] The conclusion of this syllogism seemed to be that the Arrow would be produced.

Better evidence than such statements that the government had not completely ruled out the possibility of producing Arrow is the continuing effort that was made to sell the aircraft to the U.S. A second important meeting between General Pearkes and Secretary McElroy took place in Paris in December, where both were attending a NATO ministerial meeting. Cost estimates of the aircraft had by this time been reduced to $7.8 million each to produce 100, and $3.75 million fly-away cost; this reduction had been achieved by the replacement of the ASTRA and Sparrow II systems by the Hughes MA–1 fire control system and Falcon missile.[83] Once again, however, the effort was unsuccessful; as was reported at the time, Pearkes was told that there would be no U.S. order even if substantial cost reductions were made in the Arrow.[84] The question is thus

75. Simonds, "Canada's Defence Blunders."
76. *Winnipeg Free Press*, September 24, 1958.
77. September 23, 1958.   78. September 25, 1958.
79. *Globe and Mail* (Toronto), September 25, 1958; and the *Times* (London) October 10, 1958.
80. *Debates* (1957–58), IV, 3674.   81. Cited in *Debates* (1959), II, 1307.
82. Halpenny Committee *Proceedings* (May 20, 1960), p. 126.
83. *Ibid.*, p. 136 and (May 25, 1960), pp. 144, 45.
84. Interviews; *Globe and Mail* (Toronto), December 16, 1958.

raised: if the U.S. did not refrain for economic reasons from making this purchase so much desired by its ally, and if senior military advisers were convinced of the continuing need for manned interceptors, why was the purchase not made? Was it merely the pervasive influence of the American aircraft industry which, according to Mr. Pearson, had prevented a purchase of CF-100's?[85] In fact, the reasons were more numerous, and could be arranged in order of immediacy. First in such an ordering would be technical reservations about the plane's performance. There was, among American aeronautical engineers who assessed it, no assurance that the problems of fire control had been solved; at the time of its eventual cancellation, no contract had been signed with Hughes for the MA-1 system; only estimates had been made. Also, the Arrow's range was somewhat limited for use by the U.S. Although the introduction of the Hughes systems to replace ASTRA and Sparrow resulted in some saving of space which made more room for fuel and thus increased this range, the 400-odd miles which the Arrow could fly at supersonic speeds was somewhat short for aircraft leaving from American bases.[86] The next most immediate factor was strategic. This was the period of the "missile gap," and air defense planners were hard-put to defend the proportion of resources already allocated to them against the new claims of ICBM development and ABM research. These pressures led to the cancellation of two models of the U.S. aircraft most similar to the Arrow, the F-106 models "C" and "D,"[87] and, eventually, to the cancellation of the F-108 then in development. As Canadian military advisers recognized, any chance of selling the Arrow to the U.S. depended on having it ready two years earlier. In these circumstances, the less immediate factors of the Arrow's costliness and the pressures of the U.S. aircraft industry simply did not come to bear on the decision, although either one might have been sufficient to prevent the purchase. The question remains whether American officials ever exaggerated to their Canadian colleagues the likelihood of such a purchase. While no firm answer to this question can be given as yet, there is no visible evi-

85. See above, p. 71. In fact, the U.S. *did* purchase some CF-100's, although perhaps not as many as Canadians would have liked. See Halpenny Committee *Proceedings* (May 18, 1960), p. 99.

86. *Ibid.*, p. 106. Ironically, the policy of Canadian governments of not allowing U.S. fighter bases on Canadian soil contributed to the cogency of this U.S. reasoning for not buying the Arrow, since otherwise such a long-range requirement would not have existed.

87. As Diefenbaker did not hesitate to point out to illustrate his difficulties in selling the Arrow to the U.S. *Debates* (1959), II, 1276.

dence that anyone in the upper levels ever held out such a prospect.[88]

Having again received this negative verdict from the U.S., the government now proceeded to act hastily. On February 20, the Prime Minister announced in the House that he was terminating as of that date—he had already sent the notice by telegram—all contracts for work on the Arrow.[89] Although the contract with A. V. Roe did not require the giving of notice[90] and assurance was given that "all outstanding commitments will of course be settled equitably,"[91] the company and its workers responded angrily; the former, whether out of pique or as part of a deliberate effort to pressure the government into providing alternative projects for the aircraft industry, immediately fired some 14,000 employees who were directly involved in the Arrow project.[92] The company and government each attempted to blame the other for the manner of cancellation: the government held that there had been, in effect, five months' notice, since the Prime Minister's statement of September 23 had been tantamount to a notice to cancel; the company contested this interpretation, and claimed to have been caught without warning. In fact, there was blame enough for all. It was true, as the company alleged, that the September 23 statement was by no means so clear as the government now maintained; on the other hand, in its effort to pressure the government into producing the Arrow, A. V. Roe had not used the interim period to plan for an orderly adjustment but had held out unrealistic hopes and alternatives.[93] A bitter curtain was brought down on the whole affair when the government had scrapped all thirty-seven pre-production models of the Arrow, including two which had already flown and which some had hoped would be allowed to compete for the world's speed record.[94]

The impact in Canada of the Arrow's cancellation was enormous. It was estimated that in addition to the 14,000 Avro employees whose jobs were eliminated, about an equal number in associated work was affected.[95] The Arrow was the largest project of the Canadian aircraft industry. Its cancellation affected not only A. V. Roe but also Canadair, the second of Canada's two largest aircraft

88. This paragraph is based largely on interviews.
89. *Debates* (1959), II, 1221.
90. Halpenny Committee *Proceedings* (May 20, 1960), pp. 122–24.
91. *Debates* (1959), II, 1221.   92. Newman, p. 348.
93. See the account in Eayrs, *Northern Approaches: Canada and the Search for Peace*, pp. 26, 27.
94. *Debates* (1959), V, 5389; Newman, p. 348.
95. *New York Times*, September 28, 1958, p. 29.

firms (which had had the contract for Sparrow II), and some 650 sub-contractors.[96] Newspapers were filled with protests and trade unions threatened a march on Ottawa.[97] *Maclean's Magazine,* in an editorial that became quite controversial, asked rhetorically "Is Canada itself obsolete as a military nation?" and answered with a resounding "yes."[98] One political journalist made the similarly extreme judgment that "it may not be an exaggeration to say that our position as one of the world's leading Middle Powers may have been prejudiced."[99] The discussion remained so lively that one observer was able to write, several months later, that "never in peacetime history has defence been so actively discussed by the average Canadian."[100] Happily, such consternation was not completely unrelieved. The Conservative Toronto *Telegram,* with considerable originality, called the decision "an exercise of independence by Canada without precedent in the history of our military alliance with the United States."[101]

The political implications of the action were magnified because it gave the appearance of increasing dependence on the U.S. The shadow Minister of Defense, Mr. Hellyer, said that the cancellation of what he claimed was authoritatively acknowledged as the "best manned interceptor available to the western world" would deprive Canada of its leverage within NORAD.[102] He complained that "as early as Saturday morning there were in Toronto representatives of United States aircraft manufacturing concerns ready and waiting. They telephoned our scientific personnel offering to engage them and take them south of the border."[103] Mr. Pearson, referring to the fact that the U.S. was going to share the costs of putting Bomarcs in Canada, asked if Canada was, for the first time, accepting mutual aid and wondered whether U.S. willingness to pay these costs was increased by the prospect of tying Canada more closely to the U.S. defense industry.[104] In fact, the decision did not significantly change Canada's military dependence on the U.S., for even the hundred Arrows then being contemplated were too few to avoid relying on U.S. interceptors for the defense of the bulk of Canadian air space.

96. *Globe and Mail* (Toronto), April 18, 1958; *Montreal Daily Star,* December 18, 1957.
97. *Economist,* CXC (February 28, 1959), 790, 91.
98. March 28, 1959, p. 4.
99. *Halifax Chronicle Herald,* February 25, 1959.
100. *Financial Post,* November 7, 1959.
101. Cited in *Debates* (1959), II, 1550.   102. *Ibid.,* V, 5387, 5390.
103. *Ibid.,* II, 1274.   104. *Ibid.,* p. 1293.

It was notable that the opposition did not criticize the substance of the Arrow decision, as opposed to the manner in which it was executed, although Hellyer later suggested, when it no longer cost anything to do so, that a limited number of the aircraft should have been produced.[105]

The post-mortem conducted over the Arrow decision was one of the main subjects of concern during the 1959 parliamentary session and the proceedings of the Special Committee on Defense Expenditures which was set up in 1960. In addition to reviewing the facts of the case, the debates in both these instances were concerned with determining the extent to which the decision had been based on strategic or economic factors. In discussing this issue, two distinct questions must be put: (1) How cogent were the reasons given by the government for its decision? (2) Did the government, in fact, base its decisions on the publicly-given reasons and, if not, why the discrepancy?

The consistent position of the Prime Minister and, by and large, of other government spokesmen, was that the decision was based on strategic and not economic grounds. The following passage in his February 20 announcement is characteristic:

> By the middle of 1962 the threat from the intercontinental ballistic missile will undoubtedly be greatly enhanced in numbers, size and accuracy, and the I.C.B.M. threat may be supplemented by submarine-launched missiles. By the middle sixties the missile seems likely to be the major threat and the long range bomber relegated to supplementing the major attack by these missiles. It would be only in this period, namely after mid-1962, that the CF–105 could be fully operational in the Royal Canadian Air Force.[106]

There was a strong inference in this analysis that the days of the manned interceptor in the RCAF were numbered, although, in characteristic fashion, it was not made explicit. This was strongly suggested in such phrases as that which questioned "if in fact such [interceptor] aircraft will be required at all in the 1960's."[107] Moreover, it followed logically from the government's contentions that the Arrow was cancelled not because it was too costly or technically inadequate but because of changing requirements for manned aircraft.

To be sure, this line was not consistently followed by all government spokesmen. In particular, General Pearkes—the minister who

105. Interview with Paul Hellyer. Text in *Windsor Star*, May 29, 1964.
106. See Appendix III.   107. See Appendix II.

was perhaps most accessible and most receptive to the military point of view—lapsed into contrary evaluations of the bomber threat and of the relative importance of strategic and economic factors. On July 4 and November 25, 1958, he asserted that there was a continuing threat from the manned bomber and an attendant need for manned interceptors.[108] Similarly, he sometimes broke party ranks in discussing the role played by costs: "All I can say . . . is that the cost of $12½ million for an aircraft, or even, if the alternative system of fire control had been introduced, of $7,800,000 was just a price tag which was too high to be included in the defence budgets of those days."[109] But at the critical times he, too, upheld the Diefenbaker version. For example, when asked specifically if the Arrow cancellation had been based mainly on economic grounds, he replied "I certainly would not say that."[110] He defended Mr. Khrushchev's stated view that ICBM's made the manned bomber obsolete, and even offered that view as evidence for the argument.[111] He held that by the time the Arrow would have been in operational use (1962) the manned bomber threat would "hardly exist."[112]

It is undeniable that in 1958 and 1959 the relative threats from ICBM's and manned bombers were changing, and reasonable men could differ about the rate and extent of this change, and consequently about the extent to which bomber defenses were desirable. But the argument that by the early or mid-1960's the need for manned interceptors would disappear exceeded the bounds of legitimate disagreement. First, there was an overwhelming body of testimony that bombers would still be in use then,[113] and that interceptors would be needed to counter this threat. Anti-aircraft missiles alone were not sufficient to cover the expanse involved. Second, however effective such missiles might become, so long as the early warning networks continued to be operated, there would be a need for manned interceptors to identify the numerous unidentified aircraft which appeared every day on the radar scopes.

The important point to make, however, is not that the arguments

108. *Debates* (1959), II, 1289.
109. Halpenny Committee *Proceedings* (May 17, 1960), p. 90.
110. *Debates* (1959), II, 1284.
111. *Ibid.*, p. 1280; Halpenny Committee *Proceedings* (May 20, 1960), pp. 130, 31. For an analysis made in 1958 of this Khrushchev statement, see Raymond L. Garthoff, *Soviet Strategy in the Missile Age* (New York: Praeger, 1958), pp. 222, 23. In a revised edition published in 1962 the author saw no need to change this evaluation.
112. *Debates* (1959), II, 1280.
113. See above, p. 97; Garthoff, pp. 222, 23.

lacked cogency but that they were not, in fact, the reasons for the decision. First, the evidence for this is that they were not consistent with the advice tendered the government by the Chiefs of Staff Committee. This committee never deviated from the view that some interceptor would be needed even if Arrow were not produced. The issue to them was clearly an economic one. Further, they were strongly inclined to prefer an American interceptor which could be procured more cheaply and therefore leave more funds for other defense programs; but it was recognized as a governmental responsibility to decide whether the Arrow was worth the cost, when political and prestige factors were added in.

> The Chiefs of Staff came to the conclusion that it did not make military sense to purchase aircraft at a cost of $8 million each when we could maintain aircraft with similar performance from the end of an American production line at something about $2 million. Furthermore, we could not see from where the funds were coming to finish the production of the Arrow.[114]

Second, as has already been pointed out, such arguments would have undermined the basis for the decision to install two Bomarc squadrons in Canada, since these squadrons were not scheduled to be ready until 1961; by that time, according to these arguments, the threat from manned bombers would "hardly exist." Clearly such reasoning was not seriously believed, however earnestly it may have been proferred publicly. If any doubt of this remained, it should have been removed when General Pearkes, at a later time and in a more detached atmosphere, explained the real basis for the decision:

> So the question is, how much money are we justified in spending in making an effort to defend this country against the possibility of a bomber attack? We were faced with that decision a couple of years ago when, owing to the heavy expense involved in producing and completing the development of what would have been a superb interceptor, the CF–105, had the production been completed, we decided that the cost was too high and we did not feel we were then justified in spending that amount of money on this particular weapon to defend the country against the bomber. At that time we felt justified in deciding that we should spend a much smaller amount of money on joining in the chain of ground to air missile bases which the United States was developing for the protection of their SAC bomber bases and for the protection of the main centres of industry in the northeast portion of the United States and Canada. I refer to the Bomarc ground to air missile.[115]

114. Foulkes testimony, p. 510.   115. *Debates* (1960), VII, 7649.

The question which naturally arises, therefore, is why such arguments were employed. They were clearly counterproductive. First, some valuable political capital was expended in an unsuccessful attempt to get U.S. officials to say that the Arrow would have been obsolete by the time it was operational and that this was the reason for their refusal to buy it.[116] Second, it made the decision to acquire Bomarcs appear ridiculous and impossible to defend. Third, it inhibited the government's ability to heed the future advice of the Chiefs of Staff Committee, since the known view of that committee that a new interceptor would be needed would now be extremely difficult politically to put into effect.

All of this could have been avoided, and a considerable saving achieved of mental gymnastics needed to defend contradictory arguments, by a frank admission of the fact that the Arrow was cancelled because it was too expensive for Canada to buy. Such an admission, however, required the recognition, psychologically and politically difficult, that Canada could no longer pay the price which advancing technology exacted to remain a producer of the more sophisticated military equipment. Unwilling to recognize the loss of power and prestige involved, the politically-sensitive Diefenbaker government obscured the issue. This made the future adjustment more difficult and lengthy without rendering it less painful.

THE BOEING BOMARC

Coming immediately after the Arrow controversy was another case which was politically explosive—that of the Bomarc anti-aircraft missile. A better choice to feed controversy could hardly have been designed. It was already a questionable weapon on technical grounds; the government's decision to represent it as a substitute for the Arrow involved it in that controversy; it was soon to become an inter-service and political issue in the U.S., thereby involving these factors in Canadian military planning and politics; and by virtue of its warhead, it raised the sensitive nuclear issue. How did such a weapon come to be chosen for use by Canadian forces?

The development of the weapon which became Bomarc was started in 1950; the concept grew out of work which had been going on since 1945 at the University of Michigan's Willow Run Research Center and at Boeing. (The acronym is composed of BO from Boeing and MARC from Michigan Aeronautical Research Center.) From

116. Interviews.

the beginning, it was designed to operate on an area, not point, basis, and to do so together with supersonic interceptors in a ground environment system which was being simultaneously developed and which later became known as the Semi-Automatic Ground Environment (SAGE). This system was designed to co-ordinate "the acquisition of data by ground radars, the transmission of ground radar data to computing centers, and in these computing centers the computations and functions of identification, weapon assignment, and weapon control from a centralized position."[117] Fortunately for Canada, an inter-service dispute over the ground environment system was avoided (as it was not in the case of Bomarc) since the Army's alternative to SAGE—Missile Master—had been scrapped before Canada became committed to either one.[118] The first model of the Bomarc to become operational, the Bomarc "A," was liquid-fuelled, had a ceiling of 60,000 feet and a range of 250 miles, and could use either a nuclear or conventional high-explosive warhead. The first Bomarc "A" squadrons were introduced into operational use during the latter half of 1959.[119]

By late 1957, progress which had been made in the development of solid fuels and of a low altitude seeker seemed sufficient to justify incorporating these in a later model capable of coping with the low-altitude threat, which was by that time recognized as significant. The use of solid fuel was expected to have the additional advantages of increasing the missile's range, thereby decreasing the total number of missiles required to cover a given area, and of lowering its reaction time, thereby reducing its vulnerability.[120] The Bomarc "B," as the model incorporating these developments was designated, was to have a range of over 400 miles and a nuclear warhead, as no conventional warhead had been designed for it.[121] The program of development of this model was begun in February, 1958, with the pressing operational target data set for early 1961.[122]

117. U.S., Congress, House, Committee on Appropriations, *Hearings before the Subcommittee on Department of Defense Appropriations*, 86th Cong., 2d Sess., 1960, Part 7, p. 201. (Hereafter cited as House Military Appropriations Subcommittee *Hearings*.)

118. Huntington, p. 414.

119. This information is taken from House Military Appropriations Subcommittee *Hearings* (1960), Part 7, pp. 200–208; and "The Boeing Bomarc," *Interavia*, XIII (September, 1958), 926–30.

120. House Military Appropriations Subcommittee *Hearings* (1960), Part 7, p. 201.

121. "The Boeing Bomarc," *Interavia*.

122. House Military Appropriations Subcommittee *Hearings* (1960), Part 7, p. 205.

The development of Bomarc and SAGE was closely watched in Canada, as General Pearkes announced to the House in early August, 1958.[123] On May 21, Sidney Smith had announced that American technicians would be coming to Canada to conduct surveys concerning the possible introduction of SAGE there.[124] A Canadian ground environment system, appropriately designated CAGE, had been explored by the Canadian Defense Research Board in an attempt to find a cheaper alternative than SAGE, as well as to involve Canadian industry in this project. This was subsequently abandoned in March, 1958.[125] At the same time, the stationing of Bomarc squadrons in Canada was being considered. Such a course was originally opposed on political grounds by U.S. civilian officials, who were familiar with the problems that had been caused by U.S. air bases in Newfoundland, and by U.S. personnel stationed in Canada on the radar networks. The Canadian Defense Minister, General Pearkes, who was concerned that any new air defense system should operate sufficiently far to the north to give protection to Canada's populous areas, took the political initiative by asking that some of the Bomarcs be placed in Canada. Military planners in both countries were receptive to the proposal. U.S. Air Force officers, who recognized the greater protection to the populous, industrial northeastern U.S. (and the incidental improvement in the protection afforded Southern Ontario), if two squadrons of Bomarcs originally planned for emplacement in upper Michigan and New York state were placed north of the Great Lakes, went as far as to propose where such squadrons might be placed in Canada. Such a move was mutually advantageous: the U.S. benefitted from having the bases in more isolated locations than the SAC bases originally planned; Canada profited from the consequence that any future air battle would take place over relatively unpopulated country, instead of over the populous Montreal-Toronto regions.[126] Although the Bomarc "B" was recognized from the beginning as a high-risk program, it was this model which, because of its expected superior performance, was envisaged for the RCAF. Some Canadian airmen were not enthusiastic about acquiring Bomarc, which they derogatorily referred to as "artillery." There was also some concern about

123. *Debates* (1958), III, 3237.   124. *Ibid.*, I, 309.
125. *Financial Post*, May 24, 1958; interviews.
126. Canada, House of Commons, Special Committee on Defense, *Minutes of Proceedings and Evidence* (June 27, 1963), p. 17. (Hereafter referred to as Sauvé Committee *Proceedings.*)

the cost to Canada of the Bomarc-SAGE-package (which also included expenditures for additional, "gap-filler" radar stations); this concern was manifest at the August, 1958, meeting between the delegations headed by Pearkes and McElroy. It went as far as consideration of the consequences of a refusal by Canada to accept the missiles; the consequence would be, Canadians were told, the emplacement of at least one more Bomarc squadron in the U.S., south of the Great Lakes. But the proposal received the approval of the Chiefs of Staff Committee and, having been approved by the U.S. administration, was a matter for the Diefenbaker government to decide. In approving it, the Americans had offered to man the Bomarc bases with American airmen, or to sell the missiles to Canada according to mutually satisfactory cost-sharing arrangements.[127]

This was the situation when the Diefenbaker cabinet met in September, 1958, to consider the fate of the Arrow. To the chiefs of staff, who had expected to acquire some interceptor—whether or not it was the Arrow—*and* the Bomarc, these two issues were quite distinct. They therefore opposed the joining of the announcement of the decision to acquire Bomarc with that to postpone action on the Arrow. However, the government, which did not want to appear slack in its defense effort, wanted something which would appear to be a replacement for the Arrow as Canada's contribution to NORAD. The logical replacement would have been an American interceptor; but there was no agreement for an interceptor ready at hand, as was the Bomarc deal. More importantly, it was highly preferable politically to acquire from the U.S. a missile—a product which Canadian industry did not produce—rather than an interceptor, which would appear competitive with the Arrow. Therefore, on September 23 the Prime Minister announced that it had "been decided to introduce the Bomarc guided missile into the Canadian air defence system."[128] The distinction between "A" and "B" versions of the missile was not made at this time. Indeed, Mr. Diefenbaker apparently was not aware that it was the latter version which had been settled on, or did not appreciate the difference between the two, for he said "it can be used with either a conventional high explosive warhead or a nuclear warhead."[129] On February 20, 1959, however, his statement more correctly, if not much more clearly, acknowledged that "the full potential of these defensive weapons is achieved only when they are armed with nuclear war-

127. Interviews.   128. See Appendix II.   129. *Ibid.*

heads."[130] It was also decided to man the bases with Canadian personnel, since the alternative possibility of leaving them in U.S. hands was not considered politically advisable.

The early reaction to this decision in the Canadian press and among opposition parties revealed a concern about the weapon itself, and about the consequences for Canadian economic health and political independence of accepting in the place of the Arrow an American weapon. There was a possibility, editorialized the *Globe and Mail,* that

> we may drift into a condition uncomfortably like that of certain Middle Eastern and Latin American countries which draw their entire supply of modern weapons from one of the Great Powers, and in consequence find themselves bound to support the policies of their armorer on pain of being suddenly left defenseless. A nation in that position may be independent in name, but it has no real independence in fact.[131]

Lamenting the fact that the hope entertained at the time of the first announcement of plans to acquire Bomarc that it might be manufactured in Canada had proved false, Mr. Pearson offered an explanation:

> Of course it [Bomarc] has to fit into the United States continental defence system, with SAGE, otherwise it would not be of much use to us in Canada. In that sense, this arrangement is bound to tie us more closely to United States production, United States industrial requirements. I wonder if that is why the United States is paying the cost of these Bomarc missiles in Canada. . . . Are we now, under this Bomarc arrangement, accepting for the first time mutual aid from the United States, something which we did not do during the whole course of the war?[132]

Although at this time, in early 1959, there was not yet sufficient information available to evaluate the missile technically, Mr. Hellyer, the shadow Minister of Defense, expressed some concern about the early performance of the "A," and asked skeptically what capabilities the "B" was expected to have.[133]

130. See Appendix III.   131. October 3, 1958.
132. *Debates* (1959), II, 1294. It was not only in Canada that cost-sharing came in for criticism: Senator Ellender of Louisiana, noting that Canada "does not furnish a nickel" of DEW Line and SAGE costs, concluded that "we are just a bunch of suckers. You put that in big letters." U.S., Congress, Senate, Committee on Appropriations, *Hearings before the Subcommittee on Department of Defense Appropriations,* 85th Cong., 2d Sess., 1959, pp. 992, 93. (Hereafter cited as Senate Military Appropriations Subcommittee *Hearings.*)
133. *Debates* (1959), II, 1273.

While criticisms and concern about the performance of the Bomarc "B" could not be answered so long as it was still in development, the other criticisms did not go unanswered by the government. Economic consequences of the combined Arrow-Bomarc decisions were claimed to have been ameliorated by the Development and Production Sharing program with the U.S., which was begun in 1958–59 and which established equitable principles for the sharing of Canadian industry in the production of weapons for the joint defense of North America.[134] Moreover, it was pointed out that the Bomarc agreement called for all construction work to be done and unit equipment to be bought in its entirety in Canada; and the U.S. had agreed to buy in Canada as much technical equipment as possible.[135] The charge that Canada had accepted mutual aid was met by Mr. Diefenbaker, who pointed out that the two-third/one-third cost sharing formula, under which Canada would pay only $125 million for its share of the Bomarc-SAGE-gap filler package, was the same as that devised under the St. Laurent government for the Pine-tree radar line.[136] As for the charge of increased dependence on the U.S., its truth with regard to weapons procurement was not denied; the increased reliance on the protection of U.S. interceptor squadrons, which was one factor the government cited as allowing it to scrap the Arrow, was held to be inevitable. Canada already relied on U.S. interceptors for the defense of western Canada, and would have continued to do so, even if the Arrow had been procured.[137]

The government's position as defender of the Bomarc became more difficult when, later in 1959, the weapon became the object of an inter-service dispute in the U.S. At this point, the controversy was not concerned with the weapon's effectiveness, but with the advisability of spending so much money on air defense relative to strategic missiles. In addition, the problem of duplication between the Air Force's Bomarc and the Army's Nike-Hercules missiles was cited. The two were not complete duplicates, since the Nike-Hercules, with its shorter range of about 50 miles was a "point defense" or anti-aircraft weapon, while Bomarc was an "area defense" weapon, more nearly a substitute for an interceptor than for anti-aircraft artillery.

134. *Ibid.*, pp. 1526–31. See also below, Chapter VII.
135. *Ibid.*, p. 1282.
136. For an estimate of the cost see *ibid.*, V, 5354. The text of the bilateral agreement may be found in U.S. Department of State, *United States Treaties and Other International Agreements*, XII, Pt. 2, 1375–80.
137. *Debates* (1959), II, 1283.

According to the concept of "defense in depth" both were needed, together with manned interceptors, in the air defense system.[138] Yet, at a time when estimates of Soviet bomber strength were being sharply reduced and fears of a missile gap were current, there were strong congressional and budgetary pressures to choose between the two. It was difficult to eliminate the Bomarc, since no funds were being asked for procurement of interceptors during Fiscal Year 1960, thus making the Bomarc alternative more important. The Nike program, on the other hand, was well-established and proven and consequently less politically vulnerable. There was, in addition, the interservice aspect, which made it difficult to eliminate either program completely. To ease the problem of deciding between the two, Secretary of Defense McElroy said he would not mind if Congress "held our feet to the fire" with its power over the purse-strings.[139] As it happened, two congressional committees made different choices: the Senate Armed Services Committee moved to eliminate Nike-Hercules, and the House Military Appropriations Subcommittee voted to eliminate Bomarc.[140] Faced with this difficulty, McElroy issued a clarification of his comment about "holding our feet to the fire" to the effect that this meant forcing a decision on the relative numbers of Nike and Bomarc bases, not a choice of eliminating one or the other.[141] The administration then announced a "master air defense plan," which called for the continuation of both programs in reduced numbers.[142] The appropriation which was finally passed followed the general outlines of this plan, although the sums designated for these programs were slightly smaller than those in the plan.[143]

This debate was followed closely in Canada, where its impact was magnified. The opposition, drawing largely on the published hearings of the House Military Appropriations Subcommittee, pointed out two uncertainties in Bomarc's future—the dangers that Congress might scrap it, or that it might be a technical failure. They questioned whether these uncertainties did not make it inadvisable for Canada to base its air defense program on this pig-in-a-

138. Address of General Laurence S. Kuter, Commander-in-Chief, NORAD, to NATO Parliamentarians' Conference, Washington (November 18, 1959).
139. Senate Military Appropriations Subcommittee *Hearings* (1959), p. 33.
140. *New York Times*, May 29, 1959, p. 1.
141. Senate Military Appropriations Subcommittee *Hearings* (1959), pp. 329, 30.
142. *New York Times*, June 13, 1959, p. 1; June 21, 1959, p. IV, 7.
143. *Ibid.*, August 5, 1959, p. 10.

poke, and to proceed with work on the SAGE system, which was said to be tied to Bomarc. It was pointed out that the first test of the "B" version of the Bomarc on May 26, 1959, was not successful.[144] As no very effective answers to these charges existed, none were given. General Pearkes minimized the seriousness of the congressional cuts in the Bomarc program by saying that they were directed at the "A" version, not the "B" model which Canada was to acquire, an assertion which was at best only partially true.[145] (Since only the "A" model was then in production, it could be argued that cuts in production orders would affect it more than the "B"; in fact, the Administration program proposed a slowdown in production so as to wait for greater numbers of the "B"; therefore congressional cuts in that program did affect this model. Moreover, the House Appropriations Committee's proposed scrapping of the Bomarc program would have eliminated "A" and "B" alike.)[146] He added the assurance, which should not have been necessary in a country the size of Canada had there not been the precedents of the Sparrow and ASTRA boondoggles, that if Bomarc were abandoned by the U.S., Canada would not assume responsibility for its development.[147]

Canada became more directly involved in the inter-service contest between Bomarc and Nike-Hercules when disclosure was made of a U.S. Army plan for stationing Nikes along the Mid-Canada line. Such a program would, of course, have enhanced Nike's prospects, for any attempt to curtail its production would have been then an international, not merely an interservice, issue. The tactic had already been employed by Boeing, the manufacturer of Nike's Bomarc competitor, with what was to prove remarkable success. Boeing had been very eager and willing to grant Canadian wishes for subcontracts in Canada for work on the Bomarc, once Canada became committed to the missile. It did so, knowing that the missile was then in jeopardy in Congress and that such a move would internationalize the commitment and make more difficult any future attempt to curtail the program.[148] In this event, the strategy would prove to be quite effective, as we later shall see. Speculation that the Army plan, or a variant which would have placed both Nikes and Bomarcs in northern Canada, might be adopted continued into

144. *Debates* (1959), V, 5364.
145. *Globe and Mail* (Toronto), May 30, 1959.
146. Senate Military Appropriations Subcommittee *Hearings* (1960), p. 1596.
147. *Globe and Mail* (Toronto), June 6, 1959.   148. Interviews.

August, when Secretary McElroy visited Ottawa.[149] At the conclusion of that visit, however, General Pearkes announced that no missile sites in addition to the two Bomarc bases would be introduced into Canada.[150] He said that proposals to move into Canada the Bomarcs planned for bases in the western U.S. were rejected because of the dislocation which would be caused to Pinetree, SAGE, and Bomarc sites themselves.

The Bomarc had survived relatively intact the congressional challenges to it in 1959, but another and more severe test was to follow in 1960. In an attempt to provide some objective advice for it in formulating the Bomarc program, the administration had had several studies made of the program. The first of these, the Furnas Committee Report, was undertaken in late 1958 and finished in April, 1959, in time to be considered in the master air defense plan and the congressional appropriation for Fiscal Year 1960.[151] The study had been undertaken because of concern that the compressed three-year development period for the Bomarc "B" was perhaps not a realistic goal. The committee concluded, however, that the March, 1961, target date could still be met under certain conditions. It recommended that the total scale of the program should be reduced, but that the more limited program be expedited, so that missiles might be deployed before the passing of the threat from manned bombers.[152] As a result of the 1959 congressional criticism, of a three-month retardation in the tight schedule for testing, and of the disappointing early test results of the "B" version—the first seven tests were all failures[153]—two additional studies were undertaken. First, in the fall of 1959, a panel comprising the commanders of the Air Research and Development Command, the Air Materiel Command and the Air Defense Command was established to review periodically the air defense programs under their jurisdiction, and to determine if these were compatible with the priority which had been given to Bomarc.[154] Reports were made by this group in November, 1959, and in January, 1960.[155] Second, a study of the technical feasibility of the "B" program was assigned in December, 1959,

149. *Globe and Mail* (Toronto), August 10, 1959.
150. *Ibid.*, August 12, 1959.
151. House Military Appropriations Subcommittee *Hearings* (1960), Part 7, p. 199.
152. *Ibid.*, pp. 259, 60.
153. Senate Military Appropriations Subcommittee *Hearings* (1960), p. 1533.
154. House Military Appropriations Subcommittee *Hearings* (1960), Part 7, p. 199.
155. *Ibid.*, p. 265.

to the USAF Chief Scientist, Dr. Flax, whose report was complete in early March, 1960.[156]

The results of these studies were incorporated in an important statement which was made on March 24, 1960, by General Thomas White, the Air Force Chief of Staff, regarding changes in priorities in the defense program.[157] The new program reflected a generally increased emphasis on the ICBM threat, and decreased stress on the bomber threat. The changes which this revision entailed were as follows: an expansion of the ICBM program and acceleration of the BMEWS program; improvement in the fighter-interceptor force so as to achieve improved defenses against manned bombers at an earlier date than previously planned; reduction in the number of Bomarc "B" 's to be procured, and elimination of the SAGE super combat center project, so as to provide increased funds for the other programs.[158] The final paragraph of the announcement described the effect of these changes on Canada:

> The proposed reduction in total Bomarc strength will not affect Bomarc squadrons programed for the Royal Canadian Air Force. Included within the revised air defense budget are provisions for SAGE direction and control in Canada. The Canadian Minister of National Defence has been kept fully informed throughout development of the Air Force's modified air defense plan.[159]

If these studies and program changes were designed to forestall further congressional criticisms of the Bomarc program, the move did not succeed. The House Military Appropriations Subcommittee recommended not only a reduction from $421.5 million to $40.4 million in new appropriations for the Bomarc program; it eliminated the recommended new appropriation entirely, and in addition called for the revocation of $253.6 million in unspent prior-year funds. Thus, it reduced the program by $294 million below the $381.1 million cut proposed in the administration's revised program.[160] It would have allowed only $50 million for continued testing of the missile, although the subcommittee's chairman, Congressman George Mahon, opined that the Pentagon would probably not bother to continue the tests under such circumstances.[161] Three shortcomings of the missile moved the Subcommittee to this action. First, the unsatisfactory sequence of tests, none of which had been a success[162];

156. *Ibid.*   157. *Ibid.,* pp. 197, 98.   158. *Ibid.*
159. *Ibid.*   160. *New York Times,* April 30, 1960, p. 1.
161. *Times* (London), May 4, 1960.
162. House Military Appropriations Subcommittee *Hearings* (1960), Part 7, p. 242.

second, the expected date of operational readiness had slipped, and it was not expected now before 1962,[163] and would thus not be available during what was expected to be the period of the maximum manned bomber threat; third, the missile sites would be quite vulnerable, and therefore could be knocked out easily by ICBM's in the first wave of a Soviet attack.[164]

These developments put the Diefenbaker government in Ottawa in an extremely difficult position. Prior to the revision in air defense policy which was recommended by General White on March 24, General Pearkes had given no intimation that changes were under consideration. He had greeted each announcement of the Bomarc "B" 's test failures with a report of his consultations with Secretary of Defense Thomas Gates, and an affirmation of his confidence in the eventual success of the missile.[165] Work on the installation of SAGE continued apace, unaffected by the increasing uncertainty which shrouded the future of Bomarc.[166] There were some warnings in Canada about a cutback in Bomarc—in January it was reported that the House Military Appropriations Subcommittee would be examining the proposed funds for the missile more closely than ever in 1960[167]—but the statements of the minister seemed to acknowledge no realistic possibility that the Bomarc program was in danger.

On March 24, when the administration itself proposed a drastic cutback in Bomarc funds, the impression was therefore magnified that there had been no consultation with Canada on the change. This impression was reinforced by General Pearkes's reaction to the news of the revised plan. Although the recommendations were made to the Subcommittee in executive session, the news leaked out almost immediately, and on March 25, a question was asked in the House of Commons. At first, General Pearkes refused to comment on the press report, since it consisted of speculation about a secret U.S. meeting, although he held that "Canada has been consistently consulted regarding a possible revision of the joint air defence plan."[168] Later in the day, he read to the House the text of a U.S. Department of Defense statement (which was simultaneously made public in Washington), about the content of, and reasons for the proposed changes.[169] These events prompted the opposition to

163. *Ibid.*, pp. 220, 242.   164. *Ibid.*, p. 227.
165. *Debates* (1960), I, 547; II, 1787–89.
166. *Financial Post*, January 30, 1960.
167. *Vancouver Province*, January 25, 1960.
168. *Debates* (1960), III, 2446.   169. *Ibid.*, p. 2489.

move the adjournment of the House to debate the government's air defense policy. To its astonishment, the motion was accepted. Of the several grounds for attacking that policy, the most immediate was the apparent lack of consultation with the U.S. prior to the change in policy. This seemed to be a clear breach of the NORAD agreement, which called for the "fullest possible consultation . . . regularly and consistently undertaken."[170] "We have the degrading picture of the Minister of National Defense standing up in the house . . . and reading a statement which was entitled, 'Statement Being Issued by the United States Department of Defense.' "[171] Mr. Pearson pointed out that there was a difference between being consulted and being informed, the latter being the term used in the DOD statement to describe the Canadian role.[172] On March 27, General Pearkes had rendered himself even more vulnerable on this score by his statements on a CBC broadcast and later in the House that in the revised air defense plan fourteen Bomarc sites—twelve American and two Canadian—were called for,[173] whereas the correct figure was ten sites, including two in Canada.[174]

In point of fact, the position of Canada in working out the revised Bomarc program was probably not so bad as General Pearkes's rather ineffective defense would lead one to believe.[175] First, General Pearkes did know in advance of the proposed revision, even if he did not take steps to prepare public opinion in Canada for it.[176] The commitment of Canada to the Bomarc was one of the main reasons, if not the only one, for the administration's decision to leave a rump Bomarc "B" program in the revised air defense plan.[177] It is difficult to believe that Canadian pressure did not contribute to the acceptance of this reason. Even the shadow Minister of Defense, Mr. Hellyer, later implied that the U.S. would have ended the program but for Canadian pressure, thereby conceding by implication the effectiveness of the pressure, even if he did not agree with its advisability.[178] There were also, at the time, press reports to this effect. On May 2, Chairman George Mahon of the subcommittee said that he had reason to think that the Pentagon wanted to give

170. See Appendix I.   171. *Debates* (1960), III, 2505.
172. *Ibid.*, p. 2499.   173. *Ibid.*, p. 2501.
174. Senate Military Appropriations Subcommittee *Hearings* (1960), p. 1562.
175. *Debates* (1960), III, 2508–15. He spent more time outlining the channels available for defense consultation with the U.S. than in demonstrating that they were being used.
176. *Financial Post*, April 9, 1960; interviews.   177. Interviews.
178. *Globe and Mail* (Toronto), April 14, 1960.

up Bomarc, and that some of the officials there were glad to see Congress take the blame for it. "But," he added, "one never knows; if the Canadian government starts putting pressure through the Senate foreign relations committee or the executive branch, we may after all have to spend money on this missile in which we have no confidence at all."[179] Although this assertion was denied by Pearkes, who called it "ridiculous,"[180] there were other reports to the same effect.[181] What General Pearkes did not know was when the revised plan would be announced, and in this he was apparently in no worse position than his U.S. counterpart, Secretary Gates, who was in Paris at the time and did not give his approval to the program until later.[182] But the political cost had to be paid by Pearkes, not Gates, for this state of affairs, during which Canada was considered generally to have been treated, in the word of the *Globe and Mail,* "shabbily."[183]

When the House Appropriations Committee exceeded the Air Force proposal and recommended scrapping the entire Bomarc program, it did so with some awareness of the consequences for Canada. One of the most determined antagonists of Bomarc on the committee, Representative Daniel Flood of Pennsylvania, said that he was familiar with the State Department's concern for the effects of the contemplated cutback on Canadian-American relations and its intervention with the Department of Defense, but was going to raise the issue anyway.[184] "I know a good deal about the conversation. I would rather be a congressman from Cuba this week than the Secretary of Defense in Canada," he observed.[185] He felt that the concern of General Pearkes was based not so much on strategic grounds as on the expected effect a cancellation would have on forthcoming by-elections in constituencies in which the Bomarcs were scheduled to be placed.[186] Senator Magnuson of Washington, who was, in effect, the Boeing representative in the Senate, predictably suggested that if Bomarc were cancelled, the reaction in Canada would be so severe that the Diefenbaker government might fall and its successor elect to leave NATO.[187] While this view received no general support, there were differences of opinion about the extent to which Congress should be concerned with Canada's interests in the matter. One

---

179. *Ibid.,* May 3, 1960.   180. *Ibid.*   181. *Ibid.,* May 6, 1960.
182. Senate Military Appropriations Subcommittee *Hearings* (1960), p. 1320.
183. March 28, 1960.
184. House Military Appropriations Subcommittee *Hearings* (1960), p. 254.
185. *Ibid.,* p. 228.   186. *Ibid.,* p. 254.
187. *Winnipeg Free Press,* May 6, 1960.

of those giving advice to the committee, Roger Hilsman of the Washington Center of Foreign Policy Research, suggested that if Canada were willing to pay for a low-priority item that the USAF could not afford, then it should be allowed to do so.[188] On the other hand, Senator Chavez, a member of the Committee, felt that "we ought to respect Canada and give her the best we have and not something that is not good enough for us."[189]

General Pearkes, acting for the government, at no time wavered in his faith in Bomarc's eventual success and in its utility for Canada, or in his determination to hold the U.S. to its commitment to complete the development of the missile and provide Canada with two squadrons. He announced plans to begin the construction of one of Canada's two Bomarc sites, even before the missile had been successfully tested.[190] When such a successful test finally occurred, he eagerly interrupted a budget debate to convey the news to the House.[191] When the announcement was made of the House Appropriations Committee's recommendation, he took the strong position that such action, if confirmed by the Senate, would constitute a violation of a year-old agreement between Canada and the U.S.[192]

The government's effort to obtain reversal of the House action on Bomarc was blessed with success, owing to several special factors. The first of these was the successful test of the Bomarc "B" which was held in mid-April and which, despite the fact that it was followed by another failure, held out promise of eventual technical success. Second, the failure of the Paris summit conference changed the political background against which military requirements were formulated, so that it seemed inadvisable to forego such an obtainable margin of defense as the Bomarc sites represented. Senator Chavez, who had earlier suggested that something better than Bomarc should be provided for Canada, now reportedly said (in an article, "Summit Collapse May Save Bomarc"): "We are ready to co-operate. Tell us what you need; we are ready to provide."[193] Third, high-level talks played a role: in June, the Prime Minister visited Washington and raised the subject in his talks with President Eisenhower. He was reportedly assured that in the final Appropriations Act, the funds for Bomarc would be restored.[194] This assurance, if in fact it was given, was well-founded. By June 6, Senator Chavez

188. *Globe and Mail* (Toronto), May 4, 1960.
189. *Round Table*, L (June, 1960), 307.   190. *Debates* (1960), III, 2514.
191. *Globe and Mail* (Toronto), April 14, 1960.
192. *Ibid.*, April 30, 1960.   193. *Ottawa Evening Journal*, May 19, 1960.
194. *New York Times*, June 5, 1960, p. 21.

was saying "you can rest assured that when the subcommittee finishes marking up the bill, the Bomarcs necessary for Canada will be there."[195] On June 9, announcement was made of the Senate Military Appropriations Subcommittee's recommendation to restore the $294 million cut by the House and an additional $75 million for equipping two Bomarc bases in the western U.S., which had been partly built but abandoned in the Department's revised air defense plan.[196] On June 28, agreement was reached in conference to compromise on a restoration of $244 million. Thereafter, the "B" program was quickly completed. The missile was successfully tested in July and August, was put into production in October, and in early December the first finished production model was turned out.[197]

These successes did not, however, remove the Bomarc issue from the Canadian political arena. Confidence in the Defense Minister had been so seriously damaged that even the Conservative *Globe and Mail* was calling for his resignation.[198] In July, a move in the House to cut to one dollar the funds for Bomarc was only narrowly defeated. In early August, the Liberal Opposition for the first time went beyond challenges for clarifications of government policy and offered their alternative defense program.[199] The parts of this program pertaining to North American defense were in clear contrast to government policy. Acquisition of Bomarc and SAGE by Canada was opposed for several reasons: their vulnerability, which was a factor of more conspicuous importance since the British had cancelled the Blue Streak IRBM the previous spring, partly on these grounds; also the estimate that the Bomarcs would not be available during the period of maximum danger, i.e., 1960–62; and the view that to accept the missiles before making a decision about acquiring nuclear warheads for them was to put the cart before the horse. To these remarks, offered by Mr. Hellyer, Mr. Pearson added an objection to the strategy on which the use of Bomarcs was based—on defending the deterrent. He held that this was a task for which the U.S., not Canada, was responsible.[200] In his view, Canada had become "the last two knots on the Bomarc tail of the defence kite,"[201] and this position should be changed by renouncing the use of nuclear

---

195. *Globe and Mail* (Toronto), June 7, 1960.
196. U.S., Congress, Senate, Report No. 1550, "Department of Defense Appropriation Bill, 1961," 86th Cong., 2d Sess., 1960, p. 30.
197. See *New York Times,* July 9, 1960, p. 42; August 12, 1960, p. 3; October 13, 1960, p. 34; and December 2, 1960, p. 32.
198. May 5, 1960.   199. *Debates* (1960), VII, 7560–73.
200. *Ibid.*, p. 7606.   201. *Ibid.*

weapons and foregoing carriers which depended on them for effective employment. As its contribution to North American air defense, Canada should acquire a modern interceptor, which according to a deal then in the discussion stage would have the additional advantage of securing for Canada a large aircraft order by the U.S. This interceptor should perform the exclusive function of identifying the unidentified objects reported daily by the radar networks.[202] These remarks were made at a time when defense issues were being fervently discussed in Canada. The publication in the spring of 1960 of James Minifie's book, *Peacemaker or Powdermonkey*, was one of the significant contributing factors to these polemics; Mr. Pearson, while rejecting the book's conclusions, felt advised to refer to it in his exposition of the new Liberal defense policy.[203]

With the announcement of this new Liberal policy, a significant debate about Canada's defense policy could at last begin. At least as far as North American air defense was concerned, it offered distinct alternatives to government policy. It recognized clearly the continuing need for interceptors to perform the function of identifying unknown aircraft; it made a strong case against procuring Bomarc by pointing out the effect of that missile's vulnerability; and it raised forcefully, for the first time, the question of nuclear weapons and offered one possible solution. Surely, the alternative policy by no means gave a definitive answer to the current defense problems. It did not explain why, if an investment were to be made in aircraft of sufficiently high performance to identify any unidentified flying object, the modest additional expense involved in arming it to destroy hostile aircraft should not also be incurred. Nor did it display any recognition that the Bomarcs, even though vulnerable, might have some utility by diverting fire away from more important targets and that the proper way of determining whether to procure them was to compare that utility with their cost, as Mr. Hellyer later recognized as minister.[204] The suggested policy of nuclear abstinence bore marks of being determined as much by moral revulsion as by a detached consideration of strategic and political issues. But

202. *Ibid.*, p. 7567.
203. The book (see note #8, Chapter III), which was written by the Washington correspondent of CBC, advocated that Canada leave NORAD and NATO and adopt a neutral posture. Military expenditures would be sharply reduced and the savings applied to programs of aid to underdeveloped countries. A subsequent book by the same author, James M. Minifie, *Open at the Top* (Toronto, Montreal: McClelland & Stewart, 1964), repeats these arguments without substantial change or improvement.
204. Sauvé Committee *Proceedings* (June 27, 1963), p. 17.

for the first time, the Bomarc dispute produced somewhat clearer lines of disagreement between the major parties, and thereby opened the way for the thorough debate on defense policy that was needed. In the NORAD controversy, there had been no partisan disagreement about the advisability of the agreement itself. In the case of the Arrow, there was no vote to reveal whether such agreement existed on the basic decision to scrap the aircraft, but it is highly likely that a Liberal government would have taken the same course. With the Bomarc, a concrete disagreement on policy appears for the first time, and with it the beginnings of a policy debate. The fact that this debate was to remain confused for some time was less important than that it was finally begun.

THE McDONNELL F–101B "VOODOO"

The third controversial decision involving North American defense which the Diefenbaker government had to face concerned the role of manned aircraft in Canadian air defense, and in particular, the acquisition of an interceptor to replace the Arrow as a follow-on for the obsolescent CF–100's and F–86's then in use. We have seen that there was never any doubt among the government's military advisers that some interceptor would be needed, whatever happened to Bomarc. How, then, does one explain the long delay from September, 1958, when Arrow's cancellation was first suggested, to June 12, 1961, when announcement was made of the planned acquisition of sixty-six F–101B Voodoos for the RCAF?

What has become the standard answer to this question is that Canada was victimized by changing U.S. strategic intelligence estimates. This is indeed a general problem, since Canada depends almost entirely upon the U.S. for information upon which to base such estimates, though the information is jointly evaluated. This is a process through which, reportedly, the influence of the relatively more conservative Canadians frequently renders the joint appreciation more accurate. However, "this joint judgment is often a compromise and has not always been accurate. As a result, it has been necessary for Canada to make considerable change and expensive adjustment to its contributions to continental defence."[205] What happened in the case at hand, according to this version, is that in 1958–59, U.S. strategic intelligence estimates were revised to stress the increasing ICBM capability of the Soviet Union—this was the

205. Foulkes, "The Complications of Continental Defence," p. 101.

revision which produced the USAF's "revised air defense plan," as well as the popular speculation about the "missile gap"—and in 1960–61, were revised again to take account of the Soviet Union's failure to shift emphasis from bombers to missiles as early or as quickly as had been anticipated. Since the first of these was commonly thought to have been the basis of the cancellation of Arrow, and since the second took place at about the same time as the decision to acquire the Voodoos, the changing intelligence estimates appeared to have the effect of inducing the RCAF to purchase an American, rather than Canadian, interceptor: "Canadians have . . . had the expensive, not to say humiliating, experience of producing for about half-a-billion dollars a fighter interceptor designed for use against bombers, only to be told that the main threat was from ballistic missiles; and have proceeded to scrap the interceptor, only to be told that there is a threat from bombers after all."[206] Again, "inevitably, public opinion in Canada was greatly disturbed by the apparent contradiction between dropping the Arrow and then, only a short time later, being urged to stock up with U.S.-built aircraft."[207]

This explanation may be neat, but it is incorrect. We have seen already that the changing bomber threat was, at best, only one of the reasons for the failure of both the U.S. and Canada to procure the Arrow. More importantly, neither the change in strategic estimates nor its effect was so sharp as this interpretation implies; it was not a question of whether the threat was from bombers or missiles, but of the relative importance of the two and, consequently, of the priority to be given anti-bomber defenses such as interceptors. It is true that the administration's proposals for Fiscal Year 1960 called for no additional procurement of manned interceptors, and that development of the F–108 and of two later models of the F–106 was cancelled. But there was never any suggestion that existing squadrons of such aircraft as the F–106 and F–101 would not be needed in the future; and in the revised air defense plan of 1960, added improvements were provided for interceptor defenses even within the context of a plan which shifted the emphasis towards the ICBM threat. What the U.S. administration decided to forego was moving into a new generation of interceptor aircraft. But for Canada, this was not the question. For the RCAF, the problem was one of re-

206. Eayrs, *Northern Approaches: Canada and the Search for Peace*, p. 34.
207. Melvin Conant, *The Long Polar Watch: Canada and the Defense of North America* (New York: Harper Bros., 1962), p. 156.

placing the CF–100's and F–86's of an earlier generation by aircraft such as F–106's and F–101's. The government's military advisers never wavered in the view that such a replacement was needed. Thus, it was not the dictates of changing strategic estimates which accounted for the long delay in a decision about the future use of interceptor squadrons in Canada. It was, as will be seen, the dictates of politics.

In an important sense, however, the political considerations were affected by the strategic ones. In particular, the government's decision to justify its Arrow decision by strategic arguments made it politically difficult to choose any of the courses which were then left to it. These alternatives were outlined for the government by the Chiefs of Staff Committee. Three possibilities were discerned: (1) Canada could concentrate on Bomarcs, get out of the interceptor business, and admit USAF interceptor squadrons into Canada to fill the gap; (2) a U.S. interceptor could be bought in adequate numbers for the RCAF; (3) the one-third or so of U.S. interceptors on alert might be rotated onto Canadian bases but not be permanently stationed there. The first of these was ruled out on political grounds, although it was briefly considered.[208] The third was never seriously considered, since it was only slightly less politically objectionable than the first, and considerably less satisfactory militarily. Therefore, the second was chosen, although it was never the quantity of aircraft that the RCAF considered satisfactory.[209] There was considerable interest in the possibility of later acquiring the sophisticated U.S. F–108, then still in development, if arrangements could be made for its manufacture under license in Canada as McElroy reportedly assured that they could.[210] Whatever the prospect for this—it proved barren when the F–108 was scrapped several months later[211]—there was general agreement that something was needed in the interim before it would become available in the period 1962–64.

For some months after the Arrow's cancellation, the controversy surrounding that decision made it politically impossible to make serious moves toward finding a substitute aircraft. The government later justified this delay on other grounds, by saying that before the end of 1959 no suitable substitute was available, and that there

---

208. *Debates* (1959), V, 5353.   209. Interviews.
210. Article by Harold Greer in *Globe and Mail* (Toronto), January 13, 1959.
211. *Ibid.*, October 16, 1959.

was no rush since the Arrow would not have become operational before the end of 1961.[212] This justification was, in a sense, correct. The joker lay in the meaning of "suitable": since it was regarded as politically impossible to buy American aircraft outright, consideration was limited to aircraft which the USAF could divert to Canada out of its own squadrons. (As the government was to learn later, there were also some political objections to the acceptance of aircraft which had already been used.)[213] This ruled out the RCAF-preferred F–106, which could not be spared, and the choice fell on the more dispensable McDonnell F–101B "Voodoo." Sixty-six of these were available for diversion to the RCAF, and this was the quantity that was offered. An address in Ottawa by USAF General Laurence Kuter, the new commander in chief of NORAD, to the effect that acquisition by the RCAF of a new interceptor was a requirement of North American defense, gave some impetus to the effort to work out satisfactory terms.[214]

The original U.S. offer was to give Canada the Voodoos. This was rejected for two reasons. First, it would have stigmatized the government with having accepted foreign aid, something which it claimed not to have done.[215] Second, it was regarded as a concession of defeat to the American aircraft lobby; even though the planes in question had already been produced, and would not therefore increase McDonnell's orders, it was thought that giving them to Canada might lead indirectly to the firm's getting other orders. The Canadians, therefore, suggested that a politically acceptable way of getting the Voodoos might be an exchange in which the U.S. would acquire Canadian-built aircraft. The Canadair-built CL–44 transport, for which there was some American official interest, was the candidate for this arrangement; it was proposed that the administration purchase it for use by the Military Air Transport Service. To balance the accounts, Canada would take over the operation of some facilities in Canada then operated by the USAF, namely the remaining American-operated stations of the Pinetree line. This would also make the arrangement more palatable, politically. In

212. Halpenny Committee *Proceedings* (May 20, 1960), p. 127.

213. According to Hellyer, the Canadian Defense Department had "become a pawnshop for second hand American hardware." *Debates* (1960–61), VIII, 8230.

214. *Montreal Daily Star*, November 18, 1959.

215. Whether or not the claim was correct depends on the definition of "aid" that is used. The U.S. had paid two-thirds of the cost of the Pinetree radar stations that were located in Canada.

spite of political pressure brought to bear on the Administration at the last minute by the U.S. aircraft industry and the reluctance of MATS to use a foreign-produced aircraft, U.S. agreement to the plan was forthcoming by July, 1960. In that month, Secretary Gates was in Ottawa for a meeting of the Canada-U.S. Ministerial Committee on Joint Defense, and an agreement on the swap deal was reached. It was still contingent, however, on the agreement of the Canadian cabinet. This agreement was delayed, to the displeasure of the U.S. Department of Defense, which had to withstand more political pressure the longer the delay. The potential political liability in Canada was minimized because the Liberals had gone on record as favoring the exchange.[216] Reportedly, there was at one point cabinet agreement on proceeding with it; but if it ever existed, it soon dissolved, after such political associates of the Prime Minister as Howard Green, the Secretary of State for External Affairs, and John Pallett, the Prime Minister's parliamentary secretary, convinced him that it would be a political liability to go through with the deal. Green was bothered by the dependence on the U.S. implied in the exchange; Pallett, representing a Toronto constituency, was not happy that compensation for cancellation of the Arrow—which would have been produced near Toronto—was being awarded in the form of an order to a Montreal firm. Thus ended the proposed exchange of CL–44's and F–101's. It was rejected not by American military or political leaders, as the most common public version would have it,[217] but by the Canadian government.

Almost immediately, officials in the Department of Defense Production began to look for an alternative way of financing the acquisition of Voodoos. By this time it had been decided that the RCAF air division in Europe was going to be re-equipped with the F–104, which was to be manufactured under license in Canada by Canadair, and that the same plane was going to be provided under mutual assistance to European members of NATO. It was therefore proposed that Canada pay part of the cost of that mutual assistance in return for an order with Canadair for the F–104's that would be sent to Europe. This had the appealing factor that Canadian and European air forces would then have standardized on the same version of the F–104, in addition, of course, to the fact that it constituted a

216. *Debates* (1960), VII, 7606.
217. See e.g., the account in Richard A. Preston, *Canada in World Affairs: 1959 to 1961* (Toronto: Oxford University Press, 1965), p. 62, which makes U.S. aircraft industry the villain of the piece.

substantial order for a Montreal aircraft manufacturer. In this form, the deal finally went through and on June 12, 1961, was announced in Ottawa.[218] It involved Canada's taking over the U.S.-operated Pinetree stations and paying $50 million of the cost of providing F–104's for Europe under mutual assistance. In return, it received sixty-six "Voodoos" and an order for $200 million worth of F–104's.

218. *Debates* (1960–61), VI, 6179–80. The text of the agreement may be found in U.S., Department of State, *United States Treaties and Other International Agreements*, XII, Part 1, 723–27.

CHAPTER V

Canadian Forces for NATO

WITHDRAWAL FROM EUROPE REJECTED

WHEN the Diefenbaker government assumed office in June, 1957, equally as pressing as the issues of NORAD and aircraft for North American defense were the impending choices about re-equipping the Canadian units allocated to NATO. The most pressing of these choices concerned Canada's Number One Air Division, which was flying twelve squadrons of obsolescent F–86's and CF–100's. However, just as the NORAD controversy caused a critical one-year delay in the decision about the future of the Arrow, so that latter issue led in turn to a postponement of the decision about the air division. General Foulkes has recalled the rationale of this delay for the benefit of the Commons' Defense Committee:

> A decision on the 104 [the aircraft which was eventually chosen for the air division] was delayed simply because the government could not settle that until it settled the question of the Arrow. I am quite sure you are much more astute in political matters than I, but it would not seem a very good plan to put forward the purchase of one type of aircraft when you consider disbanding another which was manufactured in Canada. Furthermore, it was always hoped that in some way or other the 105 might be able to be used in Europe.[1]

There was yet another reason for the delay; it was one which affected not only the air division, but also the brigade group which was Canada's contribution to the NATO ground forces; any decision to re-equip these forces had to await the more basic political decision concerning the length of time that they might remain in Europe. The forces had originally been sent to Europe in the expectation that they would be brought home and put into strategic reserve as the European countries recovered their economic and military strength. By the late 1950's, there were good reasons for making this return an early one. Canada, like its southern neighbor, was running a chronic balance of payments deficit, which it filled only

1. Foulkes testimony, p. 511.

by the politically unpalatable inflow of U.S. investment funds. The military forces in Europe cost a substantial amount of foreign exchange, which, unlike the case of the U.S., was not compensated for by large arms sales to Europe.[2] In the Fiscal Year 1960–61, e.g., $36 million was spent maintaining the brigade group in Germany and $91 million on the air division, figures which, in each case, exclude the costs of equipment and of training in Canada.[3] These were high prices to pay for the results achieved, partly because of the expense—applicable to American forces as well as Canadian—of operating units at the end of a 3000-mile supply line. Also, because Canada relied upon a volunteer army, it was required to pay its servicemen well. It was frequently pointed out that for the same financial outlay, Europeans could provide a contingent considerably larger than a brigade, perhaps as much as a division.[4] But political factors overrode for Canada, as they did for the United States, these matters of cost. It was not that the Canadian presence in Europe had a comparable psychological importance to the American presence, in spite of the claims of some Canadian officials that the smaller European countries attributed great importance to the Canadian commitments.[5] The governing factor was rather the negative one that any Canadian withdrawal might have been regarded as the forerunner of a similar American action. It was therefore resisted by Europeans, who did not want to encourage such an imminent U.S. withdrawal, and by Americans, who did not want to give the false impression that they planned to withdraw.

The nice balance of these factors, prior to the 1957 election, produced a certain vagueness in the statements of the St. Laurent government and of opposition spokesmen on the subject. As early as September, 1955, Mr. Pearson suggested in a press conference that

2. More recently this situation has been changing as Canada has increased its arms sales abroad. In 1965, Canada exported about $68 million worth of arms to countries other than the U.S., mainly in Europe. This was some $30 million more than it imported from the same countries. Although Germany is a net importer of arms from Canada, there is no offset agreement relating its arms purchases to the foreign exchange costs of Canadian forces, as with the U.S. Information taken from Canada, Department of Defense Production, *1965 Annual Report* (Ottawa: The Queen's Printer, 1966), pp. 25, 45.

3. Halpenny Committee *Proceedings* (June 3, 1960), p. 230.

4. Foulkes testimony, p. 502. General Foulkes thought that even a corps of two divisions could be provided by the Europeans for the same cost.

5. It was reported that the government felt a withdrawal of the brigade group would have a disastrous effect on Norway, Denmark, Holland and Belgium and might lead to the collapse of NATO. While this view may not in fact have been seriously entertained, its repeated expression showed at least a proneness to accept it. See the *Globe and Mail* (Toronto), January 16, 1959.

the increasing importance to NATO of North American defense might lead within two or three years to a decision to withdraw the air division to Canada.[6] The last Liberal statements on the subject prior to the 1957 election were marked by a studied ambiguity. Paul Martin, in one of his last speeches as Minister of National Health and Welfare, remarked that

> the Canadian Government is prepared to maintain that contribution in Europe as long as it is considered necessary for the protection of the Atlantic community, and as long as other members of the Organization, who have as much at stake in the security of Western Europe, are prepared and willing to carry their equitable share of the sacrifices it calls for.[7]

Such a statement could be interpreted as a continuing undertaking to maintain forces in Europe, or as a designation of the escape hatches through which the commitment might be reduced, according to the predilection of the listener. Nor was the Conservative spokesman, General Pearkes, more precise. In a July, 1956, speech in the House, he called for a re-assessment of Canada's NATO commitments in view of the changed conditions of the thermonuclear age.[8] Although the thrust of his speech suggested that he was thinking of a reduction in the European commitments, he later took exception to the interpretation that he advocated the "withdrawal" of the forces.[9]

After the Diefenbaker government took office, these uncertain statements were increasingly replaced by more definite affirmations of the intention to maintain Canada's European commitments. The first intimation of this was contained in a statement to the press by the Deputy Minister of National Defense, Frank Miller, to the effect that the air division would definitely remain in Europe.[10] Although it was not revealed at the time, this decision was given formally at the NATO Heads of Government meeting in December, 1957, since the military plan MC–70, adopted at that meeting, contained the understanding that the air division would "in due course"

6. *Winnipeg Free Press*, September 30, 1955. After they went into oppostion, Liberal spokesmen also employed the financial arguments in favor of a reduction of the commitments. See the report of a speech by Walter Gordon, reportedly endorsed by Pearson, in the *Globe and Mail* (Toronto), September 1, 1962.

7. Canada, Department of External Affairs, *Statements and Speeches*, 57/24, April 8, 1957.

8. *Debates* (1956), VI, 6206–07.

9. *Ibid.*, p. 6239. As early as 1953 he had thought it uneconomic to keep Canadian troops in Europe. *Ibid.*, 1952–53, IV, 3812–20.

10. *Montreal Daily Star*, September 25, 1957.

be re-equipped.[11] In June, 1958, in a speech introducing the President of the Federal Republic of Germany, Theodor Heuss, to the Canadian Parliament Mr. Diefenbaker gave a still ambiguous, but somewhat clearer undertaking:

> Whatever threats may be made against those nations which believe in the mission of NATO and the necessity for its continuance, Canada will maintain forces in Europe as long as international disquiet and justifiable fears require Canadian participation.[12]

A few months later, on the occasion of his visit to the Canadian forces in Europe, the Prime Minister made clear the intention to keep them there: "Canada will be represented in NATO by its army and its air force as long as Canada is required and as long as there is a task left to be performed."[13] The political arguments for staying had prevailed over the economic-military arguments for "bringing the boys home." This decision may have been unimpeachable; but it was regrettable that it was taken without reference to public debate. It is difficult to blame the Diefenbaker government for this, for the decision was as little noticed after it was taken as it was debated beforehand.[14] The government was perhaps more culpable for the exaggerated justifications it used for staying in Europe. General Pearkes, who, four years earlier had hinted at the advisability of withdrawing the forces, publicly expressed different views as a member of the government: "I would go so far as to say that our NATO allies would consider it a disastrous blow if Canada withdrew her forces from Europe."[15]

If the decision to continue the Canadian effort in Europe was clear by the fall of 1958, the scope of that effort was not so plain to see. At the Paris meeting of NATO ministers in December, 1958, Canada reportedly resisted pressures to increase its contribution of money or arms.[16] But in the Berlin crisis of 1961, Canada responded dutifully by increasing the brigade by 1,100 men to full war

11. *Debates* (1959), V, 5392.   12. *Ibid.* (1958), I, 772.

13. Address given by Mr. Diefenbaker on the occasion of a dinner given by Chancellor Adenauer in Bonn, November 7, 1958. Text from Canada, Department of External Affairs.

14. See, for example, the *Globe and Mail* (Toronto) for the days following November 6, 1958, in which only the vaguest accounts of the Prime Minister's speeches in Germany may be found. Senior officers of the RCAF, however, were attentive listeners. From these speeches of his date the beginnings of their efforts to re-equip the air division.

15. Halpenny Committee *Proceedings*, June 3, 1960, p. 231.

16. *Montreal Daily Star*, December 19, 1958.

strength.[17] It was plain that regardless of the number of men involved, the Canadian contingents in Europe would need new equipment if they stayed there for several more years. The air division was flying eight squadrons of obsolescent F–86's and four squadrons of CF–100's, both subsonic aircraft. The brigade group lacked both adequate firepower and mobility to perform its role under a strategy which relied on the early use of nuclear weapons. The remainder of this chapter relates the problems involved in finding satisfactory military roles in the alliance for the land, air, and—more briefly— sea forces of Canada, and of the further problems of acquiring satisfactory equipment with which to perform those roles. Since all three components chose roles dependent on the use of nuclear weapons, these issues are closely related to those discussed in the next chapter. There is no completely satisfactory way to disengage the issues involved in acquiring the carriers for nuclear weapons from those involved in acquiring the weapons themselves. The system followed here is to deal with the factors that are primarily military in this chapter, with those that are mainly political in the next.

The Brigade Group

From the time that it was sent to Europe in the early 1950's, the Canadian brigade group occupied a front-line position on the central front in Germany. There were certain anomalies in this situation which rendered it more bothersome as time passed. One of these was that Canada was performing a military role similar to that of the U.S., the U.K. and France but was not, like those countries, an occupying power; this was the legacy of Mackenzie King's decision in 1945 to bring the Canadians home as soon as possible. Another was the ticklish possibility, after NATO "went nuclear," that Canadian forces would both be operating on foreign soil and using foreign-controlled weapons. Neither the Americans, who controlled their own weapons although they operated on European soil, nor the Europeans, who were based on or near their own territory though they relied on warheads in U.S. custody, had both problems to contend with. But both of these situations presented problems that were comparatively intellectual and hypothetical. More concrete and immediate were certain logistical and organizational problems. These have been explained by General Foulkes:

17. *Debates*, 1960–61, VIII, 8225.

Our brigade is an independent and isolated brigade. Normally a brigade operates as part of a division and a division operates as part of a corps, and a corps operates as part of an army. However, as we have only one isolated brigade, we have to provide for that brigade all the support and facilities which would normally be provided by the division, by the corps and by the army, with the result that with that brigade at the present time has [sic] medium artillery regiment, which is not normal. We also provide an armoured regiment. The C.G.S. pointed out that he is going to require bridging, which is not normally supplied except in a corps. So we are in the position of having to meet all the requirements for a brigade as if it had a division, a corps and an army behind it, and the majority of these will have to come from Canada.[18]

Moreover, problems in the system of supply aggravated these burdens. Canada utilized the British supply system which, because of the U.K.'s manpower and financial problems, has been hard pressed to meet British requirements alone; Canadian needs have added to the difficulty. In addition, there has been an increasing use by Canadian forces of U.S.- and Canadian-made, rather than British-made, items. This has necessitated an additional Canadian system of supply. All of these difficulties have been increased by the decision to adopt a forward strategy, which has lengthened the lines of communication still further.[19]

In working out its military commitments to NATO, a country such as Canada has, according to published versions of the procedure, a great deal of leeway in choosing its role, provided it knows clearly what kind of role it wants to perform.[20] Because of the difficulties described above, the Canadian military became increasingly interested in revising the role of the brigade group. In 1960, there was discussion on the military level with West Germany and with SACEUR about the withdrawal of the brigade group from its forward position to a mobile reserve position, with West German forces taking its place on the front line. But the same political factors which have kept Canadian troops in Europe operated on this occasion to keep them in the front line, and there they remained.[21]

If they were going to stay, certain measures to increase the brigade group's firepower and mobility became necessary. Not only did this follow from NATO's adopted strategy and from the determination that "if war becomes imminent, Canada must have weapons equal

18. Foulkes testimony, p. 497.   19. *Ibid.*, pp. 496, 97.
20. See articles by General Foulkes in the *Vancouver Sun*, August 30–31, 1962.
21. Foulkes testimony, p. 497; interviews.

to those of an enemy."[22] It was dictated by the political argument, which has long enjoyed great support in Ottawa, and is as often applied to North American as to European defense, that Canada's forces must not have arms that are inferior to those of their allies who are performing similar tasks.[23]

Two needs were greatest: tactical nuclear weapons, in the form of short-range ground-to-ground missiles, were needed to translate into operational terms NATO'S nuclear strategy; and the increased troop dispersal which that strategy entailed, made more acute the need for mobility, and generated a requirement for armored personnel carriers.[24] Difficulties were encountered with both pieces of equipment selected to fill these requirements.

The chosen missile was the Lacrosse, which was being developed in the U.S. for the U.S. Army. The Canadian government's decision to acquire it was announced in October, 1958, in the wake of the turmoil caused by the first Arrow announcement.[25] Already, within three months, there were reports from the U.S. (even from the President himself) that its development was being stopped.[26] However, inquiries made by Canadians elicited from the Pentagon the assurance that development was being continued. In his statement of February 20, 1959, Mr. Diefenbaker referred to Lacrosse as well as Bomarc as weapons the "full potential" of which could only be realized with nuclear warheads, and that Canada was accordingly carrying on negotiations for their provision.[27] As late as November, 1959, there were still high-level assurances that Canada would acquire the Lacrosse, given the successful completion of tests.[28] However, the tests were not successful. As announced by General Pearkes on March 29, 1960, the weapon changed in nature and tactical employment while under development; in particular, its operation became too complex for it to be employed in forward areas. Accord-

22. *Montreal Daily Star*, June 12, 1962. The speaker was Douglas Harkness, Pearkes's successor as Minister of National Defence.

23. See, e.g., Halpenny Committee *Proceedings*, July 7, 1960, p. 449.

24. Even under a strategy which sought to avoid the early recourse to nuclear weapons, the carriers would have been equally necessary. See Neville Brown, *Strategic Mobility* (New York: Praeger, 1964), p. 198. Also, Alastair Buchan and Philip Windsor, *Arms and Stability in Europe* (London: Chatto and Windus, 1963), p. 158.

25. *Globe and Mail* (Toronto), October 3, 1958.

26. *Maclean's Magazine*, January 3, 1959.   27. See Appendix II.

28. As given by Howard Green, following a meeting of the Canada-U.S. Joint Ministerial Committee on Defense at Camp David. See *Le Devoir*, November 10, 1959.

ingly, he continued, the Canadian Army had been authorized to acquire the 762 millimeter rocket and Honest John launcher known collectively as the Honest John system.[29] While this change of weapon systems was not to be compared in its substantive importance or in its impact on opinion with the Arrow or Bomarc cases, it provided one more discomfiting reminder of the consequences of depending upon weapons that were under development in the U.S. Unfortunately, it came only a few days after the leak of the USAF's revised air defense plan, with its sharp cutback of funds for Bomarc. On this occasion, criticism was directed at the government not so much because of the country of origin of the missile, as because of the decision's implications for nuclear weapons policy and for the brigade's military role. In the announcement of the decision to acquire Honest John, no mention was made of the fact that it used a nuclear warhead. Only under questioning by the shadow Minister of Defense, Mr. Hellyer, was the statement evoked that the missile could use either nuclear or conventional warheads; even then, no indication was given of which type the government intended to acquire.[30] As for the brigade's role, Mr. Hellyer regretted the choice of Honest John over the Little John, a lighter weapon which, because it was air transportable, could have been used in the mobile reserve role then under consideration.[31] General Pearkes's reply that there was no intention that the brigade be transported by air in Europe was one of the first indications that the mobile reserve role had been rejected.[32] By the summer of 1960, Canadian troops were receiving training in the U.S. in the use of the Honest John.[33] By early 1962, the missiles were introduced into service in Europe, although no decision had yet been taken to supply them with nuclear warheads.[34]

The armored personnel carrier it intended to acquire for the brigade group was a Canadian-developed vehicle, the "Bobcat." Its development was undertaken in Canada in 1953, at a time when no other allied nation had begun a similar project.[35] By 1963, ten years later, British, American and German carriers of a comparable nature were operational—the American M-113 had been in use for two

29. *Debates* (1960), III, 2548, 49. The Honest John became the subject of a good deal of political humor, since the Prime Minister was sometimes jocularly called by the same name.
30. *Ibid.*, p. 2644.
31. Halpenny Committee *Proceedings* (July 7, 1960), p. 461.   32. *Ibid.*
33. *Ibid.*, June 3, 1960, p. 234.   34. *Debates* (1962), II, 1104.
35. Sauvé Committee *Proceedings* (October 29, 1963), pp. 607–08.

or three years. Yet the "Bobcat," after a development expenditure
of some nine million dollars, was not yet in production, and the
Canadian brigade group was still without its needed mobility.[36]
Moreover, any "Bobcats" produced, if and when they were ready,
were certain to cost substantially more than the $23,000 unit price
of the M–113, because of the comparative shortness of the Canadian
production run. Accordingly, in 1964, the development of this vehicle was stopped, and an order placed for M–113's. There were
two villains in the story of this unsuccessful development program,
as it was explained to the Commons' Defense Committee in late
1964. One was the cost-plus contract, the terms of which provided
no incentives to the developing firm, Leyland Motors (which was
later absorbed by Canadian Car Company, which was taken over in
turn by Hawker-Siddeley) to hold down development costs. The
other was inadequate financing, the necessity for seeking new funds
at various stages as a result of the rising costs of development under
the cost-plus contracts. The pace of development was also affected
by the fact that the developing company changed ownership several
times, and that it was not pressed by government officials as vigorously as it might have been.[37] When asked what measures were
being taken to prevent such boondoggles from occurring in the future, Mr. Hellyer, who was then the Minister of National Defense,
drew some morals from such experiences as those of the Arrow
and Bobcat:

> There are certain lessons open to us. One of them is that first
> of all you have no guarantee that anyone else is going to buy
> a finished product. Secondly, if you have a good idea and you
> are going to develop it, develop it with speed and go all out to
> make sure it is the first and the best. You then have the best
> chance of getting markets in other countries. What we must not
> do, and what has been done in this country once or twice, is to
> extend the design and development time so much that you lag
> behind the efforts of others who come in later and because of their
> accelerated efforts overtake you and pass you.[38]

THE AIR DIVISION

In the late 1950's, as the brigade group encountered certain military and economic difficulties which made its role in Germany increasingly difficult, so the air division's position became increasingly
awkward. The reasons, in its case, were rather political than military

36. *Ibid.*; and *Globe and Mail* (Toronto), November 20, 1964.
37. Sauvé Committee *Proceedings* (October 29, 1963), p. 608.   38. *Ibid.*

or economic. The primacy of politics, which prevented the change in role which was favored on military grounds in the former case, produced a change in the latter, even though the military argument was not convincing. At the time it was first sent to Europe, and for years thereafter, the air division helped fill a crucial gap in Western Europe's air defenses, a gap caused by the non-existence or ill-equipped nature of European air forces. As these air forces were rebuilt, they began to assume increasing responsibility for their own defense. Moreover, the basis upon which they did so was not that of an integrated system; largely because of French opposition to integration, the single commander, single ground environment and single concept of air battle which were needed on military grounds did not exist. Logistics, as well as operational control, remained national responsibilities in most of the European area, until, in 1960, a compromise was reached. This allowed an integrated system to operate in the forward area, though France remained largely under national control.[39]

Because of this emphasis on the territorial nature of air defense, this role was an increasingly uncomfortable one for the Canadian air division. Some thought was given to changing it, at the time when the F–86 and CF–100 aircraft would need replacement. Of the alternatives that were available, complete withdrawal was opposed by SACEUR's General Norstad, who valued not only the direct military contribution of the air division (whose performance was consistently ranked among the highest of the units under his command), but also the example it set for the smaller European nations as the kind of efficient military contribution that was within the capacity of small countries to make.[40] The alternative of providing air transport for a mobile reserve force, whether composed of the Canadian brigade or not, was not acceptable to the RCAF, which scorned what was considered a role of flying "air taxis"; nor was it a requirement of SACEUR.[41] There was discussion of having the division perform a number of distinct roles, each requiring a different aircraft; but General Foulkes, the chairman of the Chiefs of Staff Committee at the time, immediately ruled this out. He expected that the Canadian government would insist on manufacturing each of the aircraft in Canada for political reasons, and this would have made the cost prohibitive.[42]

39. Mulley, pp. 178ff.
40. Halpenny Committee *Proceedings* (June 24, 1960), p. 351; and interviews.
41. Interviews.   42. *Debates* (1959), V, 5400; and interviews.

As has been pointed out already, the matter was left in abeyance until the future of the Arrow was settled. This was done because it would have been bad politics to buy an American aircraft when a Canadian one was being cancelled, and also because the possibility of using the Arrow in Europe meant that a role might have to be chosen to suit the aircraft, rather than the reverse. The delay was indeed significant. The "strike reconnaissance" role (which was eventually adopted) was first recommended in 1956, when the St. Laurent government was still in office. That government received the proposal unenthusiastically and, like other defense matters, postponed it until after the election.[43] It was discussed with the Diefenbaker government, in the form of talks between General Norstad and General Pearkes, as early as November, 1957.[44] But it was not agreed upon until July, 1959, or put into effect until 1962, when the first CF–104's became operational. It was still later when they received their nuclear weapons. Military consequences of this delay are explored later; for the moment, we shall merely note its existence.

The Arrow's demise not only permitted the question of re-equipping the air division to be taken up again; it contributed to the pressures for doing so. While it was true that there was some political liability in buying an American aircraft after cancelling the Arrow, this was now offset by the fact that the RCAF was looking for a new channel for its energies and influence. The choice fell upon the air division in Europe. Air Marshal Hugh Campbell, the Chief of the Air Staff, settled upon the strike reconnaissance role with General Norstad, and arranged to bring him to Ottawa to help sell the government on the idea.[45] His visit was made in mid-May, when he specifically recommended the strike reconnaissance role for the air division[46] and reportedly also asked the cabinet to take an early decision to provide the brigade group with nuclear weapons, as it had undertaken to do in 1957.[47] It was somewhat surprising that the Government consented to this new role, not only because it involved the use of nuclear weapons, but also because it involved flying offensive missions to strike targets behind enemy lines. This marked a considerable change from Canada's accustomed, politically congenial air defense role.[48] When General Pearkes made the an-

43. Foulkes testimony, p. 499. Also, Foulkes, "The Complications of Continental Defence," p. 103.
44. *Globe and Mail* (Toronto), November 14, 1957.
45. Interviews.   46. *Debates* (1959), V, 5400.
47. *Globe and Mail* (Toronto), May 19, 1959.
48. The RCAF did perform bombing operations during World War II, and

nouncement in the House on July 2, 1959, there was, significantly, no mention that the role entailed the use of nuclear weapons.[49]

The reaction to the announcement of the decision was milder than might have been expected, in view of the facts that the role was offensive and nuclear, and that it would mean using an American aircraft. However, the latter irritant was considerably softened by the government's statement that the choice of the Lockheed F–104 Starfighter (the plane selected from the more than twenty that were considered), was dependent upon working out satisfactory arrangements to produce the plane in Canada under license.[50] This was achieved in fact, although there were last-minute pressures, emanating from Lockheed, suggesting that Canada's share in production should take the form of manufacturing one component of the aircraft for both Canadian and American use, instead of the entire aircraft for the shorter Canadian production run.[51] The Canadian rejection of these suggestions was quickly understood by the U.S. Department of Defense, and arrangements were completed for the construction of the airframes by Canadair and of the engines by Orenda for the payment of some seven million dollars in licensing fees and royalties. This was a relatively small fraction of the total cost, which somewhat exceeded $400 million.[52] It was estimated that the order would create some 6000 jobs in Canada for three years.[53] This judgment doubtlessly contributed considerably to the erosion of such opposition as there was to the decision.[54]

Some criticism was directed not at the decision itself but at the aircraft which was chosen. Mr. Hellyer pointed out that the F–104 had been accident prone, that it could not be used for the North American squadrons—as his candidate, the Republic F–105D Thunderchief, allegedly could. He also claimed that such substantial modifications would have to be made on the F–104 to render it suitable for Canadian purposes, that it amounted to developing a new aircraft—something the government had said that it would not do again, after the Arrow experience.[55] It was also reported that Republic had made an attractive offer to provide tooling at nominal cost

towards the end of hostilities it was contemplating major action of this kind in the Pacific theatre. See Stanley W. Dziuban, *Military Relations Between the United States and Canada, 1939–45* (Washington: Office of the Chief of Military History, Department of the Army, 1959), p. 271. Since 1945, however, the dominant emphasis had been given to air defense.

49. *Debates* (1959), V, 5352.   50. *Ibid.*   51. Interviews.
52. *Debates* (1959), V, 5691.   53. *Globe and Mail* (Toronto), July 3, 1959.
54. *Ibid.*, Editorial, July 4, 1959.   55. *Debates* (1959), V, 5461.

if the F–105 were chosen.[56] In point of fact, the choice had been not between the F–104 and F–105, but between the F–104 and Grumman's F–11–1F Super Tiger: these were the two aircraft with which the RCAF was happy.[57] Since either could have been produced under license in Canada, the decision was made in favor of the F–104, on the basis of the Department of Defense Production judgment that it stood a better chance of being sold in export. It had already been chosen by West Germany, and there were good prospects that other European nations might standardize on it. As has been seen in the case of the Voodoo swap, this judgment was vindicated.

The more significant criticisms were directed at the strategic aspects of the decision. Some of these concerned the delayed timing of the decision.[58] It had come too late; and there was a further delay before the planes could be put into production. This meant that by the time they became operational—the first squadrons were activated in October, 1962[59]—the existence of Soviet IRBM's in considerable numbers in Eastern Europe rendered the airfields vulnerable from which the strike aircraft were operating, and the credibility of their use was very questionable.[60] General Pearkes replied that the government had been able to negotiate a better deal by waiting until 1959 than they could have obtained a year earlier.[61] This claim, even if true, was certainly not the reason for waiting, and was not an answer anyway to the strategic argument. Another problem was created by the fact that two of the Canadian airfields from which the F–104's were to operate were located in France, and were therefore subject to the French policy of disallowing nuclear weapons not under French national control on their soil. These restrictions "were really imposed against the United States some years ago and they have rubbed off on us."[62] There were even suggestions, though probably not very realistic, that the Germans might adopt the same policy, thereby worsening the problem.[63] Those who were concerned about this problem were not reassured to hear from General Pearkes that there had been no negotiations with France about it, and that his conviction that, in an emergency, the problem could be solved by relocating the planes stemmed from nothing more concrete than his "confidence in the supreme allied commander."[64]

56. *New York Times,* May 17, 1959, p. 24.
57. Interviews.   58. *Debates* (1959), V, 5400.
59. Sauvé Committee *Proceedings* (November 14, 1963), p. 699.
60. Foulkes testimony, p. 499.   61. *Debates* (1959), V, 5393.
62. Sauvé Committee *Proceedings* (October 31, 1963), p. 631.
63. Foulkes testimony, p. 499.
64. Halpenny Committee *Proceedings* (July 11, 1960), p. 501.

The criticisms just described were not caused by a distaste for the strike role so much as by concern that it would probably not be effective. There were also those—including both such Liberals as the Leader of the Opposition and the shadow Minister of Defense, and such Conservatives as the Toronto *Globe and Mail*—who regretted the nuclear role itself, the turn toward which had "radically altered [the air division's] whole posture, and inevitably the posture of the nation."[65] These critics were not appeased by the disingenuousness and confusion of government spokesmen about the nature of the new role. The disingenuousness concerns the role's nuclear aspect. There was a reluctance even to mention that the F–104 *could* carry nuclear arms; the preference, as was noted for the first announcement of the new role, was not to mention the word "nuclear" at all. This was defended by the doubtful assertion that "it was well known that the 104 could carry nuclear weapons."[66] Moreover, when pressed, the most which was ever admitted by General Pearkes was that the plane "could" be so armed; it was never mentioned that the "strike" role was by definition nuclear, "attack" being the NATO characterization for a similar role with conventional weapons. Confusion arose about the nature of the targets which the F–104's would attack. In explaining the role to Parliament, General Pearkes said that it involved striking targets of opportunity, that short-range missiles were the preferable instruments for taking out fixed targets.[67] This was directly contradicted by the Canadian commanding officer of the air division:

> I think, Mr. Deachman, when you talk of "interdicting the battlefield" you are confusing a strike role with an attack role. A strike role, in the nuclear, doesn't go around casting these off at targets of, shall we say, targets of opportunity. Certainly not in any context that I know of. Any nuclear target is a pre-determined target. . . . All our targets, I am sure, will emanate from SHAPE itself.[68]

Finally, criticism was directed at the government's failure to demonstrate that it had solved, or even foreseen accurately, the problem of nuclear control. There was an apparent conflict, which was applicable not only to Canada, between the need in an emergency to get the aircraft off the ground as fast as possible in order to avoid pre-emptive attack, and the existing requirement that the aircraft's nuclear weapons could only be armed after receipt of authorization

65. *Globe and Mail* (Toronto), July 4, 1959.
66. Halpenny Committee *Proceedings* (July 11, 1960), p. 500.
67. *Ibid.*, p. 503; and *Debates* (1959), V, 5474, 75.
68. Sauvé Committee *Proceedings* (November 14, 1963), p. 703.

from the U.S. and Canadian governments. As a result of these several inadequately answered criticisms, the judgment of General Foulkes that "this role is unlikely to become a satisfactory and continuing contribution"[69] gained increasingly general acceptance.

NAVAL FORCES

The Royal Canadian Navy, most of which was earmarked for service under SACLANT in case of war, largely escaped during the period 1957–64 the kind of polemical review of its role and equipment which affected RCAF units in North America and Europe, and the Army's brigade group in Germany. That it did so was probably attributable not so much to enlightened naval policies as to their relative unimportance and the absence of significant change in their broad outlines. As it was the budgetary Cinderella of the services—it received only eighteen per cent of the funds spent on the three services during the decade 1951–1960[70]—there was not the same incentive for the Navy's expenditure, and therefore, its policies to be as closely scrutinized as were those of the Air Force and Army. This was perhaps reinforced by the greater difficulty which potential parliamentary critics had in comprehending naval strategy than understanding the operations of bombing or shooting down bombers.

Under the operative doctrine of balanced collective forces within NATO, the RCN was given a specialized role throughout this period, namely that of antisubmarine operations, designed to perform the traditional function of keeping open the shipping lanes between North America and Europe in the event of war. This continued to be the official justification for antisubmarine capability even after the adoption of a nuclear strategy by NATO and after evidence became available of Soviet development and deployment of nuclear-powered, missile-firing submarines. It was justified by the theory that mutual deterrence made it likely that "if war occurs we are going to be in a war something like the last ones but with modern conventional weapons."[71] There was no attempt to reconcile this

69. Foulkes testimony, p. 499.

70. See Canada, Department of National Defence, *Information for the Special Committee on Defence Expenditures* (Ottawa: Queen's Printer, 1960), p. 15.

71. Canada, Department of External Affairs, *Reference Papers,* #77. The formulation of the Navy's role in this standard statement of government policy changed between the copies of the document as revised September, 1956, and February, 1958.

view with the apparently contradictory NATO strategy for the land forces in Europe—which did not assume a long, conventional war— or even with the low priority attached to meeting the Canadian commitment to build up the brigade group to a division in case of war. The lack of shipping to carry out that commitment made it practically a dead letter.[72] This paradox was not limited to Canada, however; it rather characterized the alliance as a whole.

No compelling justification was given of the strategy upon which the antisubmarine capability was based; no effective answer was given, either, to those who questioned whether the particular collection of ships and aircraft assembled by the early 1960's for conducting ASW operations represented a well-considered policy. General Foulkes made the point:

> I am not convinced that we really know what is the most efficient and economical antisubmarine force for Canada. There has never been, as far as I know, an unbiased assessment of the relative value of carriers, tracker aircraft, frigates, submarines, helicopters, and long range maritime aircraft in this antinuclear submarine role. What has happened is we have replaced the *Magnificent* by another carrier, the wartime frigates one for one with a $30 million (I understand that figure is out of date) relatively slow escort. The Lancasters have been replaced with the Argus maritime aircraft, which needs another replacement by 1970. But is this present conglomeration of a carrier, tracker aircraft, frigates and helicopters and long range maritime aircraft the most efficient, effective and economical grouping for this task? Or is this grouping just a collection of the plans and ambitions of the air force and navy planners? I suspect it is.[73]

It was not difficult to disparage the Navy's antisubmarine capability, or to identify the problems confronting it. In addition to those cited by General Foulkes, there were budgetary constraints which prevented the acquisition of one component highly desirable in an antisubmarine force—submarines. This led to the cancellation of the order for eight very expensive general purpose frigates, which were sought largely for their contribution to this role.[74] Moreover, a high-ranking naval officer, Commodore James Plomer, made serious charges, some of which were conceded later, about the condition of such equipment as the Navy did possess.[75]

But if it was easy to question the Navy's antisubmarine role and

72. Foulkes testimony, p. 498.   73. *Ibid.*, p. 495.
74. Sauvé Committee *Proceedings* (October 15, 1963), pp. 399, 424; (November 5, 1963), pp. 666, 667.
75. *Ibid.* (October 10, 1963), pp. 337–388; (October 15, 1963), pp. 391–99.

its capacity for performing it, it was not easy to offer better alternatives. The only one which gained any currency was the proposal that Canada concentrate on providing the sealift capacity to transport troops for United Nations peacekeeping duties. Yet barring a vast increase in the demands for such troops, these tasks could be performed by the ships already in use, simply by transferring them temporarily out of the ASW role. And since few, if any, critics were prepared to suggest that the Navy be abolished or reduced to nominal size, the ASW role continued. At a minimum, the RCN's equipment for this role constituted laboratory facilities for keeping current with the latest ASW techniques. So long as the possibility could not be dismissed of the kind of conventional maritime battle implicit in the RCN's role, it was judged useful to continue that role in a limited fashion.

CHAPTER VI

The Problem of Nuclear Weapons

THREE aspects may be distinguished in the nuclear weapons issue which, like a shadow, hovered over and behind the defense debate in Canada throughout the period 1957–64. In question form, they are as follows: (1) Should Canadian forces have nuclear weapons under their exclusive control, whether acquired by manufacture or international agreement? (2) In what ways and to what extent should Canada contribute to the U.S. nuclear deterrent by taking measures under its control, such as allowing the storage of American weapons and/or carriers on Canadian territory? (3) Should Canadian forces in North America and/or Europe be provided with nuclear weapons which are not under their exclusive control? While it was chiefly the third of these which engendered a controversial national debate in Canada, the answers to the first two merit consideration here also, because of their inherent importance and the light which they throw on that debate. A fourth aspect, that of possible Canadian participation in a multinational or multilateral nuclear force, will be discussed in Chapter VIII.

A CANADIAN NUCLEAR DETERRENT?

The fact that some, albeit little, serious consideration has been given to the possibility of a Canadian program for manufacturing nuclear weapons indicates more about the status of Canadian technology than it does about Canada's defense needs.[1] As a participant in the Manhattan Project from June, 1942, Canada is among the countries with the longest experience in nuclear technology. Although co-operation with the United States was curtailed by the U.S. Atomic Energy Act of 1946, the decision was made to continue a modest but substantial program of nuclear research. In 1947, the first

1. The best example of this serious consideration may be found in Leonard Beaton and John Maddox, *The Spread of Nuclear Weapons*, (London: Chatto and Windus, 1962), pp. 98–108. Also useful is John E. Mueller, "Canada as a Non-Nuclear Power." (Unpublished paper prepared under the auspices of the National Security Studies Program, UCLA, June, 1963). This section draws extensively on these two accounts.

Canadian reactor was commissioned at Chalk River, near Ottawa. This program has continued, with the result that "Canada is as well provided [for nuclear research] as any European country in proportion to her size."[2] It has the additional advantages of possessing large deposits of natural uranium and of having, at least until the demise of the Arrow, an aircraft industry capable of producing sophisticated delivery systems. From these factors follows the judgment that "looking at this position as a whole, it does not seem too much to say that Canada could have embarked on nuclear weapons with less effort than has been expended by France."[3]

In spite of these factors, there has been no serious advocacy of a program for producing nuclear weapons in Canada. There are several reasons for this. One is undoubtedly that Canadians, as one of their military historians has observed, "are not a military people. Enjoying a sense of security in their geographical position, Canadians within the last century have displayed small interest in the problems of defense, either of the past or the present day."[4] In strict logic, there is no reason why this distaste for militarism should focus more on nuclear weapons than upon other military systems or policies; the fact remains that in Canada it has.[5] In view of this distaste, there has been no inclination to incur the costs required to produce nuclear weapons, costs which are more keenly appreciated in Canada than in countries with less developed nuclear technologies. More cogent than either the historical or economic reasons for Canada's failure to produce nuclear weapons is the argument on strategic grounds. One side of this argument is that, having no expansionist aims and no security threats which do not at the same time affect the United States, Canada has no need to contemplate major military action independent of the U.S.; the other side is that since an attack upon Canada could not be distinguished from the early stages of an attack upon the United States, the U.S. deterrent "deters attack on Canadian territory precisely to the same extent that it deters attack upon the United States itself. . . . There is no other ally of the United States of which this can be said with equal assurance."[6]

2. Beaton and Maddox, p. 99.   3. *Ibid.*

4. George F. G. Stanley, *Canada's Soldiers: The Military History of an Unmilitary People* (Toronto: Macmillan of Canada, 1960), p. 1.

5. James Eayrs has pointed out that to advocate rejection of nuclear weapons on moral grounds is to commit oneself logically to other measures, which most Canadian proponents of that policy would not favor. See *Northern Approaches: Canada and the Search for Peace*, pp. 36, 37.

6. *Ibid.*, p. 40.

So overwhelmingly one-sided were these reasons, that the Canadian government adopted its non-nuclear course after World War II not so much by deliberate choice as by unconscious assumption: there was never any question of producing nuclear weapons. Students of the subject have written that Canada rejected a nuclear policy "in 1946 by a deliberate and conscious decision."[7] Insofar as can be judged from the public record, this was not the case.[8] This version was only given explicit government endorsement in later years, when credit was sought for fostering non-proliferation, which was, by then, generally regarded as desirable.[9]

While Canada was thus univocal in foregoing a program of nuclear weapons production, its voice was not so clear on the question of whether nuclear weapons to be used under exclusive Canadian control should be sought from the United States. Various proposals that Canada seek some kind of autonomous nuclear capacity were on occasion made by private and public figures, and some of these came close to receiving official support. The most extreme of these proposals was the suggestion of the former Chief of the General Staff, Lieutenant-General Guy Simonds, that Canada build a modest "retaliatory capability based on the atomic submarine."[10] This proposal was endorsed by Melvin Conant, an American student of Canadian military policy, who argued that it was needed to stiffen Canadian resistance to possible nuclear blackmail, and that it was more compatible with Canadian pride and political tradition than the alternative policies (as he saw them) of satellitism or neutrality.[11] Both men appear to have changed their minds later, Simonds in favor of total abstention from nuclear weapons, Conant in favor of Canadian participation in a NATO multilateral nuclear force.[12]

More modest was the aim entertained by some persons, both within and outside the government service, of gaining independent Canadian control over the nuclear weapons contemplated for use

---

7. Beaton and Maddox, p. 98.

8. See Mueller; also Peter Newman in *Maclean's Magazine*, October 22, 1950.

9. "Although at the end of the war Canada could have developed the capability to manufacture nuclear weapons, it elected, as a matter of deliberate choice, not to become a nuclear power." Canada, Department of National Defense, *White Paper on Defence*. (Ottawa: Queen's Printer, 1964), p. 7.

10. *Times* (London), "Supplement on Canada," November 24, 1958, p. vi.

11. Melvin Conant, "Canada and Continental Defence: An American View," *International Journal*, XV (Summer, 1960), p. 227.

12. Sauvé Committee *Proceedings* (October 17, 1963), p. 442; and Melvin Conant, "Canada and Nuclear Weapons: An American View," *International Journal*, XVIII (Spring, 1963), pp. 207ff.

in North American air defense. The proponents of this view were concerned not so much with promoting Canadian independence and sovereignty as with enhancing the deterrent posture: "Canadian control is desirable not for reasons of prestige but because divided control weakens the capacity to deter."[13] There was some variation in the kind of Canadian control which this was thought to entail. Those who did not bear the responsibilities of office were free to propose a thorough Canadian control. If Canada acquired nuclear weapons—so ran the Liberal line at one point in its evolution—they "should be owned by Canada and should be used under Canadian authority exclusively."[14] Such was the importance attached by some people of this persuasion to unified control that they found it

> preferable, should such negotiations leading to exclusive Canadian control fail, to request the United States to assume full operational control over anti-missile and antiaircraft defences installed on Canadian territory at our initiative and our expense. Alternatively, the nuclear components might be acquired from the United Kingdom under conditions allowing for full Canadian control.[15]

The Diefenbaker government, on the other hand, did not get much farther in exploring this question than to consider rectifying a quirk in NORAD's operations whereby American interceptors could be armed with nuclear weapons in an emergency without awaiting presidential authority, while Canadian interceptors in the same command would have to await presidential release of the weapons to Canada, and authorization by the Canadian government.[16] This question was more one of civil-military than of international relations, but in that its solution would have required a change in U.S. legislation it was international. General Pearkes and Sidney Smith went as far as to discuss with committees of the House of Commons the probability that such legislation could be obtained.[17] But as the Diefenbaker government became bogged down in the more basic question of whether Canadian armed forces were to get nuclear weapons at all, nothing ever came of the proposal.

It may be asked whether any of these proposals was realistic, in view of the existing U.S. legislation which prohibited any such relinquishment of the American veto on use of American-made nuclear weapons. The answer is that for at least one of the contem-

13. Eayrs, *Northern Approaches: Canada and the Search for Peace*, p. 43.
14. *Debates* (1960), I, 139. The spokesman was Pearson.
15. Eayrs, *Northern Approaches: Canada and the Search for Peace*, p. 43.
16. Interviews.   17. *Globe and Mail* (Toronto), July 8–9, 1958.

plated changes—that designed to place Canadian and American interceptors in NORAD on the same emergency basis—there was a realistic possibility that a change in the legislation might have been forthcoming. It was publicly intimated by Secretary McElroy in Ottawa, after a meeting with his opposite numbers in August, 1959, that the Administration might seek appropriate legislation from Congress with hopes of success.[18] This possibility was later held by his successor, Thomas Gates, as well.[19] There was even some evidence that a more significant liberalization might be contemplated. For example, *The New York Times* editorially regretted the failure of the 1958 amendments to the Atomic Energy Act to place Canada on the same basis as the United Kingdom so far as nuclear collaboration with the U.S. was concerned.[20] President Eisenhower later stated, in a press conference, that he favored changing the law extensively enough to permit the U.S. to give nuclear weapons to its allies.[21] However, the statement appears to have been a more-or-less unintentional exaggeration of proposals then under consideration in the State Department to give nuclear weapons only to Britain. After a reminder from the Joint Committee on Atomic Energy that it had views on the question, the White House denied any intention of seeking changes in the law.[22]

In view of the difficulty involved in the passage of new legislation as well as the indecision about acquiring nuclear weapons under any conditions, no attempt was made by the Diefenbaker government to get these weapons under exclusive Canadian control, in spite of the fact that some of its statements were perhaps meant to be so interpreted. The debate in Canada has concerned not so much the advisability of seeking changes in U.S. legislation governing nuclear matters, as the measures which the Canadian government should properly take in this area within the limits of existing legislation.

CANADIAN ASSISTANCE FOR THE U.S. NUCLEAR DETERRENT

The least controversial category of such measures included the provision to the United States of certain Canadian resources and

18. *Ibid.*, August 12, 1959; *Montreal Daily Star*, August 12, 1959.
19. Interviews.   20. June 9, 1958, p. 22.
21. *Ibid.*, February 4, 1960, p. 12.
22. Harold L. Nieburg, *Nuclear Secrecy and Foreign Policy*. (Washington: Public Affairs Press, 1964), pp. 193, 94.

facilities. Of course, the most significant Canadian contribution to the U.S. deterrent lay in this category, namely the co-operation in the construction and maintenance of the radar early warning networks, partly by offering Canadian territory and communications channels. For the moment, however, we are not concerned with this general contribution, but with the more specific contributions which affected, or were affected by, the issues of nuclear politics in a more direct way. Two such contributions call for comment: the sale of uranium to the U.S. for military as well as non-military uses; and the granting of permission for U.S. carriers of nuclear warheads to operate in Canadian airspace, or from Canadian soil. As for the former, the relevant point to make here is not that such sales took place in large quantities to the U.K. as well as the U.S. These transactions were, on the Canadian side, economically motivated and did not need the additional, political justification that they aided the American deterrent. The politically relevant point is that Canadian governments gave their blessings to the sales, which were channeled from private producers through a public corporation—Atomic Energy of Canada, Limited—and that they not only approved these sales, but "protested very strongly"[23] when they were reduced. This is a telling rejoinder to the posture of moral rectitude sometimes struck by the Diefenbaker government in its hesitation to accept nuclear weapons. It did not go unnoticed that in contemplating the acceptance of nuclear arms, the Canadian government's position was similar to that of the "dope peddlar who is on the verge of becoming an addict. It is of some significance that the dope peddlar is generally deplored more than the addict."[24]

Lacking the economic motivation present in the case of uranium sales, Canadian governments approached more gingerly the question of enhancing the U.S. deterrent by making available to American forces Canadian territory and airspace. Permission for overflights by SAC bombers on training exercises was given by a general agreement, but the condition was attached (partly because of fears

23. General Charles Foulkes, "Future Defence in the Nuclear Era," Address to the Empire Club of Toronto, February 28, 1963. Text available from Library of Canadian Institute of International Affairs, Edgar Tarr House, Toronto. Canadian concern at the prospect of declining uranium exports, which attained a level of $300 million per year in the 1950's, was expressed, e.g., in the ministerial talks at Camp David in November, 1959. Preston, *Canada in World Affairs: 1959 to 1961*, p. 161.

24. Cited in Eayrs, *Northern Approaches: Canada and the Search for Peace*, p. 36, from the letter of J. W. Hilborn in the *Globe and Mail* (Toronto), November 23, 1959.

related to the nuclear loads of these bombers) that each flight must be cleared with Canadian authorities in advance.[25] Reportedly, the inconvenience of this arrangement at some point led SAC authorities to route their aerial alert force around Canada rather than over it.[26] Refuelling facilities for American aircraft were granted, at first only at the Goose Bay and Harmon air fields which were under a special juridical status.[27] They were extended to other air fields in Canada in 1958.[28] However, such aids to the strategic force were never carried so far as offering sparsely-populated Canadian territory as a home for American strategic bombers or missiles, or Canadian territorial waters for American Polaris submarines.[29] There is no evidence that the Canadian government's failure to make such an offer caused any concern to U.S. administrations. The political difficulties raised by the stationing of American forces abroad were evident, not only in Canada, from the experience of Americans who were in that country to work on the radar networks, but in many countries around the periphery of the Soviet Union where U.S. strategic forces had been based. It is probable that U.S. officials did not regard the military value of such bases in Canada as worth the political cost they would entail.

It is likely that there was more U.S. concern, although after the founding of NORAD it was probably not regarded as crucial, about the existing regime governing the forces of interception in North America. American interceptor squadrons, including those armed with nuclear weapons, were apparently not subject to the rule governing SAC flights that each entry into Canadian airspace must be approved in advance.[30] Neither were they permitted, however, to operate from airfields in Canada, except in case of emergency. Moreover, U.S. interceptor squadrons stationed at Goose Bay, Labrador, and Harmon Field, Newfoundland, were prevented from achieving their maximum effectiveness by being denied the permission

25. *Debates* (1958), I, 781.
26. Eayrs, "Sharing a Continent: The Hard Issues," p. 64.
27. U.S. rights at these bases stemmed from a ninety-nine year lease signed with the U.K. when Newfoundland was still a British possession but honored by Canada when Newfoundland joined the confederation in 1949. See U.S., Department of State, *United States Treaties and Other International Agreements*, III, 4271ff., and 5295ff.
28. *Ibid.*, IX, 903ff.
29. According to Diefenbaker, "That question has not been raised or considered." *Debates* (1958), II, 1425.
30. *Ibid.*, I, 1016. Exactly what principles do govern such flights is not public knowledge, however.

to keep nuclear warheads on the premises for their air-to-air missiles. Talks aimed at gaining this permission were initiated by the United States as early as 1951, even though there was some question that under the terms of the agreements in question Canadian permission was necessary. In 1960 they were said to have been "reaching the stage of very near finality in connection with the exchange of the note."[31] During the following three years it was occasionally asserted that nuclear weapons were in fact present at the bases,[32] but this was denied by both American authorities[33] and spokesmen for the Canadian government, who asserted "categorically that there are no nuclear weapons in Canada."[34] In fact this agreement, along with those aimed at the arming of Canadian weapon systems, was never approved by the Diefenbaker government.[35]

The Acquisition of Carriers for Nuclear Weapons

The most intense part of the Canadian nuclear debate occurred from 1960–63, and the fact which, more than any other, made such a debate unavoidable during these years is that before and during that period the Canadian government acquired five weapons systems which in varying degrees depended on nuclear weapons for their effective employment. Decisions to acquire each of these have been described previously in other contexts. But before describing the delay in providing them with warheads, it will be useful to review the reasons for which each required nuclear weapons, and the timing of their entries into operational readiness.

While it was not one of the five systems eventually acquired, it was the Arrow which first raised the question of nuclear armament for Canadian weapons. Senior officers of the RCAF planned throughout the period of the Arrow's development that it would eventually have the best weapon available, and this meant a nuclear weapon.[36] This was obscured by the fact that the two missiles which were considered for use with the Arrow before its cancellation were the Sparrow II and the Falcon, both of which use conventional high-explosive warheads. But there is no contradiction: this was the period when nuclear weapons design was undergoing great changes,

31. Halpenny Committee *Proceedings* (June 30, 1960), p. 397. And Foulkes, "The Complications of Continental Defence," p. 103.
32. See, for example, the *Globe and Mail* (Toronto), October 31, 1960.
33. *New York Times*, December 11, 1960, p. 50.
34. *Debates* (1962), I, 203.
35. *Ibid.*, 1962–63, II, 1033.   36. Interviews.

and lighter, more compact warheads suitable for use in air-to-air missiles were being devised. In this situation, the Sparrow II (and later the Falcon) was seen as a provisional weapon which would be replaced when the nuclear successor was developed and the requisite political accord negotiated.[37] It is doubtful how far ministers in both the St. Laurent and Diefenbaker governments were aware of these military plans. There were reports that the latter government raised the question with the U.S. in talks at the ministerial level in the summer of 1958, a time when the Arrow was the most seriously considered of the various nuclear weapon carriers.[38] It is ironic that these early initiatives appear to have been Canadian, for at the conclusion of the nuclear controversy, the appearance was given—which did not entirely conform to reality—of the U.S. thrusting nuclear weapons upon an unwilling Canada.

The Bomarc was the first weapon actually acquired by Canada which required nuclear warheads for the performance of its role. A conventional high explosive warhead was developed for the "A" model of the Bomarc, but was discarded in view of the superiority of the nuclear warhead. All American Bomarc squadrons, whether "A" or "B," employ nuclear warheads. In the case of the "B," no conventional warhead was ever developed; and this was the only weapon ever considered for use in Canada. The Diefenbaker government suggested at times that the Bomarc could use either type of warhead.[39] This was true only in the sense that a conventional warhead had existed for the "A" version or could be developed for the "B", but only at considerable cost and delay. The advantages of nuclear warheads which led to the preference for them were two: first, their "kill capacity" is greater, i.e., they have a higher likeli-

---

37. Interviews.
38. Some of these reports were denied. In particular, the reports that General Pearkes in his Washington talks with Secretary McElroy in August, 1958, raised the question of buying the MB–1 Genie missile, which uses a nuclear warhead, were denied by Sidney Smith. See the *Globe and Mail* (Toronto), August 5–6, 1958, and the *New York Times*, August 4, 1958, p. 1. There was no official comment on another article by Chalmers Roberts in the *Washington Post*, July 11, 1958, p. 1, which alleged that the Canadians, in talks in Ottawa, sought to win the agreement of Secretary Dulles to provide them with warheads but that Dulles, concerned at that stage about nuclear proliferation, was willing at most to provide for the emergency supply of such weapons, not for their stockpiling in Canada. The report sounds dubious, but if it is true, it increases the irony of the nuclear episode; for at its conclusion in 1963 it was Canada which was proposing that such emergency provisions be worked out and the U.S. which was insisting on stockpiles.
39. Halpenny Committee *Proceedings* (June 22, 1960), p. 328.

CANADA'S CHANGING DEFENSE POLICY

hood of destroying a target at a given distance from the target than a conventional warhead, so that less accuracy is required; second, the radiation produced by a nuclear explosion can render harmless or less effective the attacking warhead by "cooking" it. Since enemy bombs are expected to utilize "dead man" fuses which will detonate on impact, this capability could significantly reduce the damage from bombs intercepted in Canada's populous area.[40] The two Canadian Bomarc squadrons were emplaced in the fall of 1961 and became operational, though harmless, in mid-March, 1962.[41] They remained in this condition until early 1964, by which time the nuclear controversy had been resolved and their warheads had been delivered.[42]

The missiles for the Canadian brigade group in Europe—the Lacrosse, and the Honest John in whose favor it was rejected—were both said by Canadian government spokesmen to have the capability to use either nuclear or conventional warheads.[43] This was, in fact, beside the point. The military rationale for equipping the brigade group with either of these missiles was to provide the tactical nuclear firepower needed by troops on the front line to implement NATO's nuclear strategy. It was later admitted that the Honest John is "a most inefficient weapon for firing high explosive warheads," if one existed in fact.[44] Nevertheless, the Honest John battalion was sent to Europe, where it had joined the brigade group by early 1962.[45] Yet it, too, remained unarmed throughout the tenure of the Diefenbaker government.

In the case of the air division, its role of "strike reconnaissance" was by definition a nuclear role; and, accordingly, the version of the F-104 with which it was equipped was "designed exclusively for the delivery of nuclear warheads," although similar aircraft used by other NATO forces possessed a dual capability.[46] Delivery of

40. Sauvé Committee *Proceedings* (June 27, 1963), p. 17. One of the most spirited episodes of these 1963 hearings occurred when the existence of this "cooking" phenomenon was questioned by a group of physicists from the University of Alberta. They based their case on theoretical arguments alone and claimed access to no classified information. The government, which was privy not only to classified theoretical information but to data on experiments carried out in the United States allegedly confirming the phenomenon, held its ground. See *ibid.*, August 1, 1963, pp. 287–314 and the Committee's *Report*, p. 806.
41. *Montreal Daily Star*, March 14, 1962.
42. *Globe and Mail* (Toronto), January 16, 1964.
43. *Ibid.*, January 7, 1961.
44. Sauvé Committee *Proceedings* (October 29, 1963), p. 618.
45. *Debates* (1962), II, 1104.
46. Sauvé Committee *Proceedings, Report*, p. 804.

these aircraft began in October, 1962, and continued at the rate of one every three days. After their arrival, they remained without weapons to perform their assigned role until mid-1964.[47]

The Voodoo squadrons used by the RCAF were armed with conventional G.A.R. Falcon missiles when they were brought into Canada, even though they had used the nuclear MB–1 Genie earlier in service with the USAF.[48] The superiority of the latter followed from the same factors which applied to the nuclear warhead for Bomarc. Therefore, when these aircraft were transferred from American to Canadian use their effectiveness was reduced. In contrast to the Bomarc, F–104, and Honest John, they were armed conventionally and so were not completely useless. Yet by late 1964, these squadrons had not been armed with nuclear missiles.

The RCN and the maritime squadrons of the RCAF never became so completely dependent upon nuclear weapons as did the forces performing other roles. Yet nuclear depth charges would have increased somewhat the effectiveness of the Argus maritime aircraft and the Navy's surface craft in their anti-submarine role. Negotiations for these weapons were never undertaken by the Diefenbaker government; accordingly, they were not provided for in the agreement reached by the Pearson government and the U.S. in August, 1963.

THE GOVERNMENT DELAYS ITS DECISION

There was little evidence before 1959 for predicting that the nuclear issue would become politically explosive in Canada. In spite of the traditional Canadian anti-militarism which might have been expected to seize on the issue, and in spite of an occasionally-expressed anxiety about overflights of U.S. aircraft carrying nuclear weapons, nothing resembling an outcry had been raised on any of the occasions when a debate on the nuclear issue was appropriate. On the two most notable of these occasions (the governments' reports to the House of Commons on the NATO meetings of December, 1954, and December, 1957), there was no discussion whatsoever of the significance of the NATO decisions affecting the deployment of nuclear weapons, nor was there any criticism or support of the governments' concurrence in those decisions.[49] The significance of this is the greater since one of the governments was Liberal, the

47. *Globe and Mail* (Toronto), June 30, 1964.
48. *Debates* (1962), II, 1985.
49. *Debates* (1955), I, 628–29; and 1957–58, III, 2719–28, 2783–87.

other Conservative. The absence of debate particularly on the second of these two occasions—the NATO Heads of government meeting of 1957—was especially regrettable, since it obscured the significance for Canada of Diefenbaker's acceptance without reservation of the agreement concluded there for the establishment of nuclear stockpiles for NATO forces in Europe. This acceptance was understood by the military staff of NATO as an "indication that Canada would acquire nuclear weapons for its forces in Europe."[50] Whether Diefenbaker himself grasped this is uncertain, but the concerned cabinet ministers apparently did so. By the summer of 1958, the defense and foreign ministers were calmly discussing before a committee of the House the possibility (which they implied would very likely be realized), of Canada's obtaining nuclear weapons from the United States.[51] Finally, the RCAF's unquestioned plan that the Arrow should eventually be armed with nuclear weapons suggested, even if it was not well-known by ministers, that political objections to accepting nuclear weapons were not expected.

Nor can an explanation for the Diefenbaker government's long hesitation on this issue be found easily by reference to the background or previous career of the Prime Minister. Not only had Mr. Diefenbaker refrained from criticizing the St. Laurent government's concurrence in NATO's 1954 decision to adopt a tactical nuclear strategy; he had been prone, during these years, to stress the danger of not doing enough in the atomic field, rather than the evil of doing too much.[52] Even the indecisiveness which marked the nuclear weapons problem is hard to explain by reference to the early part of his ministry; his prompt decisions to enter NORAD, and to leave Canadian forces in Europe as long as they were desired both represented steps which the St. Laurent government had been loath to take and had postponed. Indeed, the former was criticized on the grounds that it was too impetuous. Whether or not the later indecision is to be regarded as a verifying instance of the proverb "once bitten, twice shy," it remains a fact that there was indecision and delay. The reasons for it we shall have to examine. In doing so, it should be borne in mind that the story to be told is a controversial one, one on which all the evidence is not yet in. Future revelations may amplify or modify the account which follows; it is unlikely that they will render invalid its main points.

50. Foulkes, "The Complications of Continental Defence," p. 103.
51. *Globe and Mail* (Toronto), July 8–9, 1958.
52. *Debates* (1953–54), V, 4968–69.

The question of acquiring nuclear weapons first became immediate in the fall of 1958 when the government announced its decisions to buy Bomarc and Lacrosse missiles. These announcements did not refer to the type of warheads which the missiles used; the question of acquiring nuclear warheads for them was raised privately with U.S. authorities before it was made public. In particular, it was discussed when the Canada-U.S. Joint Ministerial Committee on Defense met in Paris on the occasion of the NATO ministerial meeting in December, 1958. Agreement in principle was reached on this occasion for the provision of those weapons which the Canadian military advisers said were needed. Technical details were left to be worked out, and General Foulkes, the chairman of the Chiefs of Staff Committee, was sent to Washington.[53] In the meantime, the government decided finally to cancel the Arrow; and in his announcement of February 20, the Prime Minister referred also to the nuclear negotiations. He pointed out that "the full potential of these defensive weapons [Bomarc and Lacrosse] is achieved only when they are armed with nuclear warheads." He reported also that negotiations aimed at the provision of these warheads were underway with the U.S., and expressed confidence that formal agreement would be reached.[54] In the meantime, satisfactory progress was being made in the negotiations. The press in Washington revealed the agreement-in-principle and anticipated an imminent announcement; however, in the fashion of things to come, the government denied to the Canadian press that a draft agreement was in sight.[55] More importantly, an agreement was signed on May 22 and sent to Congress on May 27 authorizing an exchange of classified information regarding defense plans, military reactors, and defense against nuclear weapons. This was to the extent permitted by the Atomic Energy Act, as amended. Especially significant were provisions which authorized the training of Canadian forces in the use of nuclear weapons, and the supply to them of non-nuclear parts of nuclear systems.[56]

In the meantime, a change of personnel was taking place which was crucial for the outcome of the negotiations. Sidney Smith, the Secretary of State for External Affairs, died of a heart attack on March 17. For approximately three months, he was not replaced,

53. Interviews.   54. See Appendix II.
55. *New York Times*, March 8, 1959, p. 1; *Globe and Mail* (Toronto), March 9, 1959.
56. *New York Times*, May 26, 1959, p. 3.

and Mr. Diefenbaker again took the portfolio himself. He then named the former Minister of Public Works, Howard Green to the position. Mr. Green was a close political associate of Mr. Diefenbaker from British Columbia. Reportedly he had never visited Washington, and had not been overseas since returning to Canada from participation in World War I. However, it was true that he had been a member of the Standing Committee on External Affairs of the House from 1949 to 1955 and that, as a British Columbian, he had interested himself in Canadian-Japanese relations and in proposals for cooperating with the U.S. in controlling the Columbia River waters.[57] He was prone, whether out of conviction or political expediency, to making statements with an anti-American coloring.[58] Most importantly, he seized upon disarmament as the cause which it would be the primary business of his ministry to further. It was not always so. Years earlier, at the time of the Korean war, he had militantly advocated a more intense armed effort than the government of the day was making, bringing to this appeal the same moral fervor which he later showed in pressing for disarmament. By the end of his tenure in office, this was the critical issue:

> May I say that Canada is involved and is helping in an idealistic way all over the world. I mention first the field of disarmament. I deal with that first because this is the main way in which world peace can eventually be achieved. This is where effort is most worth while.[59]

The fervor of this attachment to disarmament is sufficiently mystifying as well as sufficiently important to be explored more specifically below. It is relevant to note here that since there was little enough that Canada could do to promote disarmament, it was all the more important, according to his view, that it do what it could: set a good (non-proliferating) example by refraining from acquiring or storing nuclear weapons on its soil. It is curious that Green attached more importance to keeping nuclear weapons—whether for U.S. or Canadian forces—out of Canada, where they could only be used defensively, than in refusing such weapons for Canadian forces in Europe, where their function could be called offensive and

57. Preston, *Canada in World Affairs: 1959 to 1961*, p. 6.
58. The more usual view is that Green is pro-British, but his nationalism sometimes calls this loyalty into question. See Peyton Lyon, *The Policy Question* (Toronto: McClelland and Stewart, 1963), p. 93.
59. *Debates* (1962–63), III, 3068. Other examples of "Greenery" may be found in Peyton Lyon, "Canada is Becoming a Mouse that Roars," *Maclean's Magazine*, June 18, 1960.

even provocative. He was apparently motivated more by a concern for the purity of Canadian soil than by a desire to reduce the risks of war.

There was some evidence that Mr. Diefenbaker was delaying a nuclear decision even before Mr. Green took over at External Affairs. In particular, the May, 1959, visit to Ottawa of General Norstad gave rise to reports that Norstad had felt it necessary to press the government for an early decision on the provision of nuclear weapons to the brigade group.[60] But the government's subsequent decision, as announced on July 2, to accept a nuclear role for the air division as well, seemed to be an earnest pledge of its intention to proceed with the acquisition of nuclear weapons, at the same time that it made such action increasingly important. In the summer of 1959 statements by General Pearkes made it seem virtually certain that the weapons would be obtained. "It is Government policy," he said on one occasion, "that Canadian troops should be armed as efficiently and effectively as are troops with which they are co-operating."[61] Since the allies with which Canada was working most closely were armed with nuclear weapons, the implication seemed clear that he meant for Canada to have them, too. In a television interview he also said, without qualification, that the squadrons of the air division in Europe would get nuclear weapons. This was later regarded as a slip of the tongue.[62] In the meantime, agreement was being held up by disagreement within the cabinet, for Mr. Green, at least, would not accept the draft agreement approved by the defense ministers and chiefs of staff of both countries.[63]

The logjam was temporarily broken when the Canada-United States Joint Ministerial Committee on Defense met again at Camp David in November, 1959. General agreement was reached among all parties, including Mr. Green, for the provision of nuclear weapons to Canadian forces.[64] When the delegations returned home, however, the stalling resumed as before.

It was natural that more and more questions should be directed to the government about these negotiations, which had been going on for months without any public evidence of a result. In response to these questions, Mr. Diefenbaker made, on January 18, 1960,

60. *Globe and Mail* (Toronto), May 15, 1959; *Montreal Daily Star*, July 31, 1959.
  61. *Debates* (1959), V, 5393.
  62. *Globe and Mail* (Toronto), August 7, 1959.
  63. *Ibid.*, June 30, 1960; and interviews.
  64. *Washington Post*, November 10, 1959, p. 5; and interviews.

in what was to be the first of a series of artful policy pronouncements committing him to nothing, a statement of the government's position:

> Eventually Canadian forces *may* require certain nuclear weapons *if* Canadian forces are to be kept effective. For example, the Bomarc anti-aircraft missile to be effective *would* require nuclear warheads. . . . In these circumstances negotiations are proceeding with the United States in order that the necessary weapons can be made available for Canadian defence units *if* and *when* they are required.[65] [Emphasis supplied.]

Statements of this kind, which were to continue in essentially the same form until early 1963, represented a shift in the government's official position. This was a real shift, even if it was largely conveyed by a change in tone, away from the relatively forthright position of early 1959 toward the anti-nuclear position of the Green contingent in the cabinet. It was to become characteristic that the Prime Minister refused to elaborate on the statement or to clarify in any way its carefully contrived ambiguities. However, he did acknowledge that the negotiations with the U.S. were continuing and that General Foulkes had postponed his retirement from active service a few months in order to devote himself to their completion.[66]

The fine art of delaying decision and concealing the divisions within the cabinet by using deliberately imprecise and loose language occasionally involved the government in embarrassing arguments over linguistic usage. In July, 1960, Mr. Green told a committee of the House that his department had not engaged in any negotiations concerning the use or storage of nuclear weapons, except those which were aimed at giving the U.S. permission to store such weapons for use on American interceptors at the U.S. bases at Goose Bay and Harmon Field.[67] This statement seemed to contradict earlier ones by both the Prime Minister[68] and the Minister of National Defense,[69] indicating that for some sixteen months negotiations concerning nuclear weapons for *Canadian* forces had been under way. For although the bulk of these negotiations had been handled by the military and the Department of National Defense, External Affairs *had* been involved, if only by virtue of Mr. Green's participation in the Camp David talks. This paradox was explained by General Pearkes, and the explanation confirmed by Mr. Diefenbaker,

---

65. *Debates* (1960), I, 73.   66. *Ibid.*, p. 144.
67. Halpenny Committee *Proceedings* (June 30, 1960), p. 387.
68. See Appendix III.
69. *Debates* (1959), V, 5393.

who pointed out that Mr. Green had used the word "negotiations" in the peculiar sense of an exchange of formal notes.[70] "Discussions" with the U.S. were continuing on the broad subject of nuclear weapons. Only in the case of weapons for Goose Bay and Harmon Field had they reached the point of "negotiations," at which the Department of External Affairs became involved.[71] Another of the government's favorite phrases, that of the "full potential" which Bomarc could reach only when armed with nuclear weapons, proved similarly embarrassing when analyzed by the opposition, in this statement by Mr. Pearson: "Either we wish to use a weapon which will not achieve its full potential, and that is a strange basis for military policy, or we decided in February, 1959, to acquire the nuclear warhead without which the full potential would not be possible."[72] The close scrutiny which the opposition came to devote to the phrasing of government statements on this subject was probably inevitable considering the ministers' unwillingness to provide a clear indication of policy and their inclination to use carefully guarded language. The 1960 Speech from the Throne was the first in several years which made no reference to defense or collective security.

At the same time that this verbal jousting was occurring on the public level, agreement was almost reached again in private talks with the U.S. Secretary Gates visited Ottawa in July, 1960, for a meeting of the Joint Ministerial Committee, in which one of the main items of discussion was the proposed exchange of CL–44's for F–101's. As we have already seen, this deal was agreed to on the ministerial level, only to be rejected later at the governmental level. One reason for this rejection was the unwritten part of the agreement reached on that occasion, an understanding that Canada would finally consent to arming its forces with nuclear weapons. The specific connection here was that the "Voodoos" which it was proposed to divert into Canada were already armed with nuclear weapons; their effectiveness would have been diminished if the nuclear problem were not solved by the time that they were acquired by the RCAF. That an understanding had been reached, in Mr. Gate's view, was not apparent from the communique but from his comments at a press conference at the conclusion of the talks: he "would assume" that the Canadian Bomarcs would get nuclear weapons and he "would think" that this would be done before the bases

70. *Ibid.* (1960), V, 5653; and Halpenny Committee *Proceedings* (June 30, 1960), p. 394.
71. *Ibid.*   72. *Debates* (1960–61), VIII, 8345.

were ready.[73] However, Mr. Green who was standing at his side, pointed out that the government had not yet reached a decision.[74] It never did do so, and this was one, if not the primary, reason why the swap deal was never completed.[75] A year later, when the Voodoos were brought into Canada, it was made explicit that they were to use conventional arms. General Pearkes's speeches continued to imply that a decision would be forthcoming; in his presentation to the House in August, 1960, he appeared more than ever pro-nuclear as he attacked the anti-nuclear program of the Liberals.[76] But as nothing came of the negotiations, they were soon discontinued. When Parliament was prorogued on August 10, the issue subsided for a time. The strength of the pro-nuclear element in the cabinet was diminished during the recess when, on October 11, General Pearkes was replaced by Douglas Harkness as Minister of National Defense. Harkness proved no less committed than Pearkes to the acquisition of nuclear weapons, but unlike Pearkes (and Howard Green) he was not a close associate of the Prime Minister's and therefore was somewhat less likely to be heeded. It was not long after Harkness's appointment before it became public knowledge that he and Green were working at cross-purposes: at almost the same time that Green was encouraging an anti-nuclear women's peace group in its efforts, Harkness was asking a group of reserve officers to help him combat the activities of such groups.[77]

The early months of 1961 brought no change in this stalemate. Confronted with the need to justify a two-year delay in reaching a decision, the government resorted to a variety of arguments. One was the contention that the negotiations need not be pressed urgently, because the weapons for which the warheads were intended were not yet ready.[78] This argument was sometimes taken even further. Mr. Harkness suggested that the determination that nuclear weapons would be needed in the future did not have to be made before ordering carriers for them: such orders were justified to avoid the delay caused by lead times, as long as the possibility existed that nuclear weapons *might* be needed in the future.[79] Even in 1960, the validity of this argument was doubtful, since the Voodoos

73. *Vancouver Province*, July 14, 1960.   74. *Ibid.*
75. *Financial Post*, June 17, 1961.   76. *Debates* (1960), VII, 7521ff.
77. *Christian Science Monitor*, February 11, 1961. Harkness's talk was supposed to have been off-the-record, but it did not remain so.
78. See, for example, General Pearkes in Halpenny Committee *Proceedings* (June 22, 1960), p. 325.
79. *Debates* (1960–61), VIII, 8357.

which were then contemplated for Canadian use were ready to use nuclear-tipped missiles if the political decision had been taken. By 1961, both Bomarcs and Honest Johns were almost ready to come into service, but each required, before it could become operational, a three- to six-month period for construction of nuclear storage facilities and training. By that time, the argument was clearly unjustified. Another reason adduced to justify the delay was the desire to do nothing to prejudice the chances of the disarmament negotiations: "We have taken the stand that no decision will be required while progress toward disarmament continues. To do otherwise would not be consistent."[80] Since it was never made clear what constituted "progress toward disarmament," this formulation could be made consistent with any decision, or with an indefinite delay on the other hand.

This left the impression that another reason for failure to negotiate a satisfactory nuclear agreement with the United States was American unwillingness to agree to the kind of control arrangements which the Canadian government was seeking. This impression was not derived from any explicit government pronouncement, but from vague statements about the kind of Canadian control which was sought. This was taken to mean that the government was seeking control arrangements that were not compatible with existing U.S. legislation. There were several instances of such vague formulations. For example, the January 18, 1960, statement contained the following: "Nuclear weapons will not be used by the Canadian forces except as the Canadian government decides and in the manner approved by the Canadian government."[81] On July 4, 1960, the Prime Minister also said: "If and when the Canadian government should decide to equip its forces with nuclear weapons, those weapons would be under Canadian control and would be used in Canada only as the result of a decision by the Canadian government."[82] Both of these statements—and all others he made on the subject—were compatible with the principles of joint control permitted by existing U.S. legislation as embodied in the so-called two-key arrangements which the U.S. had concluded already with other NATO allies. Mr. Diefenbaker himself admitted this at one point.[83] But he did not say if this kind of control would be satisfactory to the Canadian government; on two later occasions, he left the impression that it

---

80. Address of Diefenbaker before the Canadian Club in Ottawa, November 24, 1960; cited in *Debates* (1962), II, 1250.

81. *Debates* (1960), I, 73.   82. *Ibid.*, V, 5654.

83. *Ibid.*, VI, 6271.

would not be. First, he indicated in the House on February 26, 1962, that Canada could not get nuclear weapons unless U.S. law were revised to permit some kind of joint control which was not legal under existing law.[84] Secondly, he refused to deny (although he also did not affirm it) that a statement of his Minister of Public Works to the effect that Canada wanted *sole* control represented government policy.[85] The former statement elicited a clarification from Secretary of State Dean Rusk to the effect that under existing law, the U.S. was required to retain custody of nuclear weapons but that joint control "fully consistent with national sovereignty" could be arranged.[86] The result of this series of confusions was that the government could still accept U.S. nuclear weapons in the future under existing legal requirements for joint control without inconsistency. Yet, for the moment, this created the impression that an important reason for failure of the negotiations was the unwillingness of the U.S. to agree to the kind of control Canada sought. Why did the government strive to create this impression, since no hard evidence exists that it ever contemplated any other kind of control than the joint, two-key system which was finally accepted in 1963? Was it simply the creation of a straw man designed to support a position that was becoming, for other reasons, increasingly antinuclear? This was no doubt part of the explanation. But another part seems to have been Diefenbaker's pique at learning that Canada could not get the same kind of custodial arrangements as Britain had, since existing U.S. legislation made an exception of the British case. While a Canadian government might justifiably have felt entitled to the same degree of American confidence as that extended to the British, the point was not worth stressing in this instance; the difference in question was simply a procedural one, which did not at all affect the fundamental aspect of the arrangement. It was basically the same in both cases—the consents of both the U.S. and the allied government were necessary before the weapon could be armed.[87]

The 1961 Berlin crisis gave rise again to rumors that the government was finally ready to accept nuclear weapons.[88] Reportedly, the Prime Minister had received a letter from President Kennedy expressing his concern and the hope that there would be an early

84. *Ibid.* (1962), II, 1250–51.   85. *Ibid.*, II, 1342–43.
86. USIS press release, March 2, 1962.
87. See Peyton Lyon, *Canada in World Affairs: 1961 to 1963* (forthcoming).
88. *Globe and Mail* (Toronto), September 13, 1961.

decision.[89] Such a decision perhaps did not seem too much to hope for at that time, for the Canadian government was giving firm support—both military and diplomatic—to the U.S. and to NATO during that crisis. Ironically, it was an action of Kennedy's which provided the government with another excuse for delay. When he presented a new plan for general and complete disarmament to the U.N. General Assembly in October, the Canadian government took the position that it would be inadvisable to prejudice its chances for success by accepting nuclear weapons.[90] In the aftermath of this, one of the few clear statements of government policy was made, not, to be sure, by a cabinet member, but by the Parliamentary Secretary to Mr. Green:

> The government stand on this matter has been made quite clear. At the present time we say no, but if events should take place in the world that might require these weapons then the government would have to give reconsideration to that position.[91]

The election year 1962 found the government, which was eager to avoid injecting the nuclear issue into the campaign, even more reluctant than previously, if that is possible, to state a clear policy. Since the opposition parties' policies were not much, if any, clearer, they did not resist this obfuscation. The sleeping nuclear dog was, with certain exceptions noted elsewhere,[92] allowed to lie. Considering the divided state of Canadian opinion on the issue, it was not surprising that the politicians chose to treat it gingerly. Mr. Diefenbaker's mail, by which he put great store, was reported to be running strongly against accepting nuclear weapons.[93] On the other hand, one of the few polls that was taken (on December 1, 1961), showed that Canadians favored the equipping of Canadian forces with nuclear weapons by a two-to-one majority.[94] A year later a large, if somewhat diminished, majority still favored acquisition.[95] But, significantly, only about one-third of a sample of political and labor leaders favored this course.[96] The political calculation which explains this paradox is that the feelings of the pro-nuclear majority were not strong enough to affect its voting behavior;

89. *Winnipeg Free Press*, September 20, 1961.
90. *Christian Science Monitor*, October 11, 1961.
91. *Debates* (1960–61), VIII, 8162.
92. See Section Six of this chapter.   93. Newman, p. 342.
94. Public Opinion News Service release, December 1, 1961.
95. *Winnipeg Free Press*, December 22, 1962.
96. John Paul and Jerome Laulicht, *In Your Opinion: Leaders' and Voters' Attitudes on Defence and Disarmament* (Oakville, Ontario: Esperanto Press, 1963), p. 24.

while the anti-nuclear minority was not only quite vocal, in Canada as elsewhere, but was also presumed to be prepared to cast its votes on the basis of this issue. The minority was organized chiefly in two groups: the Canadian Committee for the Control of Radiation Hazards (the name was changed later to the Canadian Committee for Survival), which was formed in 1958; and the Combined Universities Committee for Nuclear Disarmament, begun in 1959 in direct response to the government's Bomarc decision, and later affiliated with the British Campaign for Nuclear Disarmament. In October, 1961, these groups participated in a 72-hour anti-nuclear demonstration on Parliament Hill in Ottawa, at the end of which they presented the Prime Minister with a petition bearing 141,000 signatures.[97] As the polemics became more heated, the argument was joined—on different sides—by such theoretically apolitical figures as the President of the Exchequer Court of Canada and the Vice-Chairman of the Defense Research Board.[98] The division of opinion was not along civil-military lines, for the military itself appeared to contain a significant minority opposed to acquiring nuclear weapons. This minority included a number of younger officers in the Canadian Army, who felt that "nuclear armament would produce the wrong kind of army for this country."[99] It also included an independent commentator of Canadian military affairs and retired RCAF Wing Commander, John Gellner, who did not feel that the military advantages of the weapons outweighed their political disadvantages.[100] By the summer of 1962, it included General Foulkes, who, until then, had advocated and had even run a political campaign on a pro-nuclear stand. He explained his *volte-face* by saying that, while the military arguments had not changed, the 1962 election had demonstrated that the country was out of sympathy with a nuclear policy. Therefore, the nuclear roles should be changed, with the exception of the warheads for Bomarc, which Canada was honor-bound to accept.[101] The debate was also entered

97. *Globe and Mail* (Toronto), October 6, 1961; The *Times* (London), October 10, 1961.

98. *Montreal Daily Star*, November 6, 1961, and *Globe and Mail* (Toronto), December 5, 1961. The latter, Dr. J. E. Keyston, was criticized for having violated the civil servant's ethic of abstention from public discussion of policy questions, the more so as he had on an earlier occasion taken to task a subordinate of his—Marcel Chaput—on the same grounds. See *Montreal Daily Star*, December 14, 1961.

99. *Ibid.*, January 27, 1962.

100. John Gellner, "Why Nuclear Arms Are Not for Us," *Globe Magazine*, March 25, 1961.

101. *Montreal Daily Star*, March 17, 1962; *Vancouver Sun*, August 30–31, September 7, 1962. He lost the election.

by non-Canadian participants. General Laurence Kuter, whose status as an American officer was not disregarded though he spoke as the Commander in Chief of NORAD, an international command, visited Ottawa in September, 1961. He publicly discussed the military need for the forces under his command to have nuclear warheads. While his remarks were not warmly received by the Canadian government, nonetheless they were treated better than a Soviet note urging Canadian abstention from nuclear weapons; it was rejected as constituting improper interference.[102]

A new note, or at least new emphasis, was injected into the government's statements on nuclear policy during 1962: the possibility that Canadian forces might be able to obtain nuclear weapons quickly during an emergency. The discussion of this question was begun by Mr. Diefenbaker, who stated to the press in Edmonton that "he had read a recent report that nuclear warheads could be made available in half an hour or an hour and indicated there was some credence in this report."[103] Later he suggested that this was not a new policy, that the government's standing position had been that "in the event that nuclear war was launched, nuclear weapons should be placed in the possession of Canadians."[104] But whether new or not, this raised the question of whether a Canada-U.S. bilateral agreement existed which would permit such emergency transfer of weapons. The government's answer, when asked this question, was that it did not.[105] Nevertheless, the idea must have seemed a good one, for when negotiations were re-opened with Washington in the fall of 1962, this was the kind of agreement which the Canadians sought.

The watershed in this chronicle of the government's position on nuclear weapons is the Cuban missile crisis in October, 1962. There was one last report before then that the government was about to announce a decision.[106] This was, by implication, denied by Mr. Diefenbaker within a day, when he said that policy continued to be the same as the one he had previously stated.[107] Therefore, it seems fair to say that on the eve of the Cuban crisis, which set in train forces that eventually led to a dramatic conclusion of the nuclear issue, the Diefenbaker government was no nearer a decision on the question than it had been four years earlier. Some of the

102. *Montreal Daily Star*, June 15, 1962.
103. Quoted by Pearson, *Debates*, 1962, II, 2000.
104. *Ibid.*, pp. 1250–51.   105. *Ibid.*, p. 1342.
106. Copyrighted article by Walter Gray, *Globe and Mail* (Toronto), October 16, 1962.
107. *Debates* (1962–63), I, 627.

reasons for this unconscionable delay have been mentioned already, and others are explored in the two sections that follow. But since the procrastination was so largely the responsibility of one man, it is appropriate to ask here what personal factors contributed to John Diefenbaker's indecision. A satisfactory answer to this can be provided, if at all, only by a biographer with access to more information than is presently available. Yet, perhaps it is possible at this time to offer some hypotheses for that biographer to test.

Without going so far as to say that Diefenbaker always gave priority to political over military considerations, it seems probable that he did give precedence to political aspects except when the military arguments seemed clear and persuasive. This would explain his unwillingness, during the early period of 1959 and 1960, to incur the political costs—in terms both of domestic politics and of Canada's disarmament diplomacy—of a decision to accept nuclear weapons when the carriers for them were not yet operative. It appears unlikely that he was swayed much by the possible counter-argument that Canada's diplomatic effectiveness with its allies would be reduced by a failure to perform military commitments, even when the need for those commitments might not seem persuasive to him.

Later, the issue was affected by mutual distrust that appears to have marked Diefenbaker's relations with President Kennedy from their first meeting in Washington in February, 1961, and which a second Ottawa meeting three months later did not remove. This is not the place to detail the relationship between the two men, but it is important to note that Diefenbaker resented what he considered Kennedy's effort to interfere improperly in Canadian affairs, even, he thought, to the point of conspiring to destroy his government. This resentment contributed to his unwillingness to take a decision that he recognized to be desired and expected by the U.S. administration on military grounds.

Finally, a series of events which occurred in 1962 were so damaging to Diefenbaker's physical and emotional health as to make it unlikely that he could take any decision at all on so difficult a matter. The wear of the 1962 campaign, the loss of his majority in the ensuing election, the fracture of his ankle, and the death of his close friend Senator William Brunt combined to produce a state of nervous exhaustion so marked in Diefenbaker that his colleagues were concerned to protect him from public exposure.[108]

108. On the Diefenbaker-Kennedy relationship see Newman, pp. 264–67; Arthur

Two other influences upon the nuclear issue deserve to be noted before the dramatic events of 1962–63 are considered. One was the emphasis upon the disarmament negotiations by the Canadian government, an emphasis that was as much a symptom as a cause of the indecision on nuclear weapons. The other was the equivocal, but uniformly non-nuclear, positions of the opposition parties.

CANADA AND THE DISARMAMENT NEGOTATIONS

One chief reason for the Diefenbaker government's long delay in reaching a decision on nuclear weapons was the importance which it attached, largely as a result of the influence of Howard Green, to the disarmament negotiations and Canada's role in them. This delay entailed a considerable loss of diplomatic credit and influence with Canada's allies. The question arises whether this emphasis on disarmament produced returns commensurate with the cost, or, if it did not, why such a course was followed.

This emphasis has been permitted, if not caused, by the fact that Canada has been a member of practically every forum in which disarmament has been discussed since World War II. Canada was

M. Schlesinger, Jr., *A Thousand Days* (Boston: Houghton Mifflin Co., 1965), p. 343; and Theodore C. Sorensen, *Kennedy* (New York: Harper and Row, 1965), pp. 370, 575. Diefenbaker's resentment appears to have been nourished by some implausibly trivial things. He appears to feel, for example, that Kennedy was piqued at having his historical knowledge contested by Diefenbaker (the latter pointed out that not all the naval battles in the War of 1812 were won by the U.S.) and at learning that Diefenbaker had caught a bigger fish than he, and that Kennedy therefore expressed this pique by "pushing around" the Canadians. He seems to have been strongly antagonized by the phrase "things to push for," which was written on the memo that Kennedy mislaid on his Ottawa visit and which Diefenbaker retained and used to threaten Kennedy (alleging that it contained offensive expressions, which were fallaciously reported in the press as "S.O.B.") about a year later, when he detected what he thought was a conspiracy between Kennedy and Lester Pearson to destroy his government. Pearson's part of the alleged bargain was to change his position on nuclear weapons, and Kennedy's was to destroy Diefenbaker's government, presumably by revelations about the nuclear negotiations. Subsequent events such as General Norstad's press conference, the State Department press release of January 30, the (doubtlessly false) letter from the U.S. Ambassador Butterworth to Pearson expressing his support for the election, and perhaps the McNamara statement about the Bomarcs being decoys supply the evidence to support the conspiracy theory. It is startlingly original in the superintelligence and cunning that it attributes to American policymakers.

On the changes in Diefenbaker in 1962 see Pierre Sévigny, *This Game of Politics* (Toronto: McClelland and Stewart, 1965), pp. 222–24. On the entire question of Diefenbaker's role in the defense crisis, see Peyton Lyon, *Canada in World Affairs: 1961 to 1963*, (forthcoming).

named a permanent member of the U.N.'s Atomic Energy Commission as a result of its co-operation with Britain and the U.S. in the Manhattan Project. It was subsequently a member of the Commission for Conventional Armaments, the Disarmament Commision which succeeded the first two, its five-nation Sub-Committee, and finally the ten-nation (later expanded to eighteen) Disarmament Committee. As the only non-Great Power to hold permament membership in the first four of these bodies, it enjoyed a status unmatched by another non-Great Power in any U.N. body except the Trusteeship Council. To the extent that it has played one role consistently within the negotiations, it is that of spokesman for "the other states," i.e., countries not directly represented in the negotiations.[109] While it is doubtful if Canadian negotiators considered themselves to be representatives of any other nation than Canada, much less of a group of nations, it is nonetheless a fair judgment to say that the main Canadian effort in these talks—to keep the negotiations going at times when they had been, or were about to be broken off—was in the interest, on the whole, of the "other nations."[110] When negotiations had been broken off, this effort took the form of helping to mobilize opinion in favor of bringing the Great Powers into negotiations once more usually by promoting resolutions in the General Assembly. This process was followed, for example, after the talks in 1960 had been broken off following the abortive Paris summit conference.[111] Canada also took a leading role in proposing that the Disarmament Committee be expanded on a geographical basis; the effort resulted in the Committee's expansion from ten to eighteen members in 1961.[112] When talks were under way, the policy took the form of accentuating the positive, as explained by Mr. Green: "Canada has aimed at picking out points where there was almost agreement and in stressing those points, trying to bring about agreement of those things in the belief that once the two sides agreed on a paragraph of that

109. Bernard G. Bechhoefer, *Postwar Negotiations for Arms Control.* (Washington: Brookings Institution, 1961), p. 342.

110. This was the predominant role after 1946, when Canada discovered the limits to any mediatory role that it could play. For a description of its application to 1957, see Grant R. Davy, "Canada's Role in the Disarmament Negotiations, 1946–1957." (Unpublished Ph.D. dissertation, Fletcher School of Law and Diplomacy, April 15, 1962), especially pp. 173, 400.

111. Canada, Department of External Affairs, *Canada and the United Nations, 1960* (Ottawa: Queen's Printer, 1961), p. 7.

112. Canada, Department of External Affairs, *Canada and the United Nations, 1961* (Ottawa: Queen's Printer, 1962), p. 9.

kind, it would be easier to go on and agree on something a little more difficult."[113]

If Canada did well, on the whole, in this role of promoting conciliation, it performed less satisfactorily the other role theoretically belonging to lesser powers in such negotiations—that of initiating new ideas. One reason for this paucity of novel concepts was the shortage within the Departments of External Affairs or National Defense of personnel with sufficient competence and technical expertise to make proposals which had a reasonable chance of acceptance. However, a partial rectification of this situation was made after Mr. Green's accession to the External Affairs post: General E. L. M. Burns, one-time commander of UNEF, was appointed to be the government's special adviser and representative on disarmament policy; and some of the brighter officers in External Affairs were charged with questions of disarmament. Also, Canada's very close alliance with the U.S. made difficult any new proposal too sharply divergent from the American position. For this reason, it was suggested by some observers that India would have made a more appropriate member than Canada of the Disarmament Commission's Sub-Committee, established in 1954.[114] By 1957 the government had become so sensitive to this suggestion that it offered, on more than one occasion, to withdraw from the Sub-Committee, if that should be desired.[115] There were, however, some advantages in Canada's close association with the U.S. in North American defense. For example, this association gave it a role of some importance in the "open skies" proposal, the altered form of which was revived in May, 1957. This plan was first suggested publicly by Secretary Dulles on May 14, although it was not presented to the Sub-Committee until August 2. In the meantime, Secretary Dulles had won, on a visit to Ottawa, Canadian consent to the inclusion of all or part of Canada in the proposed inspection zones. The proposal consisted of two parts: the first suggested that the "open skies" territory include all of the Soviet Union and all of North America north of Mexico; if this were rejected, a second, more limited offer called for an inspection zone consisting of all territory within the Arctic Circle, plus area in the region of the Bering Straits. Not surprisingly both proposals were eventually rejected by the Soviet Union, since they were disproportionately favorable to the Western position. However, it was suggested that the Soviet reponse might

113. *Debates* (1962–63), III, 3070.
114. Davy, p. 300.   115. *Ibid.*, p. 379.

have been more favorable if the proposal had been made by Canada, which had played only a minor role in the talks resulting from the U.S. proposal.[116] This suggestion reflected the view that Canada's strongest qualification as a participant in the disarmament talks was the fact that it was closely allied to, and yet independent of, the United States. This was thought to enable Canada to make proposals which, because of close consultation with the U.S., would be certain of American acceptance and which, because they were not made by the U.S., would at least be somewhat more acceptable to the other side.

Such a rationale came into conflict, however, with another goal of the Diefenbaker government's disarmament policy, which was to assume a posture more independent of the United States. In striving for this independent posture, Canadian disarmament negotiators, under instructions from Mr. Green, sometimes disregarded prior agreements made with their American colleagues, and thereby tended to destroy the confidential relationship that was so crucial to their diplomatic effectiveness. In this search for independence, more important than any divergence from the U.S. on disarmament proposals was the different priority which was attached to disarmament relative to military preparedness. This was a new element in Canadian policy. From 1950–55, the Canadian position had been that there should be no disarmament until the West had caught up with the Soviet Union, presumably in conventional arms.[117] From 1955–57, Canada supported U.S. positions almost as a matter of faith, and was prepared to resign from the Sub-Committee in 1957 rather than serve more genuinely as a "bridge" between Soviet and American points of view.[118] By 1961–62, the Diefenbaker government, under the influence of Howard Green, was prepared to reduce to ineffectiveness a large part of Canada's military forces rather than suffer what might have been a marginal reduction in the effectiveness of Canada's disarmament policy, which was only marginally influential at best. Why?

It would be a mistake to underestimate the peculiar and accidental circumstances which contributed to this policy—one thinks here of Howard Green's personality and his relationship to the Prime Minister. But there were, perhaps, certain general factors which permitted and even inclined the government to follow such a course. One

116. Trevor Lloyd, "Open Skies in the Arctic?," *International Journal*, XIV (Winter, 1958–59), 42–49; and Davy, pp. 417ff.
117. Davy, p. 300.   118. *Ibid.*, pp. 431, 379.

was the country's basic security and its leaders' knowledge—sometimes instinctual rather than intellectual, but knowledge for all that—that it could rely on the military protection of the U.S., whether or not it wanted or asked for this protection. From this security and the knowledge of it came the possibility of indulging in the luxury of taking measures of disarmament (in this case of nuclear weapons, "unarmament" might be more appropriate) which, for other countries, would have been reckless. A second factor was the ever-present temptation to follow a course different from that of the U.S. simply because of its being different, whenever this whim could be indulged relatively painlessly. Finally, since such painless action tended *ipso facto* to occur in a vacuum, there was a constant risk of losing an appreciation for basic power factors, and consequently overestimating Canadian power and influence. All of these appear to have been factors present in the disarmament policy of the Diefenbaker government.

THE OPPOSITION PARTIES' POSITIONS

One of the factors which contributed to the long continuance of ambiguity in the government's nuclear policy was the uncertainty which marked the positions of the opposition parties. Their failure to present clear alternatives weakened the effect of their criticisms of the government's indecision. This was especially true in the case of the Liberals, who were the largest opposition party. On the role of nuclear weapons in alliance strategy, on the appropriateness of such weapons for Canadian forces and on the nuclear control arrangements deemed best for Canada, the Liberals' position underwent significant change. The three questions are of course closely related, for the greater the alliance's need to rely on nuclear weapons, the greater the need for Canadian forces to have them (for both military and political reasons), and the broader the range of control arrangements that would be considered acceptable. A Liberal government was in office in 1954 when NATO first adopted the official strategy of reliance on tactical nuclear weapons to meet a conventional attack, and registered Canadian concurrence in this decision. When the NATO meeting at which this decision was taken came up for debate in the House of Commons, there was no discussion of alliance strategy in general, nor of the nuclear decision in particular.[119] But later that year Mr. Pearson, who was Secretary of

119. *Debates* (1955), I, 628–29.

State for External Affairs in that government, gave in the Stafford Little Lectures some insight into his thinking on the problem. The thrust of his message was the inadequacy of the doctrine of massive retaliation, and the need to replace or at least supplement it with a doctrine of "reasonable or measured retaliation."[120] A corollary point was that "the measure of force is as important as its nature."[121] He cited, apparently with approval, President Eisenhower's statement that "I see no reason why they [tactical nuclear weapons] should not be used just exactly as you would a bullet or anything else."[122] He also approved the new NATO strategy, which "should ultimately make it possible for NATO to rely less exclusively on the nuclear capacity to retaliate against the centres of Russian life and to rely more on NATO's ability to hold and throw back the invading armies."[123] It was clear in these remarks that Mr. Pearson found morally unobjectionable and militarily useful the reliance upon tactical nuclear weapons in Europe. Nothing was said at this time, however, about nuclear arms for Canadian forces. Nor was anything done during the remaining months of the St. Laurent government to carry out the nuclear strategy which Canada had approved in 1954.[124]

As late as July, 1959, when the question of whether or not Canadian forces should have nuclear arms was a lively one, Mr. Pearson, who was now in opposition, endorsed the same strategic views. Tactical nuclear weapons could almost be treated as conventional, he held, and NATO troops needed them if only because the enemy had them. In turn, Canadian troops would need to have them, if only to avoid the demoralization that would come from working with allied troops which, otherwise, would have superior arms. He now added the important, if ambiguous, condition that if the brigade group were to have nuclear weapons, surely they would be under "Canadian control and operation."[125] It was not spelled out at the time whether he wished to exclude the so-called two-key arrangement for joint control by this phrase. Under existing U.S. legislation, this was the maximum degree of Canadian control permitted. Not long afterwards, this point was cleared up: nuclear weapons, if Canada should get them, "should be owned by Canada and should be used under Canadian authority exclusively. . . . We should not

120. Pearson, *Democracy in World Politics*, p. 21.
121. *Ibid.*   122. *Ibid.*, p. 18.   123. *Ibid.*, p. 34.
124. *Globe and Mail* (Toronto), June 8, 1961.
125. *Debates* (1959), V, 5371.

get into the field of atomic weapons at all unless we have control over the atomic weapons our forces would be using."[126] He seemed to be thinking primarily of Canadian forces in Europe rather than in North America when he said this, for his rhetorical question took this form: "Are we on the same plane of equipment with the United States forces if a Canadian platoon with a nuclear mortar cannot use it except on orders from the United States forces?"[127] However, one may question the seriousness with which this course was suggested, not only because U.S. consent to exclusive Canadian control was unlikely to be forthcoming, but also because Pearson did not at the time think that Canada should acquire nuclear weapons under any control arrangements. He felt this so strongly that he went to the length of suggesting that it would be preferable for the U.S. to operate the Canadian-based Bomarcs rather than for Canada to accept nuclear warheads for them.[128] It is interesting to note that one of his reasons for opposing nuclear weapons for Canada at that time was that it would have been regrettable to accept them when efforts were being made in the disarmament negotiations to curtail their testing and use. When the Diefenbaker government later employed this argument in defense of its delay in making a nuclear decision, the Liberals were no longer impressed with its cogency.

In 1960 and 1961—at the same time, as it happened, that the government was inclining more and more towards an anti-nuclear position—the Liberals maintained their qualified opposition to Canadian acquisition of nuclear weapons. Although the taint of distaste for nuclear weapons as a genus was always present, the arguments were generally made on strategic grounds. In their speeches in the House in August, 1960, Hellyer and Pearson outlined the Liberals' new defense policies, and opposed the strike reconnaissance role, and hence nuclear weapons, for the air division on account of the vulnerability of its bases, the refusal of the French to allow American nuclear weapons on French soil, and the offensive character of the role. They opposed nuclear weapons for the RCAF in North America because of the hopelessness, in the missile age, of providing completely effective air defenses. They even proposed that the RCAF squadrons be limited to an identification, not an interception, role. For similar reasons, namely the impossibility of performing effectively an anti-submarine role regardless of arms, the RCN was also

126. *Ibid.* (1960), I, 137.   127. *Ibid.*
128. *Montreal Daily Star*, November 17, 1959.

to be denied nuclear weapons. Only for the brigade group was the question left open, although it was clear that a conventional role was regarded as preferable.[129] The latter preference stemmed from a changed assessment of the utility of tactical nuclear weapons in Europe, and of the consequent need for a stronger conventional shield. Pearson, who now endorsed a greater reliance on conventional forces in Europe, said, when asked about his new position, "I confess . . . that I have changed my mind."[130] His new concern with the dangers of an excessive reliance upon tactical nuclear weapons prompted him to endorse the proposal that all nuclear weapons of forces under SACEUR be grouped under NATO control in special units.[131] The policies outlined in these speeches by Hellyer and Pearson were endorsed in January, 1961, at the Liberal national convention, in what was generally regarded as a resolution of general opposition to nuclear weapons for Canada.[132] In fact, after as well as before the resolution, this opposition was qualified in two ways. First, it was acknowledged that under certain circumstances Canadian forces in NATO would perhaps need nuclear weapons;[133] secondly, the possibility was not foreclosed that a Liberal government might accept nuclear weapons in Canada under exclusive U.S. control.[134] The latter was regarded as an explicit change in Liberal policy; as we have seen, it was in fact consistent with what had been said two years earlier.

The qualifications on the Liberals' anti-nuclear policy took on increased importance during the early months of 1962. On March 20, Mr. Pearson, anticipating his significant *volte-face* ten months later, accused the government of reneging on a NATO commitment by refusing to provide the CF–104's with nuclear weapons. He denied that this represented a change of position for him, but it was certainly at least a change in emphasis.[135] The defense plank in the platform on which the party campaigned for the 1962 election contained another qualification to the effect that

> if the members of NATO make an agreement for a NATO nuclear deterrent under NATO collective rather than national control, then Canadian forces in NATO should not be prevented from participat-

129. For these speeches, see *Debates* (1960), VII, 756off. and 7599ff.
130. *Ibid.*, p. 7610.   131. *Ibid.* (1960–61), VIII, 8353.
132. *Globe and Mail* (Toronto), January 10–11, 1961; see Diefenbaker's interpretation, *Debates* (1962–63), III, 3134.
133. *Montreal Daily Star*, February 7, 1961.
134. *Globe and Mail* (Toronto), November 14, 1961.
135. *Debates* (1962), II, 1986–7.

ing in this agreement by acquiring the necessary NATO tactical and defensive nuclear weapons.[136]

Otherwise, the party's position continued to be anti-nuclear. Since the government had no desire to argue the pro-nuclear case at that point, the subject was not an important issue during the 1962 campaign. Inevitably, the Liberals' position was characterized by allusion to Mackenzie King as being "not necessarily nuclear arms, but nuclear arms if necessary."[137] This remained the party's position until the sequence of events beginning with the Cuban crisis of October, 1962.

At least as divided and uncertain on the nuclear issue as the Liberals was the Social Credit party. By the time of the 1963 crisis its Québec wing, under Réal Caouette, had declared itself categorically opposed to nuclear weapons for Canada.[138] The forthrightness of this stand was almost certainly an important asset to it in the 1963 election.[139] However, the English wing of the party under Robert Thompson remained somewhat unclear. It appeared at some times to favor the acquisition of defensive nuclear weapons, but not those for the strike role;[140] while at others, it advocated nuclear arms for the Canadian forces in Europe, but not in North America.[141] Since the minority Diefenbaker government depended on Social Credit support after the 1962 election, this factor was important; it was, in fact, the withdrawal of this party's support which led to the fall of the government in February, 1963.

It was the New Democratic Party which enjoyed the distinction of having the clearest policy on the nuclear question: it consistently opposed the acquisition of nuclear weapons for Canadian forces. The whole complex of military, political and moral arguments were employed to justify this stand. As an NDP spokesman, F. A. Brewin, summarized it, "such a decision [to acquire nuclear weapons] would be militarily useless, politically disastrous and morally unjustifiable."[142]

The picture that emerges from this account, with the exception of the New Democratic Party, is one of equivocation on the nuclear

136. *Ibid.* (1962–63), III, 3123.
137. *Globe and Mail* (Toronto), May 28, 1962, citing *Le Droit*.
138. *Debates* (1962–63), III, 3123.
139. See Ramsay Cook, "Foreign Policy and the Election: An Uncertain Trumpet," *International Journal*, XVIII (Summer, 1963), 374–80.
140. *Debates* (1962–63), III, 3090.
141. *Globe and Mail* (Toronto), January 16, 1963.
142. *Debates* (1962–63), III, 3141.

issue and, one which including the NDP, on balance seemed to advocate remaining non-nuclear. Precisely this same description could be applied to the government, so that opposition critics of the government's indecision were inhibited from throwing political stones by the glass houses in which they lived themselves. This stalemated position was only broken by a crisis.

NUCLEAR DÉNOUEMENT

The Cuban missile crisis of October, 1962, acted as the catalyst which eventually produced a Canadian decision on nuclear weapons. All of the details of Canada's role in this crisis are by no means clearly known; but enough is known to support the judgment that the situation caused by Canadian indecision was sufficiently danger-ous to prompt government and opposition in Canada, and the U.S. administration to take actions designed to resolve the dilemma.

The judgment that the situation was dangerous derived from the government's reluctance to consent to certain measures to increase North American military preparedness during the crisis. This im-pression was more lasting than the fact, which was critically noticed at the time and since, that the government only gave full diplomatic support to the American action on October 25, three days after Presi-dent Kennedy's speech.[143] Measures which it has been suggested the Canadian government should have taken fall into two categories. One is the alerting, or bringing to a state of increased readiness, of the Canadian forces in NORAD. The other is the granting of permission to the U.S. to take such emergency measures as arming its interceptor squadrons at Goose Bay and Harmon Field with nu-clear weapons, and the dispersal of other interceptor squadrons to Canadian airfields. Some have said that serious thought was given at one point to arming Canada's two squadrons of Bomarcs, but there was apparently never any question of doing this during the emergency. As for the other two kinds of measures, there is conflicting evidence about what was done in fact. On the former question, on October 23 Mr. Harkness was asked whether Canadian naval units or RCAF units in NORAD had been alerted; his com-ment was "by and large the answer to that question is *no*."[144] Two days later, the Prime Minister suggested that after a delay the alert had been given: "The Canadian component of the NORAD forces has been placed upon the same level of readiness as the United

143. *Ibid.*, I, 911.   144. *Ibid.*, pp. 821, 22.

States forces under NORAD operational control."[145] Speaking later at Nassau, he acknowledged that there had been a delay, which he defended by saying the U.S. had not fulfilled the NORAD commitment to full consultation with Canada.[146] A later statement from NORAD headquarters, however, said that RCAF forces were alerted at the beginning of the crisis, and that only the government's announcement had been delayed.[147] In fact, these seemingly conflicting statements can be reconciled. It appears that after a delay of one day in which there was no military action, Canadian forces were alerted on the order of Douglas Harkness on October 23; the Cabinet still had taken no action. Harkness's denial of this in the House on that day was based on a technicality, namely the fact that orders for some of the less crucial things that were done normally as part of an alert, (e.g., the cancelling of leaves) were omitted. The following day, Wednesday, October 24, the Cabinet did authorize the complete alert and orders were given accordingly; but announcement of this was deferred until the House would be in session on Thursday. In sum, after a wobbly start, Canada's performance on this point was consistent with its alliance commitments and its own security interests.[148]

On the second point, the question of government permission for U.S. military movements in Canada, the conflicting evidence concerns not whether Canada was unco-operative, but only the degree of nonco-operation that existed. A number of charges have been made, to the effect that the U.S. had asked permission several hours before President Kennedy's speech of October 22 to move nuclear warheads from Bangor, Maine, to arm its interceptor squadrons at Harmon Field and Goose Bay, and to disperse its nuclear-armed interceptors to other Canadian fields; that it expected this permission as a matter of course; that this permission never came; that permission was granted for only eight of the 640 SAC overflights for which requests were made during the crisis.[149] According to at least one report, the U.S. also asked for and was denied landing rights for SAC bombers.[150] It seems doubtful that that report is correct, but if so, the Canadian government might legitimately have refused such a request out of a wish to avoid taking, or allowing the U.S. to take, action that could be regarded as needlessly provocative. As for the other charges, it is not yet possible to say if all

145. *Ibid.*, pp. 912, 13.   146. December 30, 1962, Associated Press dispatch.
147. *Globe and Mail* (Toronto), January 3, 1963.   148. Interviews.
149. Newman, pp. 339, 40; *Financial Post*, December 1, 1962.
150. Henry M. Pachter, *Collision Course.* (New York: Frederick A. Praeger, 1963), p. 95.

are correct down to details. However, the government's refusal to deny or even to comment upon them when asked must be regarded as tacit admission that they were basically correct in establishing that the government was uncooperative. They are further supported by an attempt of Mr. Green to disengage NORAD from any consideration of the Cuban crisis, which is understandable only if he wished to avoid consenting to certain actions within NORAD as a result of the crisis.[151] The government's defense of its behavior during the crisis (even though it never spelled out what that behavior had been) lay in its assertion that it had not been consulted about the U.S. action but merely informed a few hours before the President's speech of October 22. It is true that the NORAD agreement recognizes the increased "importance of the fullest possible consultation between the two governments on all matters affecting the joint defense of North America."[152] However, it also says that the "plans and procedures to be followed by NORAD . . . shall be capable of rapid implementation in an emergency."[153] This had been granted on an earlier occasion by Mr. Diefenbaker, who pointed out that, "as I have emphasized frequently, consultation must take place beforehand, and there would be little more than clearance given during an emergency."[154]

The end of the Cuban crisis brought no immediate public change in the government's position, which, according to Mr. Green, continued to be "to decline nuclear weapons until there is a deteriorating world situation or war."[155] But pressures for a decision were increasing. American displeasure at the events of October constituted one source of pressure. Another lay in the fact that the date by which Canada had committed itself to have the first units of CF–104 squad-

151. The attempt was made in a television interview on October 24. The line of reasoning harked back to the 1957 NORAD controversy: NORAD, he held, was a part of NATO, and since NATO was not directly involved in the Cuban crisis, neither was NORAD. The subject was raised in the House the following day, but he refused to elaborate on his earlier statement. See *Debates* (1962–63), I, 919.

152. See Appendix I.   153. *Ibid.*

154. *Debates* (1958), II, 1029. There is some evidence that it was the Diefenbaker government which obstructed consultations, that Howard Green refused to take the telephone call from Colorado Springs which was intended to brief him on the crisis from the NORAD point of view. See Newman, p. 338. However, this point as well as Green's general conduct during the crisis is a matter of dispute, since there is other testimony that he favored taking the action desired by the U.S.

155. From Vancouver speech of December 4, 1962, cited in *Debates*, 1962–63, III, 3326.

rons operational was May 1, 1963; since some six months were needed after the conclusion of a bilateral agreement for the construction of storage facilities and for training, a decision was needed by November 1.[156] Under such pressure, the government asked the United States to resume nuclear negotiations on a confidential basis.

Others made more public suggestions. The national vice-president of the Progressive Conservative Association proposed a free vote in Parliament on the issue, and his proposal was endorsed by the *Globe and Mail*.[157] In early December, two Liberal spokesmen on defense policy, in what were apparently trial balloons, reversed their positions and advocated Canadian acceptance of nuclear weapons.[158] The government itself was reported to be sounding opinion, concurrently with the Liberals, with a view toward a possible policy announcement at the annual Progressive Conservative convention on January 18–19.

Into this fluid situation, a new voice was injected by General Lauris Norstad, who had recently retired as SACEUR, when he made his farewell visit to Ottawa in January, 1963. In an interview held on January 3, he expressed the view that Canada had accepted a commitment within NATO to acquire nuclear weapons, and that it would be reneging on this commitment if such weapons were not provided for the CF–104 squadrons being introduced into service at that time. He pointed out further that a bilateral agreement with the U.S. was a necessary precondition for the equipping of the air division with nuclear arms during an emergency, as well as for completing its nuclear training. All of these points seemed to be made with some reluctance, and with little awareness of their political importance. Yet inasmuch as each of them amounted to a contradiction of the government's view of the situation, the result was a political sensation. The government's reaction was somewhat muted. Howard Green and Davy Fulton, the Minister of Public Works, asserted that Canada *had* fulfilled its NATO commitments. The vagueness of that word, however, suggested that their disagreement with Norstad might be only verbal. He had not said there was a written, formal commitment, only that he regarded the undertaking to perform the strike role as tantamount to a commitment to accept nuclear weapons. Other, unidentified, government spokes-

156. *Financial Post*, December 1, 1962.   157. December 1, 1962.
158. Paul Hellyer and Charles Drury. See *Globe and Mail* (Toronto), December 15, 1962.

men contested his view that a bilateral agreement was necessary, even in an emergency, before nuclear weapons would be put into Canadians' hands. They also said that an additional three- to six-month training period would not be needed in the case of the brigade group, since the unit had already had the necessary training.[159] On the other hand, Norstad was supported by General Foulkes, who seemed puzzled at the consternation caused by Norstad's statement: "There's no official secret connected with the fact that Canada made an agreement with NATO."[160]

On January 12, another significant change was made in the political situation. The Leader of the Opposition announced himself in favor of fulfilling Canada's commitments by accepting nuclear weapons, while seeking to change the commitments themselves. In a speech delivered in Toronto, Mr. Pearson explained his new position:

> As a Canadian, I am ashamed if we accept commitments and then refuse to discharge them. . . . [The Canadian Government] should end at once its evasion of responsibility, by discharging the commitments it has already accepted for Canada. It can only do this by accepting nuclear warheads, for those defensive tactical weapons which cannot effectively be used without them but which we have agreed to use. . . . [At the same time] the Government should re-examine at once the whole basis of Canadian defence policy. In particular, it should discuss with the United States and with NATO a role for Canada in continental and collective defense which would be more realistic and effective for Canada than the present one.
>
> This examination would be concerned, among other things, with the necessity of building up NATO's conventional forces and the part Canada could play in this.
>
> Until the present role is changed, a new Liberal Government would put Canada's armed services in the position to discharge fully commitments undertaken for Canada by its predecessor. Perhaps I'm making it a little easier for the Government to reach a decision.[161]

He had been prompted to make the change, he later pointed out, by knowledge derived from the Cuban crisis about the state of U.S.-Canadian relations and from the December NATO ministerial meeting about the Allies' estimate of Canada's military performance. The beginning of deliveries of CF–104's, coming after the Honest John batallion and the Bomarcs were already in place, had convinced

159. *Ottawa Evening Journal*, January 9, 1963.
160. *Globe and Mail* (Toronto), January 11, 1963.
161. Text in *ibid.*, January 14, 1963, p. 11.

him that there was no longer any hope of changing in the short run the roles which Canada had accepted, and that they would therefore have to be fulfilled.[162] Early reaction to his speech was reported to be "very favorable."[163] While the rest of the Liberal Party showed less than Marxist discipline in following the change of line of its leader, neither did opponents of the change succeed in destroying the effect of the speech, which served to give a new character to the defense debate.

Although the pressures on it were increasing, the government failed to progress toward a similar decision. The annual Progressive Conservative convention granted the Prime Minister's request to pass no resolution, advocating either nuclear course, leaving the matter open.[164] He refrained from additional remarks on the subject until the reconvening of Parliament on January 23 permitted him to use that forum. When he spoke, on January 25, the result must have been a disappointment to anyone hoping for an announcement of a decision. "We do not want to do anything at this time to rock the boat," he said.[165] The pretext for leaving the issue open was the uncertainty introduced into alliance questions by the Nassau agreements reached between the U.S. and the U.K. in December. Both the stress placed on conventional forces, and the plans for a multilateral nuclear force were said to call into question Canada's whole defense posture: "If . . . there is going to be set up a multi-lateral nuclear force, then all our planning to date, or most of it, will be of little or no consequence."[166] Some of his remarks suggested that he might be contemplating a repudiation of Canada's nuclear role, at least for the air division: "The strike reconnaissance role has been placed under doubt by the recent Nassau declaration concerning nuclear arms, as well as other developments both technical and political in the defence field," he said, adding that it would be better to reject an unwise policy than to follow it simply because money had already been spent on it.[167] Finally, he revealed that in late October the Canadian government had asked for the discussions with the U.S. to be resumed on a confidential basis, with a view to making nuclear weapons available to Canada in case of an emergency.[168]

162. *Debates* (1963), I, 111.
163. See *The Times* (London), the *Globe and Mail* (Toronto), and the *Montreal Daily Star* for January 14, 1963.
164. *Globe and Mail* (Toronto), January 19–21, 1963.
165. *Debates*, 1962–63, III, 3137.   166. *Ibid.*
167. *Ibid.*, p. 3136.   168. *Ibid.*

The Prime Minister spoke on this occasion for almost two hours, and one of the results was that the Minister of National Defense, Mr. Harkness, did not participate in the debate. He resorted therefore to the extraordinary step of making his comments in the form of an "interpretation" of Mr. Diefenbaker's speech, which he issued as a statement to the press. More extraordinary than the procedure was the substance of the interpretation. Referring to the relevant portions of Mr. Diefenbaker's speech, he said:

> Those paragraphs state a definite policy for the acquisition of nuclear arms in these terms:
> First, our obligations to equip certain weapons with nuclear arms are reiterated, together with the determination to honour those obligations.
> Second, the strike reconnaissance role of the F–104's has been placed in some doubt by the recent Nassau declaration, as well as other developments in the defence field; thus, it is necessary for Canada to seek, on the part of NATO, a clarification of her role in NATO defence plans and dispositions; this clarification to be provided when the NATO ministerial meeting is held in Canada next May. Should NATO reaffirm for Canada a role involving nuclear weapons, Canada will equip her NATO forces to discharge her obligation.
> Third, so far as NORAD is concerned, Canada has been negotiating with the United States for the past two or three months in order that nuclear warheads will be made available for our two squadrons of Bomarcs and for the F–101 interceptor squadrons. These negotiations will be continued in order to reach a satisfactory agreement. I believe such an agreement can be arrived at in the near future.[169]

The striking discrepancy between the speech itself, which left the question very much open, and Mr. Harkness's interpretation, which indicated that a pro-nuclear decision had been taken, was immediately evident. When Mr. Diefenbaker refused to endorse the minister's interpretation of his speech (he held that the speech was quite clear, and needed no interpretation), the opposition called for Harkness's resignation.[170]

On January 30, the U.S. Department of State issued a statement commenting upon Mr. Diefenbaker's speech of January 25. With the expressed aim of "clarifying"[171] the situation, the statement in effect challenged Mr. Diefenbaker's interpretation, if not his representation, of the facts on several major points. First, it questioned

169. *Ibid.*, pp. 3319, 3320.   170. *Ibid.*, pp. 3204, 3205.
171. See Appendix IV.

the feasibility of the kind of emergency arrangements for the provision of nuclear weapons which the Canadian government had reopened the negotiations to arrange: "The Canadian government has not as yet proposed any arrangement sufficiently practical to contribute effectively to North American defense." Second, it denied any connection between the Nassau agreements and Canadian defense policy: "The agreements made at Nassau have been fully published. They raise no question of the appropriateness of nuclear weapons for Canadian forces in fulfilling their NATO or NORAD obligations." Third, it argued similarly that the need for increased conventional forces had no direct bearing on the immediate question: "A flexible and balanced defense requires increased conventional forces, but conventional forces are not an alternative to effective NATO or NORAD defense arrangements using nuclear-capable weapons systems."[172]

The issuance of this statement was disapproved by every Canadian party as an inappropriate interference in a Canadian debate; but it was noted that Mr. Diefenbaker had first broken confidence with the U.S. by revealing publicly the negotiations which the Canadian government had asked for on a secret basis. Some critics wondered whether the State Department's recourse to a public channel of expression had been made necessary by the ineffectiveness of using private, diplomatic channels.[173] Events were now moving swiftly. The government was unable to defeat an Opposition motion to adjourn the House to discuss the State Department statement and defense policy in general. On February 4, Douglas Harkness resigned. He explained to the House that when he issued his interpretation of the Prime Minister's January 25 speech, he had felt that Mr. Diefenbaker's views on the nuclear issue were acceptable. He later discovered them to be irreconcilable with his long-standing conviction that Canada should have nuclear weapons. In retrospect, he saw as a mistake his willingness to accept government delay on the issue, but explained that he had done so in the hope of eventually obtaining a satisfactory decision.[174] On the same day, a motion of no confidence was introduced in which defense policy was cited as the major, but not the only, important issue. Even at this late date, defeat could have been avoided had Mr. Diefenbaker been willing to deal with the Social Credit party, which was prepared to co-operate on

172. *New York Times*, February 1, 1963, p. 1.
173. *Debates* (1962–63), III, 3290. Pearson was speaking.
174. *Ibid.*, p. 3377.

any reasonable basis since its members were eager to avoid another election.[175] Since he was unwilling to do this, the government was defeated on February 5, and Parliament dissolved. George Hees, the Minister of Trade and Commerce, and Pierre Sévigny, the Acting Minister of National Defense since Harkness's resignation, also resigned out of dissatisfaction with the government's defense policy a few days later.

The ensuing election campaign was waged not so much on the specific defense issue as on the question of the Diefenbaker government's general competence to govern. Its handling of defense policy was a relevant, but only a partial point; however, it did loom always in the background, and intruded unexpectedly into discussions of other issues from time to time.[176] For these reasons, the story of the campaign belongs more properly to a political history than to this discussion of defense issues. Nevertheless, one event of the campaign must be noted here. On March 29, a transcript of the testimony was released which Secretary of Defense McNamara had given to the House Military Appropriations Subcommittee the previous February 6. It included the following passage:

Mr. Minshall—No hearings of this subcommittee would be complete unless I at least mentioned in passing the word "Bomarc."
Mr. Flood—You are speaking of the woman I love.
Mr. Minshall—I notice on page 55 of your statement you pointed out: 'As I pointed out last year, the Air Force's Bomarc missile suffered from essentially the same defects as manned interceptors (deleted). Nevertheless, we plan to continue the Bomarc force (deleted), since the large initial investment costs are already behind us.' If I remember correctly, including the cost of SAGE and the Bomarc missile itself, all the research and development, we put somewhere between $3 billions and $4 billions into this program. I just wonder if it is as ineffective as you now agree it is, why we even put any money into the operational cost of this weapon when it is so useless.
Secretary McNamara—The operational costs are really not extensive. Since we have put such a heavy investment in the weapons system itself and in the controls for it, the SAGE controls, it seemed wise to us to continue to deploy it at least as far ahead as we can see.
Mr. Minshall—We are trying to cut down at every corner of the budget. These sites take men to man. I am sure it will run into millions of dollars just for operations and maintenance.
Secretary McNamara—Yes, the Bomarc looks to us to cost on the order of $20 millions a year to operate.

175. Sévigny, pp. 268–70.
176. For a concise summary of the issues in the campaign, see Cook.

Mr. Minshall—That to me is an awful lot of money.

Secretary McNamara—For the protection we get I do not believe it is an unreasonable amount.

Mr. Minshall—The protection is practically nil, Mr. Secretary, as you said here in your statement. The sites are soft, SAGE is soft.

Secretary McNamara—We can correct for some of these deficiencies. We are considering further dispersal of those Bomarcs. The problem with the dispersal alternative is its costs money to disperse. We have a series of alternatives underway that we hope will allow us to increase their effectiveness. In any case, I would hesitate to cancel their deployment if we saved no more than $20 millions a year.

Mr. Minshall—You remind me of the story my good father used to tell me about Pat and Mike when they were fishing in the Niagara River about a mile above the falls. . . . Suddenly the rope came untied from the shore and they were caught in the current. Pat excitedly said, "Throw over the anchor." Mike responded, "It ain't got no rope on it." Pat said, "Throw the anchor over anyhow, it might do us some good." That is pretty much the situation here with Bomarc. They might do some good.

Secretary McNamara—At the very least, they would cause the Soviets to target missiles against them and thereby increase their missile requirements or draw missiles onto these Bomarc targets than would otherwise be available for other targets.

Mr. Flood—Here is another chance for another McNamara hard decision.

Secretary McNamara—If there were any real amount of money to be saved, I would propose taking them out, but for $20 millions a year I think we are getting our money's worth.

Mr. Minshall—In view of the statement you just made, Mr. Secretary, why do we not leave the Jupiter missiles in Italy and Turkey? If we have to draw enemy fire, that is a good place to draw it.

Mr. Flood—If we scratch Bomarc, we have stuck the Canadians for a whole mess of them and we have another problem on our border.

Secretary McNamara—As they are deployed, they draw more fire than those Jupiter missiles will.

Mr. Minshall—All I can say is, these turned out to be very expensive targets.

Secretary McNamara—They did, I agree with you fully.[177]

There is nothing obvious about the connection of either the content of this testimony or the timing of its release to the Canadian election. The period that elapsed between the date of Secretary McNamara's appearance and the public release of his testimony was quite a normal

177. U.S., Congress, House, Committee on Appropriations, *Hearings before the Subcommittee on Department of Defense Appropriations*, 88th Cong., 1st Sess., 1963, Part 1, pp. 512, 13.

one under the procedure whereby such statements are "sanitized"
to remove what is regarded as sensitive information before being
released to the public. Almost certainly, the timing of its release
was completely unaffected by events in Canada, if only because
no one could know in advance what effect it would have on the
Canadian election campaign. According to a clarification of McNamara's statement issued by the Department of Defense, the transcript of his testimony was given to the Canadian government for
comment more than a week before its release, and none was made.[178]
Similarly, the content of the statement does not appear to have
been immediately concerned with Canada. Although the text does
not make clear whether he was speaking of Bomarcs located in Canada or the U.S., the facts make clear that he was thinking primarily
of American bases: there are more Bomarcs stationed in the U.S.
than in Canada, he was defending the expenditure of U.S. and not
Canadian money, and he did not have the responsibility for maintaining or cancelling the Canadian Bomarc bases. Nonetheless, the
argument was evidently relevant to the Canadian bases, as well;
therefore, it was drawn on immediately by Mr. Diefenbaker, who
charged that the Liberals, by proposing to arm the Canadian Bomarcs, would be making Canada into "a decoy for intercontinental
missiles."[179] It was noticed by many, however, that Diefenbaker's
argument could be turned against him, since it had been his government which brought the Bomarcs into Canada. Consequently, the
net result of the McNamara statement in terms of votes was by
no means clear; but undeniably, its existence provided ammunition to
those seeking to capitalize on anti-American feeling, and thereby
increased the emotionalism surrounding the whole nuclear issue.

The fact that the Liberal government which was returned to office
did not command a majority in the House did not prevent it from
carrying out its pledge to acquire nuclear weapons. As early as
May 11, 1963, Prime Minister Pearson confirmed in the communique issued after his Hyannis Port talks with President Kennedy,
his government's "intention to initiate discussions with the United
States government leading without delay towards the fulfillment
of Canada's existing defense commitments in North America and
Europe, consistent with Canadian parliamentary procedures."[180]
Finally, on August 16, 1963, he announced that the five-year nego-

178. *Ottawa Evening Journal*, March 30, 1963.
179. Cited in Newman, p. 391.
180. Text in *New York Times*, May 12, 1963, p. 3.

tiations had been successfully concluded. Under conditions of joint control similar to that existing between the U.S. and other NATO allies, Canada was to acquire nuclear weapons for four weapons systems: the Bomarc "B", the Voodoo interceptor, the Honest John artillery rocket and the CF–104 Starfighter strike-reconnaissance aircraft.[181] There was no public outcry. The issue had been settled. But the long controversy would continue to affect Canadian alliance policy, as we shall see below.

181. *Ibid.*, August 17, 1963, p. 1.

PART III

NEW POLICIES EMERGE

CHAPTER VII

Defense Development and Production Sharing

CANADIAN thinking about defense was absorbed during the years 1957–63 with the episodic controversies which we have been considering. Little attention was given to the bases of Canadian defense policy during the long term which began when the final trauma of these years, the acquisition of nuclear weapons, had been resolved. As we have seen already, that final resolution had been delayed, in part because of the tendency for the solution of each defense issue to render more difficult the solution to the next.

To identify the reason for this tendency is to suggest one of the basic criteria for a long-term Canadian defense policy. The reason lay in the economic character and political influence of Canada's defense production industries, especially the aircraft industry. In the late 1950's, these industries were increasingly unable to provide economically and in a reasonable time the major equipment required by Canadian forces in the roles that they were filling. On the other hand, they *were* able to provide sophisticated and high-quality equipment at higher prices on later delivery dates. They were economically inefficient, relative to their U.S. competitors, but not so inefficient as to be beyond consideration. The fact that this capability was so marginal allowed other, non-military criteria to be brought to bear on decisions of whether or not to produce particular items in Canada. One of the criteria was the effect the decision would have on the Canadian industry. Political pressures on the Canadian government to buy Canadian-made weapons, which are great enough in any case, are especially intense when to decide otherwise would jeopardize the existence of an industry, as well as the jobs and prestige which go with it.[1] Another criterion was the effect

1. While the possibility of scuttling an industry by consistently denying it large contracts is a very real one, the danger from any particular adverse decision tends to be exaggerated. For example, the scrapping of the Arrow was widely regarded as a crippling blow to the aircraft industry in Canada; yet this industry did approximately the same dollar volume of business in 1962 as in 1955. See Canada, House of Commons, *Special Studies prepared for the Special Committee of the House of Commons on Matters Relating to Defence*, p. 98.

of weapons purchases on the Canadian balance-of-payments: there were strong pressures not to worsen the current account deficit which Canada chronically runs with the U.S. by increasing net purchases of military equipment from the U.S. For all these reasons, decisions to purchase U.S.-made equipment were politically difficult, even when there was no comparable Canadian item, and especially so when a Canadian substitute was available. The consequences of these factors are painfully evident in the cases described above. The NORAD controversy was aggravated, if not in part caused, by sensitivity to the increased use of U.S. equipment which a joint command was thought, correctly, to entail; development of the Arrow was continued for too long, at the expense of depriving the taxpayer and the military services of funds which could have been better spent elsewhere; the selection of a replacement for the Arrow was delayed for two years because of sensitivity to adopting a U.S. aircraft in its place; the commitment to Bomarc became politically irreversible even after it became technically unjustified, since to have scrapped it would have seemed a concession to U.S. pressure. Also, the re-equipping of the air division to fulfill its new role was delayed until that role had practically ceased to be an effective one; first, because of the hesitancy to acquire another American aircraft, and second, because of the time required to set up facilities in Canada to manufacture the F–104 there. Finally, the nuclear decision was delayed so long partly because of the unpalatable fact that not only the weapons, but the carriers with which they were to be used, were U.S.-made. This pattern has been repeated elsewhere since Canada experienced it—most strikingly in the United Kingdom— at a higher level of technology. Britain's cancellation of the Blue Streak intermediate range missile and later of the TSR–2 aircraft bear striking resemblances to the case of the Arrow; the British experience with Skybolt took the same form, if it did not have the same result, as the Canadian experience with Bomarc. All of these situations constituted real dilemmas, one horn of which involved accepting inappropriate, second-best or more costly military equipment, while the other involved taking decisions that were politically and economically painful, and which could have potentially disastrous effects.

If one rules out as politically and economically unacceptable the policy of letting the Canadian defense industry die and relying on foreign sources for most military equipment, this dilemma could be resolved in only two ways: (1) Canada's military roles could be so chosen that they entailed the use of a minimum of equipment which it was beyond Canada's means to develop and produce; and/or (2) purchases of military equipment from foreign sources could be rendered politically and economically more palatable by compensating in some way the affected Canadian defense industries. By originating the Development and Production Sharing program, the Diefenbaker government emphasized the second of these two approaches. In so doing, it provided one of the bases for developing a more stable and longer-term defense policy than existed during its tenure, though whether or not it is an entirely satisfactory basis remains to be seen. The Pearson government, as we shall see in the following chapter, continued after 1963 to follow the second of these approaches while also making increasing use of the first.

EARLY COLLABORATION IN DEFENSE PRODUCTION

The essence of the Development and Production Sharing Program was to give Canadian firms opportunities equal to their U.S. competitors for U.S. defense contracts, and thereby to offset growing Canadian purchases of military equipment in the U.S. by increasing U.S. purchases in Canada. There was ample historical precedent, going back at least to 1941, for such a program. On April 20 of that year, Prime Minister Mackenzie King and President Roosevelt, meeting in New York, took cognizance of the balance-of-payments problem created by Canada's large purchases of defense materiel in the United States. In what became known as the Hyde Park Declaration, they agreed that the problem should be solved by increasing U.S. materiel purchases in Canada and recognized, in more general terms, the "general principle that in mobilizing the resources of this continent each country should provide the other with the defense articles which it is best able to produce, and, above all, produce quickly, and that production programs should be coordinated to this end."[2] These were not merely idle words. The $200–300 million worth of purchases by the U.S. in Canada, the goal mentioned in the declaration for the following twelve months, was achieved and even surpassed. Each of the two countries spent, during the course of World War II, some $1.25 billion in the neighboring country for military goods.[3] Equally as important as the scale of the program was the fact that it was achieved by measures which

2. *U.S. Department of State Bulletin,* IV (April 26, 1941), 494.
3. Dziuban, p. 292.

reflected, by and large, the general principle recognized at Hyde Park. A Joint Materials Coordinating Committee and a Joint Defense Production Committee were established to set priorities and allocate strategic materials between the U.S. and Canada, and to co-ordinate the productive capacities of the two countries. Canada participated in the U.S. priorities system with a status similar to that of U.S. agencies, so that its orders were filled as quickly as U.S. orders. Moreover, export licenses for shipments to Canada were virtually eliminated.

In May, 1945, at U.S. instance, the two countries agreed to continue to base their co-operation on the principles of the Hyde Park Declaration for the remainder of the war and in the peacetime reconversion.[4] But under conditions of demobilization, there was little need or will to continue such close co-ordination; as a result, little was heard of the May, 1945, notes (which were not made public until 1948). Also of little significance was the Joint Industrial Mobilization Planning Committee, established in 1948. Only when the two countries began the process of rearmament did the incentives to resume their collaboration in defense production revive, and then in unequal measure in the two countries. On October 12, 1949, the Permanent Joint Board on Defense decided to initiate a new program for reciprocal military procurement, based upon objectives similar to those of the Hyde Park Declaration: to augment U.S. sources of supply; to increase the dispersal of industrial facilities; to foster industrial standardization of equipment; and to help Canada earn the foreign exchange to pay for her military purchases in the U.S. In a New York speech in February, 1950, Prime Minister St. Laurent sought to press forward with this program by speaking of Canadian desires for larger and more numerous U.S. defense contracts.[5] He was rewarded three months later, when the Secretary of Defense issued a directive instructing the military departments to procure between $15 and $20 million worth of military equipment in Canada during Fiscal Year 1951. The outbreak of the Korean war in the following month, however, called for a firmer and clearer statement of the basis for this kind of collaboration. As a result, the two governments on October 26, 1950, exchanged notes embodying a "Statement of Principles for Economic Cooperation." This

4. "North American Defense," *Round Table* No. 160 (September, 1950), p. 329.
5. "North American Defense," *Round Table* No. 160 (September, 1950), p. 331.

statement included, in addition to an affirmation of the general principle endorsed in the Hyde Park Declaration, two more specific
undertakings:

(1) In order to achieve an optimum production of goods essential
for the common defense, the two countries shall develop a coordinated program of requirements, production, and procurement.

. . . .

(5) Barriers which impede the flow between Canada and the
United States of goods essential for the common defense effort
should be removed as far as possible.[6]

These principles, and the administrative arrangements designed to
carry them out, were embodied in the U.S. Armed Services Procurement Regulations. More specific obstacles were set aside when
the U.S. Army and Air Force exempted Canadian supplies from
the "Buy American" Act, when Canadian equipment was included
on U.S. procurement lists, and when Canada was accorded special
and more liberal treatment on questions involving security and access to classified information.

As a result of these measures and, more importantly, of the increase in pace of rearmament after June 25, 1950, reciprocal military purchases between Canada and the U.S. far exceeded the
amounts envisioned in the spring of 1950. U.S. purchases in Canada
in Fiscal Year 1951 amounted to some $100 million, rather than
the original goal, $15–20 million. In the succeeding fiscal year the
amount reached $300 million. Canadian purchases in the U.S. in-
creased even more sharply: between April 1, 1951, when records
of the Department of Defense Production were begun, and December
31, 1952, Canada spent some $850 million on defense purchases
in the U.S.[7] This gross imbalance suggests that the opportunity for
Canadian firms to sell to the U.S. military services was more theoretical than real. However, it would not be fair to attribute the
meagerness of these sales to U.S. unwillingness to buy Canadian
goods, or to administrative obstacles putting Canadian firms at a
competitive disadvantage. The imbalance was rather the result of
the incipient stage of Canada's restored defense industry at this
time. During this period of rapid rearmament, the U.S. needed Canada's industrial capacity, and even such articles as advanced aircraft,

6. *U.S. Department of State Bulletin*, XXIII (November 6, 1950), 743.
7. *Debates* (1960), I, 457.

which were later to be so politically sensitive, were purchased in Canada. But Canadian industry was not yet able to meet the needs of Canadian rearmament, much less to fill sizable orders from the U.S.

In order to help restore and maintain a defense industrial base in Canada, the Department of Defense Production was established in 1951. Under C. D. Howe's active leadership, it succeeded in this effort; by the mid–1950's, Canadian industry was producing a wider range of more sophisticated military equipment than it ever had. Canada had produced no aircraft engines during World War II, but by 1957 it was producing the R–1340 and R–1820 piston and Nene, Orenda and Iroquois jet engines. It had developed an advanced electronics industry. It was selling to the U.S. at least six kinds of aircraft: the F–86 and CF–100 fighters, Harvard and T–34 trainers, and Beaver and Otter transport aircraft. In short, while it remained dependent upon the U.S. for many of its military needs, by the mid–1950's Canada was in a position not only to produce most of the military equipment needed for its own forces, but also to compete on a selective basis for U.S. orders. Thus, one of the important preconditions for the establishment of a meaningful, comprehensive division of labor between Canada and the U.S. in defense production was fulfilled. Ironically, however, it was attained only at the time when the political will necessary for such a program was disappearing. After Korea, both governments reverted to the peacetime assumptions that domestic industry should be favored in defense contracting. This was more pronounced and consequential in the case of the United States, as was seen in its refusal to participate in the development of the Arrow, at a time when an aircraft of that type appeared to be needed by both countries and when no comparable U.S. aircraft was yet in sight. U.S. defense contracts in Canada diminished from 1953–58 to an average of only about $35 million annually.[8] A reluctance to achieve the most economical division of labor also existed in Canada, however, in the form of excessive proneness to undertake projects which were not economically feasible in a country of its size.

Progress continued to be made in two other areas of collaboration which eventually contributed to greater measures of integration. The first of these was the standardization of industrial and military items. This was recognized as one of the principles agreed upon in 1947 as the basis of U.S.-Canadian post-war defense collaboration:

8. *Debates* (1960), I, 916.

(3) Encouragement of common designs and standards in arms, equipment, organization, methods of training and new developments. As certain United Kingdom standards have long been in use in Canada, no radical change is contemplated or practicable and the application of this principle will be gradual.[9]

The qualification concerning U.K. standards was only natural for Canada, which encountered continuing difficulties as it changed more and more to U.S. standards after World War II. It was therefore a keen advocate of tripartite standardization among the U.S., Britain, and Canada and welcomed the important decision to establish a unified screw-thread among the three countries in 1948, a measure which was absolutely necessary if more extensive forms of standardization were to follow.[10] Hundreds of additional standards were subsequently agreed upon between services of two or more of the "ABC" countries (Australia later became the fourth), not only in materiel, but in such areas as organization, operational procedures and communications, and logistics.[11] It was sometimes observed that integration advanced further between the same service in these different countries than among different services within the same countries.

The other area in which collaboration became increasingly close is that of defense research. Like the standardization program, it stems from the close research collaboration among the three countries during World War II and is largely tripartite. It was brought up to date in 1957, following Prime Minister Macmillan's visit to Washington in October, when senior scientists of the three countries established the Tripartite Technical Cooperation Program, encompassing research in ten specified fields.[12] The main effect of the program has been an increased flow of information, including that which is classified (within limits), and some consequent avoidance of duplication. The cooperation is not equally close among all countries in all fields, but is probably closest in the case of Canada and

9. *U.S. Department of State Bulletin*, XVI (February 23, 1947), 361.
10. Foster Lee Smith, "Canadian-United States Scientific Collaboration for Defense," *Public Policy*, XII (1963), 307.
11. *Ibid.*, pp. 318–19.
12. *Ibid.*, p. 309. The fields were Nuclear Materials, Nuclear Warheads, Nuclear Power and Propulsion, Biochemical and Radiological Warfare, Weapon Delivery Systems, Ballistic Missile Defense, Undersea Warfare, Aircraft and Aeroengines, Electron Tubes and Infrared. By April, 1962, collaboration in the first four had ceased, but seven additional fields had been added: Radar Techniques, Electronic Parts and Materials, Military Space Research, Nuclear Weapons Effects (U.S.-Canada only), Ordnance, Materials and Electronic Warfare.

the U.S. The collaboration takes place through a variety of channels. The Canadian Defense Research Board and military services maintain liaison officers in Washington and at important development centers in the U.S. to keep them informed of the state of U.S. military research. The U.S. and Canadian Armies divide research projects systematically on a case-by-case basis. U.S. research contracts are often let to non-profit organizations, principally universities, in Canada. And U.S. firms often collaborate directly with their Canadian subsidiaries and subcontractors.[13]

Origins and Functioning of the Development and Production Sharing Program

Two distinct elements led to the incorporation of many of the principles of defense collaboration into a program sufficiently well-established to lead to a significant division of labor in defense production in 1958–59. The first is the idea that Canadian contractors should be given an equal chance to bid on equipment that is used on joint installations located on Canadian territory. This territorially-based principle had already been recognized as it affected the use of Canadian labor and Canadian construction firms. But as no earlier U.S. or joint military installations in Canada had involved large outlays on equipment, the question of allowing Canadian industry's right to bid on such items first arose in 1951, when extension of the Pinetree radar network into Canada was contemplated. In the exchange of notes which constituted an agreement on this project, the principle was affirmed:

> (3) So far as practicable, construction of the installations required for the extension will be carried out by Canadian agencies and contractors with Canadian labour and materials. Electronic and other equipment manufactured in Canada will also be used, as far as practicable.[14]

The question of what was "practicable" was elaborated in the next such agreement, that governing the construction in Canada of the Distant Early Warning system, when the principle was again affirmed.

(4) Provision of Electronic Equipment

> The Canadian Government reaffirms the principle that electronic equipment at installations on Canadian territory should, as

13. *Ibid.*, pp. 314–324.
14. U.S., Department of State, *Treaties and Other International Acts*, V (1954), Part 2, 1721.

far as practicable, be manufactured in Canada. The question of practicability must, in each case, be a matter for consultation between the appropriate Canadian and United States agencies to determine the application of the principle. The factors to be taken into account shall include availability at the time period required, cost and performance.[15]

The practical effect of this principle was not great; only $8.8 million worth of electronic subcontracts were let in Canada in connection with the DEW Line.[16] The principle's acceptance was nonetheless one of the important parts of the background to a later program which would have a significant practical impact.

The second element in the rationale of production sharing was the acceptance, by both the U.S. and Canada, of the view that the military integration embodied in the NORAD agreement of 1958 was incomplete if it did not extend to defense production. This judgment was reached by civil servants of the two countries independently of the specific decisions on military equipment that were made in Canada between the spring and fall of 1958—the cancellation of CAGE, then of Arrow, and the adoption of SAGE and Bomarc.[17] Their views may (or may not) eventually have become government policy had those decisions been different; the fact that the decisions went as they did undoubtedly contributed to the pressures on the political leaders of both sides to come to an understanding on defense production.

Indeed, the effect of those decisions was to make some such understanding a virtual political necessity in Canada; for they implied, as later was made explicit, that Canada would no longer attempt to develop major weapons systems for Canadian forces. This made it imperative that the Canadian defense industry, if it was not to perish, should gain access to the U.S. defense market. The political force of this argument, as well as its equity, were quickly appreciated in the U.S. A congressional delegation commissioned to report on sources of U.S.-Canadian friction visited Canada in the latter half of 1958, and included in its report a recommendation that Canadian defense contractors be given readier access to U.S. orders.[18] The subject was discussed at the highest level in July, 1958, when President Eisenhower and Secretary Dulles visited Ottawa. An agreement was reached that enabled Mr. Diefenbaker to say in his Sep-

15. *U.S. Department of State Bulletin*, XXXIII (July 4, 1955), 23.
16. *Debates* (1960), I, 916.   17. Interviews.
18. U.S., Congress, House, 85th Cong., 2d Sess., *House Report 1766*, "Report of the Special Study Mission to Canada." (Hays-Coffin Report), p. 15.

tember 23 announcement that "the USA Government . . . are now prepared to work out production sharing arrangements with us."[19] After July, the matter was referred to a bilateral committee at the deputy minister-assistant secretary level, and this committee began detailed substantive talks in October.[20] By the time the ministers of the two countries met in Paris in December, the arrangements were ready for their approval. When this had been given, the matter went to President Eisenhower, who approved the agreement on December 30. The arrangements were given practical effect by unilateral action of the U.S., which incorporated in DOD Directive 2035.1, entitled "Defense Economic Cooperation with Canada," the administrative changes of which the program consisted.[21]

Although reports of the agreement found their way into the press, official announcement was withheld until the final decision on Arrow was rendered, since the Diefenbaker government had obvious reasons for wanting to sweeten that pill with news of the new production sharing opportunities.[22] Clarification of such cryptic references to production sharing as that of September 23 was eagerly awaited. Not only the general principles of the program and its long run implementation were important, but also its meaning for several impending decisions. One of these was the question of a U.S. purchase of the Canadair CL–44 transport, a purchase expected to amount to some $400 million if it were carried out. Another was the share which Canadian industry would have in producing the SAGE computers and Bomarcs that were to be put in Canada. In September, the Prime Minister had said that talks would be held "on the best way for Canadian industry to share in the production programmes related to such missiles and associated equipment . . . and to share in the production of the equipment required for the expansion of the radar network and the introduction of these semi-automatic communication and control operations."[23] This statement was interpreted by some to suggest the possibility that entire Bomarcs might be built in Canada under license.[24] In fact, this was never a serious possibility, but arrangements were being considered for subcontracting some of the Bomarc work into Canada. By a

19. Appendix I.   20. *Debates* (1959), II, 1527.

21. See Armed Services Procurement Regulation 6–504 for the provisions contained in the NSC document which Eisenhower approved, in Canada, Department of Defence Production, "Canada-United States Defence Production Sharing." (Ottawa: Queen's Printer, September, 1960), p. 79.

22. *Financial Post*, January 17, 1959.   23. Appendix I.

24. *Debates* (1959), II, 1293.

curious but astute quirk, Bomarc's American manufacturer, the Boeing Company, was as receptive to this proposal as anyone involved. Its reasoning, later borne out almost exactly by events, was that the missile was even then in jeopardy in Congress, but that its chances of survival would be improved to the extent that another country was committed to its construction and use; for any attempt to scrap the missile would then become an international incident.[25]

Shortly after the government's announcement of the Arrow decision and related features of the air defense policy on February 20, the production sharing program for the first time was outlined in the House by the Minister of Defense Production, Mr. Raymond O'Hurley.[26] Those who were hoping that it would include sizable, politically-conceived orders for Canada for the particular projects then under way, such as SAGE and Bomarc, were disappointed.[27] It is true that some $5.7 million worth of subcontracting for Bomarcs was done in Canada, and claimed by the government as an achievement of the program.[28] It is also true that the Canadian negotiators sought, unsuccessfully, to get U.S. agreement to the use of Canadian electronic equipment in the SAGE system, provided only that it was technically satisfactory (i.e., even if it were not economically competitive).[29] However, the thrust of the government's program lay not in the winning of particular contracts, but in the establishment of certain general rules which it hoped would secure for Canadian industry fair access to U.S. defense contracts over the long term.

This contrast between political and non-political content of the production sharing program bears mentioning because it reflects a real dilemma. In order to gain general access to the U.S. defense market, Canadians were opposing the U.S. political pressures which resisted outside incursions. Therefore they stressed the desirability of non-political, economic competition which would place U.S. and Canadian firms on equal footing. But in order to sustain the Canadian aircraft industry, larger orders than those which could be won under such non-political criteria have been needed. Therefore, it has been necessary in these instances to reach political agreement with the U.S. on the desirability of such action. Significantly, some of the

25. Interviews.   26. *Debates* (1959), II, 1526–31; and V, 5656–64.
    27. For examples of the expressions of disappointment, see the *Globe and Mail* (Toronto), February 24, 1959; *La Presse*, March 10, 1959; *Le Devoir*, March 6, 1959; *Ottawa Evening Journal*, March 23, 1959; *Financial Post*, May 9, 1959.
    28. *Debates* (1959), II, 1519.   29. Interviews.

largest defense orders in Canada since 1959 have been in this category of the uneconomic or noneconomic—in the sense that other than economic criteria were determining the decision. For example, the decision to produce under license in Canada, rather than to buy from the U.S., the F–104's for the air division; and the subsequent order for additional numbers of these aircraft for the Mutual Defense Assistance Program. There is another way in which the program's economic principles come into conflict with political realities: production-sharing requires effective integration of defense industries with the United States, yet for political reasons, Canada's foreign policy must at times at least strive to be independent of, and thus to some degree different from, that of the U.S.

The essence of the production-sharing program, as it was first described in 1959, and as it has remained ever since, is the removal of obstacles which prevented Canadian firms from bidding for U.S. defense contracts on an equal basis with their U.S. competitors, and the consolidation of these gains by embodying them not only in U.S. Armed Services Procurement Regulations, but in the behavior of procurement agencies and of U.S. and Canadian firms. The program resembles previous U.S.-Canadian collaboration in defense production, and yet it goes considerably further than anything done before. It resembles previous directives in the objectives which are proclaimed: increased integration of U.S.-Canadian military production, removal of obstacles to reciprocal procurement and to the flow of defense goods between the two countries, greater standardization, greater dispersal of production facilities, increasing exchange of information, and the determination of Canadian capabilities to meet U.S. requirements.[30] It also added two objectives which were not recognized before: to ensure the most economical use of defense funds, and to accord equal consideration to the business communities of both countries.[31] The basic policy goal which lay behind these proclaimed objectives, couched as they were in regulation language, was the same as it had been in 1941 and in 1950: to increase U.S. defense orders in Canada. Similarly, some of the obstacles to be removed in order to accomplish this had been set aside before, but not as effectively as was now contemplated. There were several of these obstacles to consider. One was the "Buy American" Act, which imposed upon foreign suppliers in general a six to twelve

30. Canada, Department of Defense Production, "Canada-United States Defence Production Sharing," pp. 62–64.
31. *Ibid.*

per cent penalty, as compared with American contractors. Another was the body of duties which in the past had been imposed on some defense articles, especially on those which were made under subcontract with a U.S. firm. Security restrictions prevented giving Canadian firms access under the "need to know" rubric so long as there was no Canadian requirement for the article, and thereby denied them the knowledge needed to bid on specifically American requirements. Even within the limits of unclassified material, Canadian firms were not always able to find out readily what U.S. military requirements actually were.[32] Foreign suppliers were also prohibited from bidding on contracts which the Department of Defense had "set aside" for certain favored categories of U.S. suppliers: those in labor surplus areas, small businesses, depressed industries, and those furnishing articles for the Military Assistance program.[33] These were all obstacles which administrative regulations perpetuated. There was an additional obstacle which was not so readily identifiable but which was perhaps even more serious: the unfamiliarity of the U.S. military services with Canadian sources of supply, and of Canadian firms with the potential of the U.S. market.

Sufficient progress was made by the production sharing program in lowering these obstacles that the claim could be made that "basically the program provides for Canadian firms to be given equal opportunity to compete with U.S. firms on the basis of price, quality and delivery for a wide range of U.S. procurement."[34] Almost every one of the above limitations was specifically altered, in order to except Canada from its application. The restrictions of the "Buy American" Act, as they applied to Canada, had previously been waived by some U.S. services. They were now virtually eliminated as they concerned contracts between Canada and any U.S. military service. The only exception was the case of contracts for construction materials or construction to be done within the U.S.; as we have seen, this restriction was paralleled by Canadian insistence on using its own labor and materials for similar work in Canada.[35] Similarly, Canadian materials were exempted under the program from all U.S. duties, with very few exceptions. In addition to construction materials, these exceptions include supplies for contracts of less than

32. *Debates* (1959), II, 1526–31; and V, 5656–64.
33. Canada, Department of Defense Production, "Production Sharing Handbook." (Ottawa: Queen's Printer, 1964), pp. 53–55.
34. *Ibid.*, p. 7.
35. Canada, Department of Defense Production, "Production Sharing Handbook," pp. 28, 29.

$10,000 or for subcontracts of less than $5,000.[36] More flexible security arrangements were made so that Canadian industrial personnel possessing Canadian clearance could gain access to classified U.S. projects subject to approval of the relevant U.S. service. Simplified procedures were arranged for oral or visual access to the classified data, although exchange of documents continued to be handled on a government-to-government basis.[37] Arrangements were made for the provision to Canadian firms by the Naval Supply Depot of such unclassified information as U.S. specifications and standards, information which might not be included in solicitations they might receive but which would have to be known in order to respond.[38] Other measures of a primarily administrative nature, such as those providing for reciprocal inspection, reciprocal auditing, and listing of each country's products on the other's Qualified Products List, attended to the detailed problems involved in the execution of the program.[39] Of the restrictions described above, only the four "set aside" categories remained substantially unchanged by the production-sharing program with Canada.

One of the important and novel features of the production-sharing program, relative to previous collaboration of this kind, has been the vigor with which it has been administered. From the beginning of the program, the Canadian government deemed it essential that an energetic effort be made to familiarize U.S. procurement agencies with the capabilities of Canadian industry on the one hand and, on the other hand, Canadian contractors with the prospects and procedures involved in bidding on U.S. defense contracts. To achieve the latter, an expanded promotion and information program in the U.S. was undertaken. The Department of Defense Production, which administers the program, set up offices in eleven U.S. cities located in defense-industrial areas, in addition to the existing offices of the Foreign Trade Service of the Department of Trade and Commerce.[40] The DDP officers in these locations were given "the specific task of encouraging U.S. defense procurement agencies and industry to use Canadian products,"[41] a task which it seeks to perform by guiding them to the particular Canadian firms which might be able to fulfill their requirements. On some occasions, the Invitations for Bids are submitted to the DDP itself, and it relays the specifications to Canadian companies which might be in a position to respond.[42]

36. *Ibid.*, p. 33.   37. *Ibid.*, pp. 56–59.   38. *Ibid.*, pp. 20, 21.
39. *Ibid.*, pp. 62–70.   40. *Ibid.*, pp. 23–26.   41. *Ibid.*
42. Halpenny Committee *Proceedings* (July 14, 1960), p. 553.

More recently, the U.S. Defense Supply Agency has established an office in Ottawa to assist further in the administration of U.S. defense contracts in Canada.[43] For the most part, however, the emphasis has been upon preparing Canadian industry to undertake the sales effort itself and to rely upon it to find its own buyers. This was done by preparing a handbook describing U.S. procurement procedures, and distributing it widely to Canadian firms. The handbook describes in some detail such questions as how a firm can get on U.S. Bidders' Mailing Lists, how to keep informed of current U.S. requirements, the kind of sales effort needed to turn an Invitation for Bid into a contract, U.S. legislation affecting cross-border trade, and the types of services provided to the contractors by the Canadian government.[44] In addition to the liaison function described above, these services include monitoring the submission of bids by Canadian industry and, in the case of prime contracts, acting as the contractual agent between the Canadian firm and the U.S. (or other foreign) procuring agency.[45] The Canadian Commercial Corporation, a Crown Corporation which was established in 1946, is the DDP's agent in such cases. Its participation in production-sharing contracts "ensures that the country procuring defense supplies in Canada will enjoy the same standards of price, quality and delivery in respect of any such procurement as would the Canadian government were it procuring the supplies on its own behalf in comparable circumstances."[46]

In the early stages of the production-sharing program, it was appreciated that the removal of the aforementioned obstacles to greater trade in defense supplies would not suffice. Canadian firms, in order to share an equal competitive position, must be involved in the development stage of some of the articles in question. The advantage enjoyed by the firm which develops an item in competing for the production of that item remains important, even when competing firms have equal opportunities to offer bids. This appreciation led the Canadian government to grant subsidies to some Canadian firms that were in competition with the U.S. firms which had been involved in development of the articles in question; the subsidies were

43. Canada, Department of Defense Production, "1965 Annual Report." (Ottawa: Queen's Printer, 1966), p. 24.

44. Canada, Department of Defense Production, "Production Sharing Handbook." (Ottawa: Queen's Printer, October, 1964).

45. *Ibid.*, p. 9; and Canadian Commerical Corporation, "Annual Report, 1963–64," p. 4.

46. *Ibid.*, p. 4.

designed to compensate the Canadian firms for the pre-production costs of tooling-up, which, in the case of their competitors, had been charged off to development.[47] Such subsidies could help to remove the cost differential between firms which had and those which had not participated in development; but they could not eliminate the advantages in expertise and time leads. Gradually, a program was developed to solve this problem more satisfactorily by increasing the number of instances in which the Canadian firms themselves might participate in the requisite research and development. This inclusion of development projects was the second important innovation in production-sharing of the program begun in 1959. The innovation was an important one because, even more than production sharing, it was a politically bold undertaking for the U.S. Department of Defense. It was difficult enough to allow Canadian firms to bid on an equal basis for U.S. production orders. To aid them in this effort by financing their development projects with U.S. money was, therefore, a big step. This was true even more since the skills acquired by Canadian firms in the process would make them more effective competitors in other projects besides the one that was U.S.-financed.

There have been three types of collaboration in development between the U.S. and Canada: (1) projects financed by the U.S. and performed by Canadian firms to meet U.S. requirements; (2) projects performed by Canadian firms to meet U.S. requirements, but financed wholly by Canada, or jointly by Canada and the U.S.; and (3) projects performed in Canada for which there is no current U.S. requirement, but which are speculatively financed by the Canadian government. Projects of the first type are handled similarly to cases of production-sharing. U.S. requirements are monitored by DDP, which passes on to appropriate Canadian firms those requirements which it feels they could develop an item to fill, with or without government assistance. Their responses are evaluated by the U.S. services on the same basis as replies from U.S. firms: technical capability, price and delivery are the criteria. The second case, in which Canadian financing plays a role, arises when the project is of such a low priority, or the U.S. service is so pressed for funds that Canadian funds are needed to make up the difference. In such cases, DDP accepts the normal risks of development, but there is a bilateral understanding that competitive development will not be undertaken elsewhere by the U.S. service unless the Canadian

47. Halpenny Committee *Proceedings* (July 14, 1960), p. 547.

project does not meet its technical, time or fiscal standards.[48] Moreover, Small Business "set asides" have not been applied thus far to production orders for equipment developed in Canada. The chances are high therefore that successful development will be followed by a production order. One of the Canadian weapons that was most successful in winning foreign orders, the Caribou aircraft, was financed in this way. The Canadian share of such jointly-managed projects originally reached 100% in some cases. But some problems resulted in these instances, since the U.S. service representatives who monitored the programs technically had no incentive to hold down costs. They tended to demand such high requirements that the prices rose to unacceptable levels. Therefore, the program has been changed to require that the U.S. Department of Defense shall contribute not less than 25 per cent of the funds for any joint project.[49] The third category, that of projects solely Canadian-financed, does not, properly speaking, represent development sharing; it does illustrate the policy of the DDP to use all means to encourage promising Canadian developments in this field. The Department's contributions to Canadian- and jointly-financed projects have risen steadily during the years of the program's existence, from $1.8 million in the fiscal year 1959–60 to $22 million in the calendar year 1965.[50]

RESULTS

In evaluating the achievements of the Development and Production-Sharing program, it is important to note the modesty of the program's terms of reference. First, it is limited as to the kind of expenditure which is included:

> The classes of contracts included in the defense production sharing category are applied research and development, preproduction, production, licence agreements and technical assistance, installation (other than construction), and repair, overhaul and modification. The production sharing figures do not include contracts for "off-the-shelf" general procurement, construction, basic raw materials, fuel and lubricants, or services (such as transportation, rentals, and maintenance of fixed installations).[51]

48. Smith, pp. 325–330.
49. U.S. Army, Regulation No. 1–25, "United States–Canadian Defense Development Sharing Program," pp. 7–9.
50. Halpenny Committee *Proceedings* (July 14, 1960), p. 543; and Canada, Department of Defense Production, "1965 Annual Report,", p. 23.
51. Canada, Department of Defense Production, "Thirteenth Report: January 1 to December 31, 1963." (Ottawa: Queen's Printer, 1964), p. 23.

This is a limitation not of scope, but of definition, designed to ensure that the figures included under the program will bear some relation to the program's objectives. But other stipulations of the two governments limit those objectives themselves. First, it is frankly admitted that the program does not aim at the economically optimum situation in which weapons would be procured from the source which could provide them most appropriately and most cheaply, without regard to nationality:

> I want to emphasize that, as Minister of Defence Production, my procurement policies are governed by the duty, imposed by parliament, to develop and maintain the production resources needed in Canada to support our defence policy. This means that, wherever possible, we look to Canadian industrial facilities for the production of the weapons and equipment needed for our national defence. We also examine the supply requirements of the services to see how they can contribute to the creation of new Canadian industrial skills and facilities and the improvement of existing resources. This is absolutely basic to our operations. In our current purchasing for the Canadian forces we are looking to Canadian sources for the vast bulk of our needs.[52]

Since Canadians themselves had recognized on earlier occasions[53] the invalidity of using national security as a grounds for foregoing trade with the U.S. in strategic materials—supply from the other North American country being virtually as secure as domestic supply—this procurement policy was aimed in fact at the protection of Canadian defense producers. The U.S. was equally unwilling to see procurement policy determined only by the principles of economy and military efficiency. It is not easy to demonstrate, but is accepted as fact by civil servants who administer the production-sharing program, that there is a level of sophistication above which weapons for U.S. forces will not be procured from abroad except for political reasons weighed at the highest levels. A more concrete instance of this U.S. reluctance to go too far is the requirement, which the Kennedy administration attached to the production-sharing program, that a "general balance" be maintained in cross-border military procurement.[54] While the meaning of this phrase has never been made explicit, it is not regarded as inconsistent with significant imbalance in the figures for a single year. Canadians were not pleased to be bound by this requirement, but considering their great

52. Halpenny Committee *Proceedings* (July 14, 1960), p. 544.
53. Cited in Eayrs, "Sharing a Continent: The Hard Issues," pp. 69, 70.
54. For a statement of this requirement, see *Debates* (1963), I, p. 769.

dependence on U.S. sources of supply, it is doubtful if they could realistically hope for much more over the long term, even on an entirely competitive basis.

Another limitation of the program, and one which is revealing, is its bilateral character. Canada's earlier attachment to Article II of the North Atlantic Treaty, and its difficulty at that time in making clear which economic activities it wished to see co-ordinated by NATO that were not managed already by other agencies, would have suggested that it welcomed co-operation in military production on a NATO-wide basis. In fact, this course was never seriously advocated by Canada; when the U.S. briefly considered making the production-sharing program a multilateral one, it was opposed by Canada on the grounds that it would make the program administratively unmanageable.[55] More recently, Canada sought to expand its bilateral co-operation in defense production with Britain, France and West Germany. It has been also somewhat more active in trying to promote Canadian weapons within a multilateral NATO framework. But there is no aspiration or expectation that it is an alternative policy to maintaining and increasing access to the U.S. defense market. There is no clearer example of the way in which the proclaimed ideology of Canada's alliance policy—to promote multilateralism, to counter U.S. influence with European ties—often tends to dissolve when vague generalities must be translated into detailed programs.

Having qualified in so many ways the results which might be expected from the program, it should be said immediately that the program has been quite successful within those terms of reference. The volume of reciprocal military procurement reached levels never before attained in peacetime. U.S. military spending in Canada during the first seven years of the program, 1959–65, totaled $1,174 million. This represented an average of almost $170 million annually, compared to the $35 million yearly average between 1953–58. Canadian defense expenditure in the U.S. during the same period amounted to $981.6 million.[56] Even more striking are the figures representing the numbers of inquiries received from the U.S. by Canadian defense contractors, of quotations submitted by them, and of contracts resulting. Numbers in all three categories have increased logarithmically since 1957–58. In that fiscal year, about 1000 inquiries were received; some 650 quotations were submitted; and 540 contracts resulted. In the fiscal year 1963–64 the corresponding figures were approxi-

55. Interviews.
56. Canada, Department of Defense Production, "1965 Annual Report," p. 23.

mately the following: 14,000 inquiries; 3,600 quotations; and 1,900 contracts.[57] The number of Canadian firms doing business under the program was over 300.[58] Many of these firms were doing work under subcontract from U.S. prime contractors; such subcontracts began to comprise a substantial part of the total value of such Canadian contracts, whereas prior to 1959 they were not sufficiently numerous or important to be distinguished in the statistics.[59] Moreover, the recent balance in military trade across the border has been heavily in Canada's favor. Owing largely to the Vietnam war, "In 1965, U.S. production-sharing procurement in Canada reached a new high of $259.5 million,"[60] as against Canadian purchases in the U.S. of $130.1 million; and this trend continued in the early months of 1966.

It is true that the U.S. expenditures in Canada during this period included sizable outlays for projects which were determined more by political means than by the military and economic criteria of the production-sharing program. The $200 million order for F-104G's built in Canada as part of the military assistance program was the largest of these. The construction of F-104's under license in Canada for the air division does not appear in the production sharing figures. But the $430 million expenditure it involved was made in Canada rather than the U.S. as the result of political choice, not a determination of the most efficient source. Therefore, the figure showing the balance of purchases across the border is more favorable by that amount (correctly, by some fraction of that amount, since some parts were obtained from the U.S.) than it would otherwise be. All of this indicates that in spite of the production-sharing program, whole Canadian industries continue to depend on the large orders placed, at least partly, on the basis of political influence.

The critical question for the future is therefore not what the volume of business under the program has been, as much as whether its stabilization can be promoted. This can be done either by consolidating, in both countries, the political will to make it work, or, by enlarging the portion of contracts which are awarded on an eco-

57. Figures taken from Canadian Commercial Corporation, "Annual Report 1963-64," p. 7.
58. Sauvé Committee *Proceedings* (July 30, 1963), p. 265.
59. *Debates* (1960), I, 456-7.
60. Canada, Department of Defense Production, "1965 Annual Report," p. 23.

nomic-military rather than political basis. It is by no means clear what the answer to this question will be, but there have been some promising developments. For example, there have been instances in which Canadian firms have returned without comment, or have failed to return at all, Invitations for Bids from U.S. firms or procurement officers. According to U.S. procurement practices, such action would constitute a kiss of death eliminating the firm from consideration for any future work. But allowance was made for the Canadians' inexperience in the field, and their bids continued to be solicited.[61] Again, in 1963 and afterwards, the U.S. Army ordered a sizable number of Caribou aircraft in Canada because it was considered the best aircraft available to meet an existing requirement. The action marked something of a breakthrough and demonstrated to Army procurement officers that they could buy some important items in Canada without encountering the disapproval of their superiors. There remained, however, the disapproval of Congress, which repeatedly threatened to reduce the funds available for the purchase of Caribous.[62] It is because of the greater susceptibility of Congress than the Services to the pressures of U.S. firms and trade unions that the program has been given a minimum of public notice. In the U.S., progress has been sought quietly.

Some progress, though uneven, has also been made in Canada. The government's purchase of U.S.-made M–113 armored personnel carriers in place of Canadian Bobcats marked a victory for the "cost-effectiveness" school, of which the Liberal Defense Minister, Mr. Hellyer, was a devotee. It is true that the decision to produce the F–5 tactical aircraft in Canada, as well as its timing, seems to have been designed largely to give a fillip to Canada's aircraft industry, and in particular to the firm of Canadair, which had come to rely heavily on government business. But at least by having chosen a relatively simple and inexpensive aircraft, the added cost of setting up a second, Canadian production line was minimized. By 1966, the favorable balance accumulated by Canada gave the government relative freedom to make purchases from the U.S. in accordance with the principles of production-sharing without excessive worry about the political effects in Canada. Should it choose to supplement Canada's airlift capacity by purchasing more C–130's or C–141's, or to replace the declining squadrons of Voodoos with American aircraft, this fact will be of considerable benefit.

61. Smith, p. 332.   62. *Globe and Mail* (Toronto), October 12, 1963.

At the program's inception, it was appreciated that its success depended on the achievement of some basic changes of behavior:

> There are signs of intangible benefits, too, which may in the long run outweigh in importance the defence orders which are obtained . . . Successful production sharing requires some fairly radical changes in deeply-rooted commercial habits and attitudes within both Canadian and United States industry. The Canadian manufacturer discovers that United States industry is not entirely the threat which he had regarded it as being; it is, in fact, a market of enormous potential. The United States prime contractor learns, by direct experience, that there are efficient sources of supply readily available to him in Canada.[63]

By 1966, such a change of attitude seemed indeed to be occurring, as attested to by the increasing extent to which firms (and less markedly, procurement agencies), were placing across-the-border orders of increasing numbers and value. More importantly, it appeared that these firms and procurement agencies were becoming dependent on their trans-border sources of supply, even to the point that if the two governments wished to curtail such purchases, they would find it increasingly difficult to do so. To the extent that this change had occurred, the program was placed on a stable and continuing basis, notwithstanding the fact that it was embodied in nothing more formal than administrative regulations. The continuation of the program was one necessary ingredient in the answer to the more general question of what defense policy Canada could perform with usefulness, stability and satisfaction.

63. *Debates* (1960), I, 457; the speaker was the Minister of Defense Production, Raymond O'Hurley.

CHAPTER VIII

Return of the Liberals

REVIEW OF DEFENSE POLICY

THE acquisition of nuclear weapons and the establishment of the Development and Production Sharing program removed from the agenda the two most critical problems which, until mid–1963, had prevented any general examination of Canada's purposes in alliances and consequent military needs. The Pearson government that was elected in 1963, after it had "tidied up the past"[1] by acquiring nuclear weapons, was able to turn again to the search for a general defense policy comparable in stability and satisfaction to that which existed from 1949 to 1957. Its first action toward this end was the appointment—in fulfillment of a campaign pledge—of a parliamentary Special Committee on Defense, composed of members of all parties. This action departed from the past inclination of Canadian governments, both Liberal and Conservative, to resist the formation of such committees. Moreover, the Committee's terms of reference included the powers to call independent witnesses and to examine not only defense expenditures but also policy, thus insuring that the scope and significance of its investigations would exceed those of such groups appointed in the past. Between June 18 and December 11, 1963, the Committee held forty-five meetings, including fourteen in Europe and two in the U.S., heard numerous witnesses from outside as well as within the public service, and received written submissions as well as oral testimony on various aspects of defense policy. That these investigations were deemed helpful was suggested by the fact that the government followed the recommendation of the Committee that it be reconstituted in 1964;[2] and it was later given permanent status. Simultaneously with the committee's early deliberations, a general review was conducted within the Department of National Defense of all aspects of defense policy and all existing commitments. In order not to prejudice the outcome

1. "The Man Behind Canada's Bold Look at Tomorrow," *Armed Forces Management* (June, 1964), p. 47.
2. Sauvé Committee *Proceedings, Report*, pp. 791–810.

of these reviews, action was suspended on all major procurement programs then under consideration. The Minister, Mr. Hellyer, justifiably felt that in the past "policy was being set by the equipment procured";[3] and he was determined that future options should not be restricted by an early and relatively unconsidered commitment to expensive procurement programs. The particular programs affected by this order were plans for the acquisition of additional CF–104 aircraft as replacements for the existing squadrons in Europe and for the construction of eight general purpose frigates with anti-submarine, anti-aircraft and troop-carrying capabilities. Of the two, the latter project was by far the more important because of its great cost: $452 million by the official estimate, which was perhaps excessively optimistic.[4] It was eventually decided to cancel both of these programs.[5]

The Sauvé Committee's proceedings both produced a great deal of information about Canadian defense policies of the recent past, and provided an occasion for consideration of future policy. There was, on the whole, a striking agreement between the government's tentative indications of what its policies would be and the suggestions of non-governmental, independent witnesses before the Committee. In the meantime, the departmental review was progressing satisfactorily; in March, 1964, it culminated in the publication of a White Paper on Defense, the first such document since 1959,[6] and one which purported to outline Canada's defense policies for the next decade.[7] The White Paper and the later elaborations of it describe policies that differ in important respects, both general and specific, from preceding ones. They outline a new "philosophy, [which] put simply, is that Canada can make its greatest contribution to collective defense and world order by developing well-equipped flexible, conventional forces, and providing the strategic mobility to move them quickly to meet emergencies anywhere in the world."[8]

REORGANIZATION

The most dramatic of the changes announced in the White Paper concerned the organization of the defense forces. It was decided

3. "The Man Behind Canada's Bold Look at Tomorrow," p. 46.
4. Sauvé Committee *Proceedings* (October 15, 1963), p. 399.
5. *Ibid.* (November 5, 1963), pp. 666, 667.
6. Canada, Department of National Defense, "Defence, 1959." (Ottawa: Queen's Printer, April, 1959). This was criticized by members of the opposition for being couched in generalities and not providing clear guidelines to policy.
7. Canada, Department of National Defense, "White Paper on Defence." (Ottawa: Queen's Printer, March, 1964). Hereafter cited as White Paper.
8. *Debates*, February 21, 1966, p. 1562 (Hellyer).

to integrate all three services "under a single Chief of Defense Staff and a single Defense Staff. This will be the first step toward a single unified defense force for Canada."[9] This step, like other aspects of the new policy, was an attempt to correct recognizable defects of previous policies and organization. Under the previous system, the autonomy of each member of the Chiefs of Staff Committee—the three service chiefs, the chairman of the Defense Research Board, and the chairman—provided him with an effective veto against decisions of that committee that were not to his liking, and assured him of direct access to the minister. For his part, the minister was not adequately equipped or staffed to be able always to co-ordinate initiatives coming from these five men and from the associate minister. As a result, the principles of unified and civilian control were not very effectively practiced.

The principal sufferer from this lack of co-ordination and control was the Army, which was less capable than the other services of finding and executing a self-contained, independent role. In particular, it was ill-suited for service except in an international, integrated structure because the preference of the other services—especially the Air Force—for other roles deprived it of the support, reconnaissance and transport it needed to operate as a national contingent. Canadian forces, for example, in both UNEF and ONUC were dependent upon U.S. air transport for their effectiveness; the RCAF, meanwhile, took a nuclear strike role of doubtful utility and even more doubtful appropriateness for Canada. This problem resulted in several anomalies in the production and procurement of equipment. For example, the STOL short-range transport, the Caribou, a De Havilland aircraft, has been one of the most successful exports of Canada's defense industry, and large numbers have been sold to the U.S. and abroad. Only a very few, however, were purchased by Canadian forces. Although the Army wanted them, it had no air corps of its own, and the RCAF was reluctant to use its procurement funds on that type of aircraft.

So long as Canada's defense policy was based on the doctrine of "balanced collective forces," according to which a country made a specialized contribution of the kind most appropriate for it to the alliance, on the assumption that it would be used only as part of a collective effort, this situation was to be expected. But the White Paper, though it did not explicitly reject that doctrine, implied a sharp turn away from it. While it continued the assumption that, outside of North America, action by Canadian forces would be

9. White Paper, p. 19.

within a NATO or United Nations context, there appeared to be
an increasing conviction that the Canadian contingents in such operations should be balanced, autonomous forces rather than specialized
parts of an international force. The White Paper envisages, for example, that the air "squadrons stationed in Europe [will] be associated, ultimately, more directly with the army brigade group."[10]
Similarly, the acquisition of transport and support aircraft will give
Canadian contingents in peacekeeping forces the ability to operate
autonomously.

Another reason for integration, in addition to the desire for better
co-ordination, was economy. This ever-laudable goal had a particular
relevance at the time. From a peak of 43 per cent in 1954, the
portion of the defense budget spent on the procurement of equipment
had fallen to 13 per cent in the estimates for the 1963–64 fiscal
year.[11] Hellyer's goal to raise this to 25 per cent could only be
achieved—within a defense budget fixed, for political reasons, at
about $1.5 billion—by reducing expenditures on operation and main-
tenance and integration seemed the most likely means of achieving
this. Ultimately, it was hoped to save $100 million annually by
eliminating 10,000 jobs, and to apply the saving to equipment purchases, thereby increasing procurement funds by 30 per cent. After
the process had been under way for some two years, only about
1,000 jobs had been eliminated in fact, although the Minister nonetheless claimed to have achieved in that period a saving of $144
million—a claim that certainly could be disputed by investigating
the way in which "savings" were measured.[12] In any case, the portion
of the budget devoted to purchases of new equipment, though improved, remained far below the goal of one-quarter that Hellyer
had set for himself.[13]

This effort to increase expenditures for equipment was part of
a more comprehensive policy of the Pearson government to give
to Canadian producers a more satisfactory role than in the past
in providing equipment for Canada's forces. The problems that had
arisen in the past stemmed from the conflict between, on the one

10. *Ibid.*, p. 22.
11. "Why Canada is Welding Its Three Military Services into One," *Armed
Forces Management*, June, 1964, p. 53.
12. *Debates*, February 17, 1966, p. 1417; and February 21, 1966, p. 1564.
13. On December 22, 1964, the government announced a program of procurement costing $1.5 billion over five years. Assuming that the budget remains
at the same figure each year—and it is unlikely to be less–the portion for
equipment would be 20%.

hand, the aspiration to perform important roles demanding sophisticated equipment, and, on the other, the desire to have this equipment designed and/or produced in Canada, although it was not always possible to do so economically or in reasonable time. There appeared to be three parts of the Pearson government's program to end this dilemma. First, there would be a greater effort than in the past to choose military roles for which the requisite equipment was within the ability of Canadian defense industry to produce quickly and economically. "Canada's defense policy must be geared to its industrial resources," said Mr. Pearson some months before taking office.[14] Later, his Minister of Defense Production, Mr. Drury, acknowledged that he felt responsible for upholding this view in the cabinet.[15] Second, once the roles were chosen, Mr. Hellyer insisted that "the new force concept must be equipped with the best possible 'hardware' regardless of country of origin,"[16] although he acknowledged that "where the capabilities are approximately equal, we certainly would favour Canadian production."[17] Third, various inducements were offered to Canadian industry to gain their support for this policy of re-emphasizing the importance of competitiveness. The most significant of these was of course the Development and Production Sharing program, which had been well-established by the time the Liberal government took office, and which held out the hope that Canadian orders lost to U.S. competitors might be replaced by U.S. orders of an equal or larger volume. Another was the drive to increase the portion of the defense budget spent on equipment and thereby to increase the absolute amount of procurement that would be placed each year. Finally, through establishing a long-term defense policy that would not be subject to frequent and basic change, and through an improved program of communication with Canadian industry about the requirements dictated by that policy, it was hoped to enable Canadian firms to be in a position to compete more effectively for orders of the Canadian government.

> We are going . . . to take industry into our confidence to a much greater extent than has been possible in the past. . . . They have to make long range plans too, and we intend to brief them, to give them the maximum amount of information that we can.[18]

14. *Debates* (1962–63), III, 3124.
15. Sauvé Committee *Proceedings* (July 30, 1963), p. 278.
16. Paul Hellyer, "What the White Paper Means to the Air Industry," text available from Canada, Department of National Defense, p. 1.
17. Transcript of "Inquiry," March 30, 1964, p. 15.
18. *Ibid.*

In order to attain these goals of improved co-ordination and economy, halfway measures were not sufficient. Previous efforts to achieve unification, none of them entirely successful, had begun, in Canada as elsewhere, from the bottom and worked up. This was tried in Canada in the late 1950's, when medical and chaplain services were unified; but it did not progress very far.[19] Improved co-ordination at the top of the chain of command had been attained when, at the end of World War II, separate service ministers were replaced by one Minister of National Defense; and at the beginning of the Korean war, a separate chairman of the Chiefs of Staff Committee was appointed, although he was not given the authority to resolve differences among the service chiefs.[20] The continued inadequacy of this system led the Royal Commission on Government Organization, which had been created by the Diefenbaker government, to recommend that additional powers of co-ordination be invested in the Chairman, Chiefs of Staff.[21] Addressing itself to this recommendation, the White Paper concluded that "this solution does not adequately resolve the basic issues. If a single command structure is not established, co-ordination by the committee system will remain with all of its inevitable delays and frustrations."[22] It was accordingly decided to establish a unified command which would eventually extend to operational levels, and even go so far as to make likely the adoption of a single uniform. The legislation embodying the first stage of this integration came into effect on August 1, 1964. It abolished the old positions of Chairman, Chiefs of Staff and chiefs of the individual services, and replaced them with an organization consisting of the following: Chief of the Defense Staff, Vice Chief of the Defense Staff, Assistant Chief of the Defense Staff, and four functional chiefs—for Operational Readiness, Personnel, Logistics and Engineering, and Comptroller General.[23] In the summer of 1965, the integration of defense headquarters was completed on schedule; it was announced that the next stage would be the formation of six functional commands, a reduction from the eleven commands organized along service lines. By

19. Foulkes testimony, p. 524.   20. *Ibid.*, pp. 523–25.
21. Canada, Royal Commission on Government Organization, IV: *Special Areas of Administration.* (Ottawa: Queen's Printer, 1963), pp. 69–74.
22. White Paper, p. 18.
23. Subsequently the positions of Vice-Chief of the Defense Staff and Chief of Operational Readiness were combined, and the name Assistant Chief of Defense Staff was changed to Deputy Chief, Plans. *Debates* (February 21, 1966), p. 1563.

early 1966, all of these had been formed and at least had begun to assume their new responsibilities.[24] Before the process reaches the stage of a single force with one uniform and rank structure—the point referred to as "unification," as distinct from the "integration" achieved so far—additional legislation will be required. This will provide an occasion for debate, both within the defense establishment and within Parliament, to evaluate the progress to date.

There was a striking, if not perfect, degree of concurrence in the goals of this program, even among the service chiefs. This enthusiasm was enhanced by the fact that it was viewed as an experiment in defense organization which other countries might, with profit, emulate. Nine of Canada's allies, including the United States, were sufficiently interested in the experiment to establish study groups to evaluate it and to appraise its relevance for them.[25] The government's awareness of this demonstration effect seemed to suggest the hope that Canada's distinctive experiment in defense organization could give a significance to its alliance contribution which its diminishing relative strength was taking away. According to Mr. Hellyer, "we, as the laboratory for world-wide defense reorganization, can either advance or retard the inevitable move of other nations in this direction. It is a heavy responsibility and we mean to discharge it with as many thorough, all-embracing thought-processes as we can muster."[26]

NEW COMMANDS, ROLES, AND EQUIPMENT

The changed outlook reflected in the White Paper is nowhere more evident than in the concept which found expression in *Mobile Command*, the largest of the new functional forces. That document describes plans for:

> . . . two Canadian-based brigades to be re-equipped and retrained as a mobile force as well as for rotational service with the NATO brigade. Although stationed in Canada, they will be available for use where and when required. In order to achieve maximum flexibility, these two brigades will be equipped to permit their effective deployment in circumstances ranging from service in the European theatre to United Nations peace-keeping operations.[27]

24. *Debates*, February 17, 1966, p. 1417.
25. *Hamilton Spectator*, September 4, 1965.
26. Address by Group Capt. William Lee to Gananoque Rotary Club, "The New Look in Defence," October 5, 1964, p. 14, citing Hellyer.
27. White Paper, p. 22.

The goal of flexibility was dictated by the view that a country of Canada's size and resources could no longer afford to invest in expensive weapons systems that were useful only for one mission, which changing strategic or political conditions might render inappropriate. The exclusively nuclear role of the expensive CF–104's, which were of increasingly doubtful utility, provided a good example of what to avoid. The adoption of this goal signified another departure from the doctrine of balanced, collective forces.

The flexibility of the mobile force was to be enhanced further by the formation of another, smaller brigade as a special service force, equipped with air-portable and air-droppable equipment, that would be trained for a variety of roles. By 1966, plans were announced for a second special service brigade, to be supplemented by an additional airborne battalion group.[28] From 1965, this increasing mobility enabled Canada to provide one battalion, the Black Watch, to NATO's Allied Mobile Force, which was charged with reinforcing the defense of the Norwegian flank; of the six national contributions that constituted the AMF, only Canada's was based outside Western Europe. The commitment to this role was strengthened by the announcement in April, 1966, that the next commander of the force would be a French Canadian, Major General Gilles Turcot.[29] At the NATO ministerial meeting of July, 1966, Mr. Hellyer suggested that as the area of responsibility of the AMF was expanded to include the Turkish flank, Canada might enlarge its contribution to two battalion groups.[30]

To enable these Canadian-based forces to operate as independent national units, it was necessary to provide them with their own air support and air transport. The former need led to an order for 125 copies of an advanced version of the Northrop F–5 Freedom Fighter, to be produced in Canada under license by Canadair. The total cost of the aircraft—together with spares, equipment, weapons and ammunition for a year—was $215 million, considerably cheaper than the F–4 Phantom, which seems to have been the most seriously considered alternative.[31] Air transport was to be provided by the second of the six functional commands, the *Air Transport Command.* To equip it for the role, orders were placed for twenty-four C–130 Hercules long-range transports and fifteen Canadian-produced

28. *Debates* (February 17, 1966), p. 1418.
29. *Globe and Mail* (Toronto), April 14, 1966.
30. *Ibid.*, July 30, 1966.
31. *Ibid.*, article by John Gellner, March 4, 1966.

Buffaloes for medium range movements to semi-improved air strips.[32]
The transport capability thus provided was still rather more modest
than the government's rhetoric: the estimate was given to the Sauvé
Committee that forty to fifty Hercules would be needed to transport
one brigade of men with light equipment across the Atlantic within
a three- to four-week period. Although Canada's existing sea lift
capability could be used to supplement this, the possibility existed
that a still greater investment in air transport would be found necessary to fulfill the government's ambitions; yet no funds were allocated for this in the procurement planned until 1969.

The *Air Defense Command* retained under the new organization
its responsibility for what formerly had been the *pièce de résistance*
of Canada's military effort, the contribution to North American defense. Yet, the role itself dwindled in importance in the early 1960's.
The prospects for active air defense, where the greatest contribution
had previously been made, were seen to depend upon whether the
U.S. decided to deploy in the future an anti-ICBM system. A decision
to do so would involve Canada intimately; indeed, it was already
involved in research into certain aspects of the problems of defense
against missiles. As long as no such decision was taken, however,
a "downward trend in continental air defence forces" was foreseen.[33]
Accordingly, no major expenditures were planned for the acquisition
of new equipment for this purpose; and existing equipment was
gradually phased out as it ended its operational life. As the number
of Voodoos in active service diminished, they were consolidated into
three squadrons from the previous five.[34] Various of the less essential
radar stations, and the entire Mid-Canada line were closed down.[35]
There was an appreciation, however, of the need to maintain some
active anti-bomber defenses, since failure to do so (to give the
bombers a "free ride," as it was called), would go far to reverse
the relative advantages of bombers and missiles in an attacker's
force.[36] The judgment was therefore reached to continue to operate
the two squadrons of Bomarcs. Mr. Hellyer put aside his former
opposition to the weapon, and concurred in the view of Secretary
McNamara that, while the weapon had not been worth the funds
invested in it, once these had been spent it was worth the modest

32. *New York Times*, December 23, 1964, p. 10.
33. White Paper, p. 14.   34. *Montreal Daily Star*, January 11, 1964.
35. *Times* (London), March 11, 1964; and April 5, 1965.
36. See Sutherland, "Canada's Long Term Strategic Situation"; and Klaus
Knorr, "Canada and Western Defence," *International Journal* XVIII (Winter,
1962–63), pp. 1ff.

expenditures required to keep it operational.[37] There was no early decision about the acquisition of aircraft to succeed the "Voodoo" in an air defense role, although the continuing need for an aircraft to perform the identification function suggested that by the time of the Voodoo's obsolescence, a replacement would be found. There was some apprehension in Canada that the extension of the NORAD agreement, which would come up for renewal in 1968, would be required more by Canada than by the U.S., which might find it dispensable.[38] This fear of a weakening American commitment to the joint command was reinforced by the announcement that new anti-satellite missile systems of the U.S. would be under national, not NORAD, control.[39] But the recent completion of an underground headquarters for NORAD at Colorado Springs, at great cost, as well as the strengthening of SAGE by the introduction of a system for "Back-Up Interceptor Control" (BUIC) suggested that it was highly unlikely that the United States would suddenly renounce NORAD.[40]

Under the new organization responsibility for antisubmarine warfare operations was vested in the *Maritime Command*, composed of the RCN and those elements of the RCAF that engaged in ASW. This command was also to provide sealift capacity as needed by Mobile Command. The ASW role appeared for a time to hold great expectations, the basis for which was the advances in research and operational effectiveness allegedly being made by the Defense Research Board and the RCN. These were claimed to be significant both in absolute terms—that is, in affecting the balance between submarine and antisubmarine forces—and relative to the achievements of other nations in the field, including the U.S. According to Mr. Hellyer:

> we are now in a period where our ability to detect and potentially cope with attacking submarines is improving remarkably. There have been dramatic improvements in the last few months and this trend will likely continue for some months or years to come, to the point where the imbalance between the submarine and the ability to detect it and potentially deal with it will be considerably different than it has been in the past.[41]

37. Sauvé Committee Proceedings, July 2, 1963, p. 44.
38. Foulkes, "Complications of Continental Defence," p. 132; and article by George Bain in *Globe and Mail* (Toronto), May 27, 1965.
39. *Winnipeg Free Press*, May 25, 1965.
40. *Debates*, February 17, 1966, p. 1419.
41. Interview with Paul Hellyer, text in *Windsor Star*, May 29, 1964.

Based upon this judgment, increasing expenditures were made upon equipment for an antisubmarine force: destroyer escorts; maritime aircraft, both fixed-wing and helicopters; conventional submarines. The idea of constructing two or three nuclear-powered submarines was entertained, but rejected; development of an ocean-going hydro-foil was undertaken. Studies were begun to determine which combination of these weapons would provide the most effective antisubmarine force. In the meantime, as much effort was concerned to improve techniques through research and development as to build an effective operational force. This was suggested not only by the continued failure to acquire nuclear weapons for the Navy, but also by the questionable relevance of the kind of antisubmarine activities which the fleet was prepared to carry out. The White Paper itself noted that "the relevancy of developing a capability against missile-launching submarines will be determined largely by the deployment or non-deployment of anti-ballistic missile systems."[42] Some critics, if not the chiefs of staff, questioned whether the alternative role of defending the "North Atlantic sea communications against submarine attack"[43] was a sufficiently likely requirement to justify such large expenditures. It was not difficult for the government to justify the continuing expenditure of small amounts of money in order to keep abreast of research and development in ASW and to participate in the modest operational force, without which submarine attacks might seem more tempting to the Soviets. This was the naval version of the "free ride" argument used to justify anti-bomber air defenses, even in the missile age. But there were legitimate grounds for closely watching the costs of the ASW program in order to ensure that the service's desire to utilize the "large capital investment in this capacity"[44] (ASW) should not lead it to advocate expenditures that were not militarily justified. The alternative role most commonly suggested for the Navy continued to be the provision of additional sealift capacity for transporting and supplying intervention forces for peacekeeping duties;[45] but the government was explicit in giving higher priority to the antisubmarine effort.[46] Perhaps the difficulty and frustration involved in the search for a satisfactory role for Canada's naval forces were responsible for the fact that the only significant opposition to the government's plans for integration occurred in the Navy. Both the

42. White Paper, p. 23.   43. *Ibid.*, p. 14.   44. *Ibid.*, p. 23.
45. Sauvé Committee *Proceedings*, November 22, 1963, p. 757.
46. *Ibid.*, October 8, 1963, p. 321.

commander and deputy commander of the Maritime Command—Rear-Admiral William Landymore and Rear-Admiral M. G. Stirling, respectively—left office in July, 1966, to protest what they regarded as excesses in the movement towards a unified national defense force.[47]

Canada's two units based in Europe, the brigade group and air division, remained outside the six commands to report directly to the Chief of the Defense Staff.[48] Both were confirmed in their existing roles by the White Paper. The decision to leave the brigade group in its position on the central front appeared to give the lie to the announced intention to associate it in the future more closely with the air division. Independent students of Canadian defense policy suggested that it might profitably be pulled out of its forward position into reserve with a view eventually to forming with the air division a mobile force for the protection of NATO's northern and southern flanks. There were varying conceptions of the mode of operation of such a force, but for the most part they envisaged that it would be based, at least initially, in Europe.[49] There can be little doubt that the primary reason for the government's choice was political, although it was partly justified in military terms; "its presence . . . has a political significance for the Alliance, and its withdrawal from front-line positions at this time could be misinterpreted—by both our European allies and the Soviet bloc."[50] Moreover, as if to render credible the announced intention to leave the brigade in its present role, it was given additional new equipment. Not only were the Honest Johns armed and armored personnel carriers ordered, but additional tanks, anti-tank missiles and heavier artillery were provided. The disparity between utterance and action on this point was similar to the paradox on nuclear policy—that a government attempting to diminish the importance of nuclear weapons in Canada's defense posture should acquire nuclear weapons for four carriers. Both were readily explicable as relating to two different time periods: the short term, in which no basic policy changes could be made, and the more distant period in which preferred roles could be negotiated. Indeed, the placing of the two units outside the six new commands was expressly described as a transitional

47. *Globe and Mail* (Toronto), July 22, 1966.
48. *Training Command* and *Materiel Command* complete the list of six.
49. See Sauvé Committee *Proceedings*, October 17, 1963, p. 439; and October 22, 1963, p. 507.
50. White Paper, p. 21.

measure, suggesting that the units' roles were also transitional. Yet at least in the case of the brigade group, the possibility existed that the short term might turn out to be, as it had in the past, longer than expected.

As for the air division, that its strike role should be of limited duration was ensured by the government's decision not to replace its aircraft as they dropped out of service. This trend was strengthened by General de Gaulle's resolve to evict foreign bases from French soil, a policy which led to a Canadian decision to move the air division's headquarters from Metz and to remove from France the two squadrons of CF–104's stationed at Marville and Grostenquin. The six squadrons based in Germany continued in the strike-reconnaissance role, although the government equipped them with a conventional as well as nuclear capability, in line with its policy of reduced emphasis on nuclear weapons.[51]

NUCLEAR ISSUES AND NATO DIPLOMACY

Out of this congeries of actual and preferred roles and procurement decisions, the faintly perceptible outlines of a more general pattern may be discerned. There are two elements in this pattern: first, a diminishing willingness to shape Canada's military forces according to the strategic requirement of its alliances and even a shift from alliances towards the U.N. as the preferred collective agency for Canadian action; and secondly, a corollary substitution of minor for major war as the main type of conflict for which those forces were to be prepared. This should not be taken to mean either that a major part of Canada's forces would not continue to be assigned to or earmarked for alliance use, or that Canadian participation in peacekeeping was expected to be more frequent and/or more extensive in the future than in the past. The equipment possessed by Canadian forces in 1964 at the time of the White Paper's publication would alone suffice to insure their commitment for several years to the performance of roles primarily designed to deter major war. And as the accompanying chart shows, priority attached in the past to alliance contributions had not prevented Canadian participation in peacekeeping operations to a significant degree; therefore, the intention to emphasize such participation in the future did not necessarily mean a diminution in the importance attached to the alliances.

51. *Ibid.,* p. 22.

CANADIAN MILITARY PARTICI
TRUCE-SUPERVISING ACTIVI

Operation	Service Involved
United Nations Military Observer Group in India and Pakistan (UNMOGIP)	Army RCAF
United Nations Truce Supervisory Organization (UNTSO)	Army Navy
United Nations Command, Korea	Army
International Supervisory Commissions in Vietnam, Laos and Cambodia (I.S.C.)	Navy Army RCAF
United Nations Emergency Force in Palestine (UNEF)	Navy Army RCAF
United Nations Observer Group in Lebanon (UNOGIL)	Army
Organization of the United Nations in the Congo (ONUC)	Army RCAF
United Nations Yemen Observer Mission (UNYOM)	Navy Army RCAF
United Nations Temoprary Executive Administration (UNTEA)	RCAF
United Nations Forces in Cyprus (UNFICYP)	Navy Army RCAF

Source: Canada, House of Commons, *Special Studies Prepared for the Special Committee of the House of Commons on Matters Relating to Defence* (Ottawa, Queen's Printer, 1965), p. 63.

The change was rather a subtle one: it marked the approach of the White Paper more than its content, and was in some cases more apparent from programs that were not undertaken than from those that were. The novel approach consists in the determination independent of alliances of the kind of roles which Canada should be performing and the *subsequent* negotiations with alliance partners. Previously, most roles, both in North American defense and in NATO had been worked out privately in collaboration with the allies before they were openly debated in Canada; the results sometimes proved

Period of Participation	Personnel Involved	Annual Approximate Cost to Canada
Jan/49 (Cont.)	9 Officers 8 all ranks	$ 89,000
Jul/49 (Cont.) Jul/50 Sept/53	18 Officers 3 Destroyers	$177,000 —
Jul/50 Sept/53	22,500 all ranks (1 Officer, 10 R remaining)	— $ 20,000
Jul/54 (Cont.) Jul/54 (Cont.) Jul/54 (Cont.)	2–3 Officers 16 all Ranks 2–4 Officers	$ 33,000 $818,000 $ 42,000
Dec/56 Feb/57	HMCS MAGNIFICENT Sealift	
Nov/56 (Cont.) Nov/56 (Cont.)	858 all Ranks 86–275 all Ranks	$3,930,000 $612,000
Jun/58 Jan/59	70 all Ranks	$ —
Aug/60 Jun/64	250 all Ranks	$1,424,000 (Subject to Reduction)
Jul/60 (Cont.)	6–19 all Ranks	$256,000
Jul/63 Jun/63 Jun/63 Sept/63	1 Petty Officer 5 Officers 56 all Ranks	— — —
Sept/62 Apr/63	13 Officers	—
Mar/64 Sept/64 (Estimated)	HMCS BONAVENTURE 1150 all Ranks 100 all Ranks	$1,500,000 (three months) (Estimated)

unsatisfactory because the roles that were most useful to allies turned out to be inappropriate for Canada. In a television interview with Mr. Hellyer, this change was spelled out:

> Mr. Troyer: In the past, Defence Ministers, governments and indeed, senior military administrators have often taken refuge in NATO commitments and NATO reviews to avoid making comments on proposed changes. We seem now to have reversed this operation and to have decided that we will announce the changes we are going to make and negotiate with NATO later. Does this imply greater independence from NATO on Canada's part?

Mr. Hellyer: In a sense it probably does. I think that it's an advance indication of the roles that we intend to negotiate for future time periods.

Mr. Troyer: This is the first time we've made public our vowed [sic] intentions to change our role.

Mr. Hellyer: Yes, I believe this is so.[52]

This new approach was rather significant for the balance between forces for alliance or U.N. contributions. In the past, the precedence of the former had meant that peacekeeping operations had to be undertaken by forces the shape of which was determined primarily by alliance commitments. Now, however, those commitments were to be made only after the development of a coherent policy in which such factors as the requirements for peacekeeping forces would be taken into account; the precedence was largely reversed. This fact is somewhat obscured by the statement of priorities found in the White Paper, which gives a higher importance to "forces-in-being as part of the deterrent in the European theatre" than to "forces-in-being for UN peacekeeping operations"; for higher in priority than either are "forces for the direct protection of Canada which can be deployed as required," from which peacekeeping contingents would be drawn in fact.[53] This reversal meant that the needs of peacekeeping forces would now receive more sympathetic consideration in the planning of defense policy. The importance of this change should not be exaggerated. Previous experience had shown that requirements for peacekeeping forces varied so widely that little advance planning more specific than the maintenance of well-balanced, versatile forces could be done effectively. A specific battalion designated by Canada for such activity, for example, had never been called upon, while more specialized requests of an unpredictable character had been received several times.[54] Nevertheless, some recognizable deficiencies, such as the shortage of transport, could be remedied by such a change in priorities.

Moreover, the change is important as an indication of a changed assessment of the utility of alliances. Prior to 1957, at least, it had been assumed tacitly that influence within an alliance could best be maximized through making military contributions designed to fill important needs of the alliance as a whole; the resultant roles

52. Transcript of "Inquiry," March 30, 1964, pp. 8–9.
53. White Paper, p. 24.
54. Sauvé Committee *Proceedings*, July 25, 1963, pp. 238–39.

were often similar in character to those of Great Powers, although the scale was of course much reduced. But there was growing recognition that the relative smallness of Canadian contributions made them less than indispensable, and that Canadian influence was correspondingly low.[55] The appeal of the peacekeeping role was that smallness—provided it was not taken to the point of military ineffectiveness—was an advantage. The very point of such operations is that frequently the intervention of Great Powers in the underdeveloped world is politically unacceptable. Therefore, the general utility to the West of these actions by such countries as Canada might be expected to entitle them to an influence not in danger of infringement by the Great Powers, in the same way as is that influence which stems from direct alliance contributions.

None of the undertakings or preferences announced in the White Paper revealed more about the changed Canadian view of alliances than did the failure to participate actively in the diplomatic effort to resolve the most serious problem confronting NATO in the early 1960's—that of nuclear control. This was particularly evident, for example, in Canada's virtual abstention from the debate about the U.S. proposal for the establishment of a multilateral nuclear force. This project, if consummated, would have fulfilled almost every item on the traditional Canadian check-list of desirable characteristics for alliance undertakings: it would tie the U.S. and Europe more closely together; it could be viewed at least as a hindrance to nuclear proliferation, especially to Germany; it would increase collective participation in U.S. strategic policy; and it would offer the smaller countries if not an equal, presumably, a meaningful role in the formulation of important policies and decisions at a cost that they could afford. Yet, under neither the Diefenbaker nor Pearson governments was there any official expression of interest in the proposal. In the case of the former, the obsession of both opposition and government was with the question of nuclear warheads for weapons already acquired. Therefore, it was not to be expected that serious consideration would be given at that time to Canadian participation in such a project. In fact, there was little public mention of the subject in Canada during these years, except

55. In the estimation of Leonard Beaton, who was one of the independent witnesses interviewed by the committee, Canada's influence in NATO was not great: "I don't think Canada has got a say in NATO in Europe to any significant extent which derives from her contribution. I think Canada is making a contribution which is very small and very efficient but I don't think that, politically, Canada can say much. . . ." *Ibid.*, November 22, 1963, p. 759.

for the brief period between the Nassau Conference in December, 1962, and the fall of Diefenbaker's government. During this time, the Prime Minister maintained that the impending decision about the MLF rendered unnecessary any Canadian decision about other nuclear weapons. Somewhat more surprising was the almost total absence of debate on the question after the Pearson government entered office. By virtue of the previous utterances of its members that government might have been expected to approve the MLF wholeheartedly. Not only did it fail to urge Canadian participation; it also failed to bring the question to public attention as an issue worth serious consideration; neither did it give the appearance of attempting to influence, through diplomatic channels, the outcome of the proposal. There was little public effort to elicit from the government information on the issue.[56] When they were asked, ministers were reluctant to address themselves to the issue, as indeed they were to the whole complex of strategic-political differences existing within the alliance in 1963–64.[57] On the occasion of the visit of President Kennedy's envoy, Livingston Merchant, to Ottawa to explain the proposal, the statement of government policy was ambiguous and hesitant:

> While we will give this proposal consideration . . . I do not think that it will be likely that we would wish to add to our existing responsibilities and commitments by participating in this kind of multilateral nuclear force. But this is a matter which will be given the consideration it deserves.[58]

As late as April, 1964, this statement was referred to as the government's standing policy on the subject.[59] By the fall of 1964, the Canadian view had been made explicit that a multinational approach was preferable to the MLF as a solution to NATO's strategic and political problems.[60] However, even after a concrete proposal embodying such an approach had been made, in the form of the British proposal for an Atlantic Nuclear Force, Canada played no significant role in the diplomatic effort to find a satisfactory compromise. Later, in the fall of 1965, it joined the deliberations of the Special Commit-

56. The Chief of the Naval Staff, for example, was not asked about the MLF when he appeared before the committee. *Ibid.*, July 4, 1963, pp. 59–83. Only in the fall of 1964 did a debate, and then a muted one, begin to appear. See Peyton Lyon in *Maclean's Magazine*, November 2, 1964.

57. See Sauvé Committee *Proceedings*, July 25, 1963, pp. 242–44; and November 5, 1963, p. 682.

58. *Debates* (1963), I, 790.   59. *Ibid.* (1964), II, 1706.

60. *Globe and Mail* (Toronto), September 16, 1964.

tee of Defense Ministers—the so-called McNamara Committee—to discuss ways of improving joint planning and consultation on questions involving nuclear weapons. But whether through Canadian choice or not, its participation in the working groups established by that committee was limited to those dealing with exchange of information and intelligence, and with channels of communication among governments during crisis situations. It did not participate in the group which dealt with the more central question of collective planning in peacetime of the use of nuclear weapons in case of war.[61] Finally, there was little debate in Canada about the political and military advantages and disadvantages of constructing some kind of North American anti-ballistic missile system, a decision which was recognized to be very consequential for Canadian defense policy. Obviously, the decision to construct or refrain from constructing such a system would be primarily American. Yet, considering Canada's stake in the decision, and considering the strong, if not entirely persuasive, arguments that existed for concluding an international agreement not to construct such systems, as well as the catalytic role that Canada could conceivably play in securing such an agreement, it is somewhat surprising that there was no public indication of any Canadian effort to influence the outcome of the issue.

One of the reasons for this relative silence on questions of central importance for the future character of Canada's alliances stands out above all others: the desire, indeed the political necessity, to avoid reviving the recently-ended trauma about the acquisition of nuclear weapons. This requirement was apparently held by the Pearson government to enjoin it not only from taking positions which might entail the acquisition of additional nuclear weapons, but also from participating actively in diplomatic initiatives concerned with nuclear issues.

Far from aspiring to affect the outcome of these significant alliance questions, Canadian diplomacy in NATO during 1965 and early 1966 appeared to have the much more modest, if more realistic and understandable, goal of serving Canadian domestic policy. No doubt the effort of Canada's representatives at the NATO ministerial meetings of December, 1965, and June, 1966, to mediate between France, on the one hand, and the U.S. and U.K., on the other, was motivated in part by concern over avoiding a split in the alliance, even over the basic issues dividing it. Yet the Canadian gov-

61. *New York Times*, November 28, 1965, p. 1.

ernment showed no willingness to change its position on these issues, in order to achieve a more neutral status, to enhance its effectiveness as a mediator; on the basic points at stake, it remained, as it had for years, solidly opposed to De Gaulle. As late as February, 1966, Prime Minister Pearson insisted that NATO's international command was necessary, and that Canadian forces would only participate in the defense of Europe under such a command.[62] Canada showed so little sympathy for France's nuclear ambitions that it was refraining from a profitable sale of uranium ore because of the latter's unwillingness to submit to international inspection and the confirmation that the ore would be used for peaceful purposes.[63] In view of these substantive differences, it seems reasonable to consider that Canada's conciliatory gestures towards France were really conciliatory gestures towards Québec, and served primarily a domestic political purpose. The purpose is legitimate and important, but it is difficult to see how it was served by Canada's military contributions to NATO, which even appeared to conflict with it.

62. *Montreal Daily Star*, February 23, 1966.
63. *New York Times*, February 14, 1966, p. 1.

CHAPTER IX

Summary and Conclusions

THE makers of Canada's defense policy in recent years have faced a problem which, although for the most part they have probably not perceived it, goes far to explain the specific difficulties that they have encountered. This problem—certainly a happy one as problems of international politics go—is that their degree of national security has had relatively little to do with Canadian defense policy. Security has been primarily a function of the strategic balance between the U.S. and the Soviet Union, and of the geographical nexus tying Canada to the American side of that balance. Defense policy, for Canada, has been primarily a means of influencing the Western end of that stalemate, particularly at its American core; it has been a way of helping to shape the terms of the military collaboration which geography ensures will exist in some form between the U.S. and Canada. Canada is perhaps unique in the degree to which its defense policy serves nonsecurity objectives; but in varying and less marked measure, the same problem characterizes the policy of other smaller allies of the United States. It is this fact which gives to the Canadian experience a somewhat more general signifi-cance than it would otherwise have. What makes a serious problem of this situation is the extreme difficulty of determining the character and size of the defense force needed to attain the non-security goals, and the inherent difficulty of evaluating its performance.[1]

A country such as Canada, that is attempting by means of mili-tary contributions to an alliance to gain some voice in the operation of the strategic-political balance affecting its security, may adopt any or all of three strategies for doing so. To the extent that the objective to be promoted is merely the continued existence of the alliance or the growth of multilateralism, it may be furthered by undertaking and faithfully fulfilling military commitments, on how-ever reduced a scale, within the multilateral framework. As the Sauvé Committee noted in its report, "by respecting its commitments to NATO, Canada influences the other members of the Alliance

1. Cf. James Eayrs, "Military Policy and Middle-Power: The Canadian Experi-ence," p. 70.

to respect theirs. One should not minimize the mutual influences which are exerted in any alliance."[2] If the objective is more ambitious and includes the ability to exert a general influence upon the structure and the military and political policies of the alliance, then the contribution must be militarily significant. Its significance may stem from either quantitative or qualitative factors; it must either constitute a relatively great portion of the alliance's power, or, if it is not large, it must possess some distinctive characteristics which render it useful to the other alliance members.

From about 1949 to 1957, Canada's defense policy turned all three of these approaches to its national advantage. Its "alliance-mindedness" in making and carrying out military commitments helped in the establishment and successful operation of the multilateral framework whose existence was deemed useful to Canadian interests. Moreover, in terms of both size and distinctiveness, its military contribution was favored by factors which gave it a relatively great influence within the alliance. One of these factors was Western Europe's weakened condition, as the result of which Canada's rather modest military contribution in absolute terms, represented a sizable portion of allied strength. The second was the strategic importance of Canadian territory at a time when long-range bombing between the U.S. and the Soviet Union first was becoming practicable—by the Canadian route. Both factors were, of course, temporary. The first was rapidly diminishing in value in the late 1950's; and the second became markedly less important after intercontinental missiles became an operational possibility in 1957.

The result of these changes was an unhappy conflict between Canada's old aspiration (which for a brief time had been successfully realized) to exercise within the alliance a general influence going beyond specific Canadian interests, and the new reality of the rising cost of such influence. The initial Canadian response, which was far from deliberate, was to pay the increasing cost in order to retain the influential position. This cost was measured not only in financial terms, but in terms of the readiness to perform roles requiring the most advanced weapons. Such a policy could only be successfully pursued as long as its underlying assumption was valid: that the kind of military tasks which it entailed could be performed by Canada at a cost that was both politically and economically acceptable. This assumption ceased to be true after 1957, not only because of Europe's resurgence and the waning importance of Canadian territory, but

2. Sauvé Committee *Proceedings, Report,* p. 802.

also because of the increasing sophistication of the advanced weapons which such a role entailed. Their production was rendered uneconomic for any but the largest countries; while to use the weapons and *not* produce them in Canada proved unacceptable for political reasons.

The government of John Diefenbaker entered office in 1957, in the midst of this changing situation. This coincidence may have been fortuitous. Or, the change in political atmosphere that led to the Conservative victory may have been caused at least partly by the same international factors—Canada's diminishing influence and the frustrations associated with that—which produced the dilemma in defense policy.[3] In any case, the presence in office at this time of a government which started as inexperienced and proved to be inept made a situation that was already difficult more painful and prolonged than it need to have been. Ironically, the mishandling of defense issues was permitted by the same factor which helped create the initial problem: it was only because Canada's military forces were so marginal to its security that a Canadian government could permit itself the luxury of emasculating those forces for primarily political reasons. To be sure, Canadian diplomatic effectiveness suffered more than Canadian security. But since the former goal was less crucial and less tangible than the latter, its neglect was somewhat more understandable.

The first defense issue to become controversial during the Diefenbaker years was the decision to form an international North American Air Defense Command. Since it became controversial less because of substantive differences than because of the way the government mishandled its presentation to Parliament, it is significant only as an illustration of the scarcely concealed sensitivity underlying Canadian-American military collaboration, and for the way in which political feelings that it aroused affected other issues.

The next issue was the proposed acquisition by Canadian air defense forces of a modern interceptor and of Bomarc missiles. The involved series of events which led to the scrapping of the Canadian-developed CF–105, and to the substitution of an American aircraft and the American-produced Bomarc, left a widespread impression among Canadians that they had been victimized by the political power of the U.S. aircraft industry, operating by way of the Ameri-

3. See the testimony of the current U.S. Ambassador to Canada, Livingston Merchant. U.S., Congress, Senate, Committee on Foreign Relations, *Review of Foreign Policy, 1958,* May 16, 1958.

can government. However understandable the temptation may be
to locate the blame in this quarter, a look at the facts shows that
it was unjustified in this particular case. What victimized Canada
was rather its old nemesis: the disparity in size and power between
it and the U.S. The effect, in this case, was to make it exceedingly
difficult for Canadian industry to compete in terms of cost and delivery dates with its counterpart south of the border for items above
a given level of sophistication, a level which experience showed
the Arrow to exceed. As for the other means of air defense, the decision to put Bomarcs in Canada was initiated by the Canadian government, which had no choice therefore but to live with the precarious
course of the missile's development in the U.S. Far from scrapping it
without regard to Canada's order, the Americans continued its development very largely because of that order. Finally, Canada acquired
an American interceptor rather than the Arrow, not because it was
victimized by changing U.S. intelligence estimates, but because the
former aircraft was available sooner and on terms that were more
economically advantageous. The U.S. administration may be blamed
only if one feels that it had an obligation to see Canada's Arrow project through to completion regardless of cost and its own military
needs; or, if one thinks the U.S. should have been quicker than its
allies to foresee the defense production problem, and therefore should
have taken the initiative in 1955 to establish a program for development and production sharing. While such action would have been
farsighted indeed and perhaps beneficial in the long run to the U.S. as
well as to the allies in question, it would have been expecting a great
deal of magnanimity by the standards of the day.

The Diefenbaker government was still on the rebound from the
Arrow experience when it undertook, for the Canadian air division
in Europe, the new role of strike-reconnaissance. This has never
proved satisfactory politically. In retrospect, it appears that the government woke up in 1959 and 1960 with some surprise and displeasure to the fact that it had committed itself to a variety of
nuclear roles, including that of the air division. It neither renounced
the commitments nor acquired the weapons needed to make them
effective—it reacted by delaying. The reasons for this delay still
are not entirely clear, but several factors seem to have contributed
to it. The question was politically sensitive, and this would have
made the government wary of it in any case. Its wariness was increased perhaps by the memory of the previous controversies of
defense policy—NORAD and Arrow. Diefenbaker's personal relationship with Kennedy seems to have reinforced his suspicion that

the Americans would, if they were permitted, "push the Canadians around," and his determination to resist this; in 1962, various personal experiences confirmed him in this state of mind. Finally, there are the negative, or permissive, reasons that Canadian security was not seriously endangered by such indecision, and that the equivocal positions of Canada's opposition parties similarly reduced the pressures for a decision.

The Cuban missile crisis was the catalyst which finally led to a resolution of this problem caused by nuclear indecision. The crisis also represents in miniature a basic problem of Canada's defense policy: the political frustration of having to accept and help to execute decisions taken in Washington which it is hardly able to influence, but which vitally affect its security. As in the case of the defense production problem, it is difficult to see how this difficulty can be alleviated by the United States; it seems to be an inherent feature of the disparity in power between the U.S. and its allies. This problem, which of course is applicable also to other allies of the U.S., does not excuse Canada's lack of co-operation—which could have been more serious than it was—during the crisis; but it does make it somewhat more understandable.

Although the Diefenbaker government did not resolve the specific defense problems that contributed to its downfall, it did initiate one program which provided the basis for a more stable, long-term defense policy once those problems were solved. This was the Defense Development and Production Sharing program, which went a long way toward creating an integrated North American market in defense production, and which promised to give subsequent Canadian governments more freedom to choose equipment that was economical, effective and appropriate for Canadian forces. The program's continuation by the Pearson government was basic to its revised defense policy.

That government, which first set about restoring Canada's diplomatic effectiveness by honoring the nuclear commitments undertaken in the preceding years, took other measures to adapt its policy to the changed conditions which had caused such difficulties for its predecessor. In the White Paper which outlined Canada's defense plans for the 1960's, it announced the intention to make Canadian forces more well-balanced, flexible, integrated, mobile, and conventional in the future than in the past. Implicit in the new policy was a decision to give up any effort to attain influence within its alliances by making contributions of a kind or a scale comparable to that of Great Powers. There was instead an implied emphasis upon the benefits which could be derived from certain distinctive aspects of Canadian forces. The experiment with a united defense organization was one such distinctive aspect; Canada's qualifications for performing peacekeeping tasks in the interests of other members of the alliance was another. The reduced ambition implied in this change marks a realistic and appropriate response to changed conditions. But it would be unfortunate if, in its studied avoidance of contributions entailing the use of advanced weapons, the government overreacted and abstained from all diplomatic activity concerning the role of advanced weapons in its alliances. One thinks, especially, of proposals for nuclear sharing and for an antiballistic missile system, in both of which Canada is qualified to play a distinctive role.

In two respects, the Canadian experience described here is relevant to other countries, and especially to the European allies of the United States. First, and more specifically, Canada's successes and failures in attempting to relate its armament industry to its alliance policy are instructive case studies in a problem which faces all industrialized countries except the largest ones. The United Kingdom, in particular, would have done well to heed the Canadian experiences of 1958–60 with the Arrow aircraft and Bomarc missile; it later repeated them with Blue Streak, Skybolt, and the TSR–2. Canada's experience with the Development and Production Sharing program may similarly be regarded as a case study in the possibilities and limits of solving the defense production problem by gaining access to the U.S. procurement market. While the unwritten requirement of that program that the most advanced weapons will continue to be produced in the U.S. will make it unacceptable to Europeans as a complete solution to their problem, it may be regarded nonetheless as a partial answer, again as is suggested by the recent efforts of the U.K. to increase its military sales to the U.S. Second, and more generally, Canada's primary need has been to work out a basis for collaborating constructively with the United States for mutual defense in a satisfying way, and with a stability that changing political, strategic and technological factors do not easily destroy. The identical need of NATO's European members ensures that Canada's experience is relevant for them. The many unique factors of Canadian-American relations limit the relevance, to be sure. But as technological developments shrink distances and diminish the importance of geography, at least from a strategic point of view, Canada's problems become less and less unique.

APPENDIX

APPENDIX I

NORAD AGREEMENT

Department Announcement

On May 12, 1958, Canada and the United States concluded an exchange of notes regarding the principles to govern the future organization and operations of the North American Air Defense Command (NORAD). The notes were signed by Acting Secretary Herter for the United States and Ambassador N. A. Robertson for Canada. The Canadian note sets forth the principles to be adopted under this agreement. The United States reply expresses concurrence with the principles and agrees that the exchange of notes shall constitute an agreement between the two governments.

Announcement of the establishment of an integrated Canada–United States Air Defense Command was made August 1, 1957. Since that time NORAD has been operating on an interim basis, with headquarters at Colorado Springs, pending the conclusion of the formal governmental agreement between the two countries. Gen. Earl E. Partridge, USAF, and Air Marshal C. Roy Slemon, RCAF, who have been serving as commander in chief and deputy commander of NORAD respectively, will continue in their present capacities.

Text of Canadian Note[1]

Washington, D.C.
12th May, 1958

No. 263

Sir, I have the honour to refer to discussions which have taken place between the Canadian and the United States authorities concerning the necessity for integration of operational control of Canadian and United States air defences and, in particular, to the study and recommendations of the Canada-United States Military Study Group. These studies led to the joint announcement on August 1, 1957, by the Minister of National Defence of Canada and the Secretary of Defense of the United States indicating that our two Governments had agreed to the setting up of a system of integrated operational control for the air defences in the continental United States, Canada and Alaska under an integrated command responsible to the Chiefs of Staff of both countries. Pursuant to the announcement of August 1, 1957, an integrated headquarters known as the North American Air Defence Command (NORAD) has been established on an interim basis at Colorado Springs, Colorado.

For some years prior to the establishment of NORAD, it had been recognized that the air defence of Canada and the United States must be considered as a single problem. However, arrangements which existed

1. Source: *U.S. Department of State Bulletin*, XXXVIII (June 9, 1958), 979–80.

between Canada and the United States provided only for the coordination of separate Canadian and United States air defence plans, but did not provide for the authoritative control of all air defence weapons which must be employed against an attacker.

The advent of nuclear weapons, the great improvements in the means of effecting their delivery, and the requirements of the air defence control systems demand rapid decisions to keep pace with the speed and tempo of technological developments. To counter the threat and to achieve maximum effectiveness of the air defence system, defensive operations must commence as early as possible and enemy forces must be kept constantly engaged. Arrangements for the coordination of national plans requiring consultation between national commanders before implementation had become inadequate in the face of the possible sudden attack, with little or no warning. It was essential, therefore, to have in existence in peacetime an organization, including the weapons, facilities and command structure, which could operate at the outset of hostilities in accordance with a single air defence plan approved in advance by national authorities.

Studies made by representatives of our two Governments led to the conclusion that the problem of the air defence of our two countries could best be met by delegating to an integrated headquarters the task of exercising operational control over combat units of the national forces made available for the air defence of the two countries. Furthermore, the principle of an integrated headquarters exercising operational control over assigned forces has been well established in various parts of the North Atlantic Treaty Area. The Canada-United States region is an integral part of the NATO area. In support of the strategic objectives established in NATO for the Canada-United States region and in accordance with the provisions of the North Atlantic Treaty, our two Governments have, by establishing the North American Air Defence Command (NORAD), recognized the desirability of integrating headquarters exercising operational control over assigned air defence forces. The agreed integration is intended to assist the two Governments to develop and maintain their individual and collective capacity to resist air attack on their territories in North America in mutual self-defence.

The two Governments consider that the establishment of integrated air defence arrangements of the nature described increases the importance of the fullest possible consultation between the two Governments on all matters affecting the joint defence of North America, and that defence cooperation between them can be worked out on a mutually satisfactory basis only if such consultation is regularly and consistently undertaken.

In view of the foregoing considerations and on the basis of the experience gained in the operation on an interim basis of the North American Air Defence Command, my Government proposes that the following principles should govern the future organization and operations of the North American Air Defence Command.

1. The Commander-in-Chief NORAD (CINCNORAD) will be responsible to the Chiefs of Staff Committee of Canada and the Joint Chiefs

of Staff of the United States, who in turn are responsible to their respective Governments. He will operate within a concept of air defence approved by the appropriate authorities of our two Governments, who will bear in mind their objectives in the defence of the Canada-United States region of the NATO area.

2. The North American Air Defence Command will include such combat units and individuals as are specifically allocated to it by the two Governments. The jurisdiction of the Commander-in-Chief, NORAD, over those units and individuals is limited to operational control as hereinafter defined.

3. "Operational control" is the power to direct, coordinate, and control the operational activities of forces assigned, attached or otherwise made available. No permanent changes of station would be made without approval of the higher national authority concerned. Temporary reinforcement from one area to another, including the crossing of the international boundary, to meet operational requirements will be within the authority of commanders having operational control. The basic command organization for the air defence forces of the two countries, including administration, discipline, internal organization and unit training, shall be exercised by national commanders responsible to their national authorities.

4. The appointment of CINCNORAD and his Deputy must be approved by the Canadian and United States Governments. They will not be from the same country, and CINCNORAD staff shall be an integrated joint staff composed of officers of both countries. During the absence of CINCNORAD, command will pass to the Deputy Commander.

5. The North Atlantic Treaty Organization will continue to be kept informed through the Canada-United States Regional Planning Group of arrangements for the air defence of North America.

6. The plans and procedures to be followed by NORAD in wartime shall be formulated and approved in peacetime by appropriate national authorities and shall be capable of rapid implementation in an emergency. Any plans or procedures recommended by NORAD which bear on the responsibility of civilian departments or agencies of the two Governments shall be referred for decision by the appropriate military authorities to those agencies and departments and may be the subject of intergovernmental coordination.

7. Terms of reference for CINCNORAD and his Deputy will be consistent with the foregoing principles. Changes in these terms of reference may be made by agreement between the Canadian Chiefs of Staff Committee and the United State Joint Chiefs of Staff, with approval of higher authority as appropriate, provided that these changes are in consonance with the principles set out in this note.

8. The question of the financing of expenditures connected with the operation of the integrated headquarters of the North American Air

Defence Command will be settled by mutual agreement between appropriate agencies of the two Governments.

9. The North American Air Defence Command shall be maintained in operation for a period of ten years or such shorter period as shall be agreed by both countries in the light of their mutual defence interests, and their objectives under the terms of the North Atlantic Treaty. The terms of this agreement may be reviewed upon request of either country at any time.

10. The Agreement between parties to the North Atlantic Treaty regarding the status of their forces signed in London on June 19, 1951, shall apply.

11. The release to the public of information by CINCNORAD on matters of interest to Canada and the United States will in all cases be the subject of prior consultation and agreement between appropriate agencies of the two Governments.

If the United States Government concurs in the principles set out above, I propose that this note and your reply should constitute an agreement between our two Governments effective from the date of your reply.

Accept, sir, the renewed assurances of my highest consideration.

N. A. Robertson

The Honourable John Foster Dulles,
  Secretary of State of the United States,
  Washington, D.C.

Text of U.S. Note

May 12, 1958

Excellency: I have the honor to refer to your Excellency's note No. 263 of May 12, 1958 proposing on behalf of the Canadian Government certain principles to govern the future organization and operation of the North American Air Defense Command (NORAD).

I am pleased to inform you that my Government concurs in the principles set forth in your note. My Government further agrees with your proposal that your note and this reply shall constitute an agreement between the two Governments effective today.

Accept, Excellency, the renewed assurances of my highest consideration.

For the Secretary of State:
Christian A. Herter

His Excellency
  Norman Robertson,
    Ambassador of Canada.

APPENDIX II

PRIME MINISTER DIEFENBAKER'S
STATEMENT OF SEPTEMBER 23, 1958

The Prime Minister, the Right Honourable John Diefenbaker, announces today that in recent weeks the Government has fully reviewed the Canadian Air Defence programme in the light of the rapid development that has taken place during the past year in missiles for both defence and attack. In doing so it has had detailed advice from its military experts on the nature of attacks on North America that might be expected should a major war take place. A number of changes in the air defence programme have now been decided upon.

The Government has concluded that missiles should be introduced into the Canadian air defence system and that the number of supersonic interceptor aircraft required for the RCAF air defence command will be substantially less than could have been foreseen a few years ago, if in fact such aircraft will be required at all in the 1960's, in view of the rapid strides being made in missiles by both the USA and the USSR. The development of the Canadian supersonic interceptor aircraft, the CF–105 or the "Arrow" was commenced in 1953, and even under the best of circumstances it will not be available for effective use in squadrons until late in 1961. Since the project began, revolutionary changes have taken place which have made necessary a review of the programme in the light of anticipated conditions when the aircraft comes into use. The preponderance of expert opinion is that by the 1960's manned aircraft, however outstanding, will be less effective in meeting the threat than previously expected.

It has therefore been decided to introduce the Bomarc guided missile into the Canadian air defence system, to be used in defence against hostile bombers. This is a long range, anti-aircraft missile guided from the ground with the aid of the same radar system as that used in guiding interceptor aircraft. It can be used with either a conventional high explosive warhead or a nuclear warhead. Two Canadian bases for firing such missiles will be established in the general northern Ontario and Quebec areas. The use of this missile will be in accord with the approved policy of NORAD for the air defence of the North American continent. Other Bomarc bases may be located in Canada in the later development of the programme but priority is being given to the two mentioned. Most of the industrial areas in Canada considered to be potential targets of air attack will be within the defensive range of the two projected Bomarc bases or others under NORAD control and located in the northern USA.

Negotiations are under way with the USA to work out arrangements for obtaining these Bomarc missiles and the necessary equipment for maintaining, testing and launching them. Discussions will also be held on the best way for Canadian industry to share in the production programmes related to such missiles and associated equipment.

The Government has also approved the extension and strengthening

225

of the Pinetree radar control system, which was constructed, and is being operated, jointly by the USA and Canada. Several additional large radar stations will be constructed. These and the existing stations will be supplemented by a considerable number of small intervening stations.

In order that the Pinetree radar system may be able to deal more effectively with the increased speed and numbers of aircraft to be controlled and with the introduction of the Bomarc guided missiles, the Government has decided to install the "SAGE" electronic control and computing equipment in the Canadian air defence system. This will be integrated as a part of the North American SAGE system under NORAD. Discussions are being initiated with the USA authorities for the supply of the large electronic computers needed for the operation of this system and to arrange for Canadian industry to share in the production of the equipment required for the expansion of the radar network and the introduction of these semi-automatic communication and control operations.

The nine Canadian air defence squadrons already equipped with the CF–100 aircraft will continue in their present role pending their replacement with Bomarc weapons or squadrons with later types of aircraft. The whole complex of missile and aircraft defence will be worked out, as changes are made, on an integrated North American basis under NORAD operational control.

In view of the introduction of missiles into the Canadian air defence system and the reduction in the expected need for a manned, supersonic, interceptor aircraft, the Government has decided that it would not be advisable at this time to put the CF–105 into production. The Government believes, however, that to discontinue abruptly the development of this aircraft and its engine, with its consequent effects upon the industry, would not be prudent with the international outlook as uncertain and tense as it is. As a measure of insurance with present tensions as they are, therefore, the Government has decided that the development programme for the Arrow aircraft and Iroquois engine should be continued until next March, when the situation will be reviewed again in the light of all the existing circumstances at that time.

Although both the Arrow aircraft and the Iroquois engine appear now to be likely to be better than any alternatives expected to be ready by 1961, it is questionable whether in any event their margin of superiority is worth the very high cost of producing them by reason of the relatively small numbers likely to be required.

As a further consequence of the reasons given above, the Government has decided that it would be clearly unwise to proceed with the development of a special flight and fire control system for the CF–105 aircraft known as the ASTRA and of a special air-to-air missile to be used as its armament known as the SPARROW. The contracts for the development of the ASTRA fire control system and of the SPARROW missile are now being terminated. In the meantime, modifications of the CF–105 will be made during its development to permit the use of a fire control system and weapon already in production for use in USA aircraft engaged in North American defence. The important savings achieved by cancelling the ASTRA and SPARROW programmes and substituting these alternatives now in production would amount to roughly $330 million for a completed programme of 100 aircraft.

The total cost to the Canadian Government of developing the Arrow aircraft and its associated elements up to the beginning of September has been $303 million. To finish this development of the CF–105 and its components, including ASTRA and SPARROW, and to produce enough to have about 100 aircraft for squadron use would cost about another billion and a quarter dollars-approximately $12 and a half million per usable aircraft. By substituting the alternative fire control system and missile for the ASTRA and SPARROW the cost could be reduced to about $9 million each.

Commenting on these announcements, Mr. Diefenbaker said that the Government has had to make highly difficult decisions on the basis of the best judgment as to probabilities in matters of uncertainty and importance, and opinions of military and other experts. Ensuring peace by the maintenance of an effective deterrent against aggression must clearly have priority over other considerations including cost but in working out a defence programme regard must be had to the relative effectiveness and cost of various means of achieving the essential objective.

While Canada's role in the coming age of missiles is entirely a defensive one, it will clearly involve this country in considerable disruption from time to time in production as well as in changes of the role of the defence forces. The Government regrets the difficulties incident to such changes but finds them inescapable if regard is to be had to the changing needs which result from the rapid evolution in weapons.

It now seems evident that in the larger weapon systems now required for air forces, Canadian work in the design, development and production of defence equipment will have to be closely integrated with the major programmes of USA. The USA Government recognizes this and they are now prepared to work out production sharing arrangements with us. To accomplish effective integration of defence production resources of Canada and the USA will require time and continuing efforts in co-operation.

Canadians are proud of what the Canadian aircraft industry has accomplished for defence. The Arrow supersonic plane has already thrilled us with its performance, its promise and its proof of ability in design and technology. The Iroquois engine too is a fine technical achievement and its development has led to many industrial advances. Excellent scientific and technical teams had been created for these projects. However, it will be recognized, I believe, that as the age of missiles appears certain to lead to a major reduction in the need for fighter aircraft, Canada cannot expect to support a large industry developing and producing aircraft solely for diminishing Canadian defence requirements.

The Government deeply regrets the unemployment that will be involved in the termination of the ASTRA and SPARROW projects and in the AVRO plant at Malton. It is hoped that our defence industry will be able to share effectively with the USA industry in one part or another of the major programmes in the air defence of the North American continent and thereby provide alternative employment in the field of missiles and electronics.

In common with Canadians, the Government recognizes the accomplishments and technical quality of the work done, but to continue vast expenditures on aircraft and equipment which military and other expert opinion does not support as the best way to achieve the defence essential to our security would not only be wasteful but unjustifiable.

It is regrettable that in Canada's contribution to a full and effective part in the air defence of the North American continent adaptation to changing techniques and the nature of potential threat to this continent makes necessary from time to time changes in the requirements of deterrent power.

APPENDIX III

PRIME MINISTER DIEFENBAKER'S
STATEMENT OF FEBRUARY 20, 1959[1]

Mr. Speaker, with the leave of the House I should like to make a somewhat lengthy statement on the subject of one facet of the national defence of Canada because, after all, the effectiveness or otherwise of the measures taken for national defence until international peace under law is obtained constitutes the passport either to survival or destruction. The announcement I wish to make has to do with the decision regarding our air defence which was foreshadowed in the statement made by me to the press on September 23 last.

The government has carefully examined and re-examined the probable need for the Arrow aircraft and Iroquois engine known as the CF–105, the development of which has been continued pending a final decision. It has made a thorough examination in the light of all the information available concerning the probable nature of the threats to North America in future years, the alternative means of defence against such threats, and the estimated costs thereof. The conclusion arrived at is that the development of the Arrow aircraft and Iroquois engine should be terminated now.

Formal notice of termination is being given now to the contractors. All outstanding commitments will of course be settled equitably.

In reaching this decision the government has taken fully into account the present and prospective international situation, including the strategic consequences of weapon development and the effects of the decision I have just announced upon Canada's ability to meet any emergency that may arise.

Work on the original concept of the CF–105 commenced in the air force in 1952, and the first government decision to proceed with the development and with the production of two prototypes was taken late in 1953. The plane was designed to meet the requirements of the R.C.A.F. for a successor to the CF–100 to be used in the defence of Canada. At that time it was thought some five or six hundred aircraft would be needed by the R.C.A.F., and their cost was forecast at about $1,500,000 to $2 million each.

From the beginning, however, it was recognized by the previous government, and subsequently by this government, that the development of an advanced supersonic aircraft such as the 105 and its complicated engine and weapon system was highly hazardous, and therefore all decisions to proceed with it were tentative and subject to change in the light of experience. This was known to the contractors undertaking the development, to the air force, and to parliament.

The development of the Arrow aircraft and the Iroquois engine has been a success although, for various reasons, it has been much behind the original schedule. The plane and its engine have shown promise

1. Source: Canada, House of Commons, *Debates*, (1959), II, pp. 1221–24.

of achieving the high standard of technical performance intended, and are a credit to those who conceived and designed them and translated the plans into reality.

Unfortunately these outstanding achievements have been overtaken by events. In recent months it has come to be realized that the bomber threat against which the CF–105 was intended to provide defence has diminished, and alternative means of meeting the threat have been developed much earlier than was expected.

The first modern long range bombers with which Canada might be confronted came into operation over five years ago, but the numbers produced now appear to be much lower than was previously forecast. Thus the threat against which the CF–105 could be effective has not proved to be as serious as was forecast. During 1959 and 1960 a relatively small number of modern bombers constitutes the main airborne threat. It is considered that the defence system of North America is adequate to meet this threat.

Potential aggressors now seem more likely to put their effort into missile development than into increasing their bomber force. By the middle of 1962 the threat from the intercontinental ballistic missile will undoubtedly be greatly enhanced in numbers, size and accuracy, and the I.C.B.M. threat may be supplemented by submarine-launched missiles. By the middle sixties the missile seems likely to be the major threat and the long range bomber relegated to supplementing the major attack by these missiles. It would be only in this period, namely after mid-1962, that the CF–105 could be fully operational in the Royal Canadian Air Force.

The United States government, after full and sympathetic consideration of proposals that the U.S. air force use the Arrow, reached the conclusion that it was not economical to do so. Already the U.S. air force has decided not to continue with the further development and production of U.S. aircraft having the same general performance as the Arrow. The development of interceptor aircraft that is now proceeding in the United States and abroad is on different types.

Since my announcement of last September much work has been done on the use of a different control system and weapon in the Arrow. These changes have been found to be practical. Although the range of the aircraft has been increased it is still limited. It is estimated that with these changes the total average cost per unit of 100 operational aircraft could be reduced from the figure of about $12,500,000 each to about $7,800,000 each, including weapons, spare parts and the completion of development, but not including any of the sum of $303 million spent on development prior to September last.

The government has taken no decision to acquire other aircraft to replace the CF–100, which is still an effective weapon in the defence of North America against the present bomber threat. The Minister of National Defence and the chiefs of staff are now engaged in further studies of the various alternatives for the improvement of our defences.

Canadian requirements for civilian aircraft are very small by comparison with this huge defence operation, and frankness demands that I advise that at present there is no other work that the government can assign immediately to the companies that have been working on the Arrow and its engine. This decision is a vivid example of the fact that a rapidly changing defence picture requires difficult decisions, and the government regrets its inevitable impact upon production, employment and engineering work in the aircraft and related industries.

As all in this house will appreciate, this decision has been a very difficult one for the government to take, not only because of the immediate disturbance it is bound to cause to those who have been working on the Arrow and related items but because it means terminating a project on which Canada had expended a very large amount of money and in which Canadians have demonstrated the high level of their technical work. However much I might hope that the project be continued in the sense of pride of achievement to avoid immediate dislocations which are regrettable, defence requirements constitute the sole justification for defence procurement.

Having regard to the information and advice we have received, however, there is no other feasible or justifiable course open to us. We must not abdicate our responsibility to assure that the huge sums which it is our duty to ask parliament to provide for defence are being expended in the most effective way to achieve that purpose.

Now I wish to turn to another aspect of defence. As previously announced the government has decided to introduce the Bomarc guided missile and the Sage electronic control and computing equipment into the Canadian air defence system, and to extend and strengthen the Pinetree radar control system by adding several additional large radar stations and a number of small gap filler radars. Canadians will be glad to know that agreement in principle with the United States defence department has now been reached on the sharing of the costs of this program.

Under this arrangement Canada will assume financial responsibility for approximately one-third of the cost of these new projects. The Canadian share will cover the cost of construction of bases and unit equipment, while the United States share of approximately two-thirds of the cost will cover the acquisition of technical equipment. Such division of functions is necessary for the reason that the United States is well advanced in the planning and implementation of this program and the development of the technical equipment required for it. By dividing the sharing of costs uniformity of construction will be ensured and the dangers of differences in technical equipment will be avoided.

With regard to the construction of bases in Canada, work will be carried out as a practical matter by Canadian construction companies employing Canadian labour and material. It is intended that the bases when complete will be manned by Canadian military personnel.

As for the technical equipment which is to be financed by the United States, both governments recognize the need for Canada to share in the production of this equipment. Within the principles of production sharing the United States government and the Canadian government expect that a reasonable and fair share of this work will in fact be carried out by Canadian industry. To that end a number of groups of officials representing both countries have been established to initiate the production sharing activities and to deal with the problems involved. I might add that early next week the Minister of Defence Production will make full information available to the house in this connection.

Now, sir, while time is required to work out all the necessary details between our governments, considerable progress has already been made and several contracts have been placed.

The production-sharing concept also covers the broad range of development and production of military equipment for North American defence generally. Procedures are currently being evolved between officials of the two governments whereby greater opportunities than have existed in the past will be afforded Canadian industry to participate in the production of technical equipment related to programs of mutual interest.

Under the irresistible dictates of geography the defence of North America has become a joint enterprise of both Canada and the United States. In the partnership each country has its own skills and resources to contribute, and the pooling of these resources for the most effective defence of our common interest is the essence of production sharing. Believing that parliament and the people of Canada are determined that this nation shall play its full part in terms both of quantity and quality in deterring and resisting aggression, the government intends that the Canadian forces will be well equipped and well trained for the Canadian share of these tasks in a balanced, collective defence.

In keeping with that determination careful thought is being given to the principles that in our opinion are applicable to the acquisition and control of nuclear weapons. The government's decisions of last autumn to acquire Bomarc missiles for air defence and Lacrosse missiles for the Canadian army were used on the best expert advice available on the need to strengthen Canada's air defence against the threat to this continent, and on its determination to continue an effective contribution to the NATO shield.

The full potential of these defensive weapons is achieved only when they are armed with nuclear warheads. The government is, therefore, examining with the United States government questions connected with the acquisition of nuclear warheads for Bomarc and other defensive weapons for use by the Canadian forces in Canada, and the storage of warheads in Canada. Problems connected with the arming of the Canadian brigade in Europe with short range nuclear weapons for NATO's defence tasks are also being studied.

We are confident that we shall be able to reach formal agreement with the United States on appropriate means to serve the common objective. It will of course be some time before these weapons will be available for use by Canadian forces. The government, as soon as it is in a position to do so, will inform the house, within the limits of security, of the general terms of understanding which are reached between the two governments on this subject.

I wish also at this time to give the house an indication of certain basic considerations in the government's thinking on the question of the acquisition and control of nuclear weapons. The first important consideration is the government's belief in the importance of limiting the spread of nuclear weapons at the independent disposal of national governments. My colleague the Secretary of State for External Affairs stated in the external affairs committee on July 29 last that it took but little imagination to envisage the dangers of the situation if the know-how with respect to the production of nuclear weapons were disseminated in numerous countries of the world. The prospect of further dissemination of such techniques continues to be a matter of fundamental concern to the government. As a contribution to this objective, it is the policy of the Canadian government not to undertake the production of nuclear weapons in Canada, although we believe that Canadian scientists and technicians are quite capable of producing them.

Second, we intend to leave no avenue unexplored in the search for an acceptable agreement on disarmament with the Soviet Union, even though we must reluctantly admit the need in present circumstances for nuclear weapons of a defensive character. The objective of disarmament must ever be kept in view, even though in the experience of the past it may be capable of only partial realization. For example, we believe that agreed zones of inspection in the Arctic to guide against surprise attack would be steps necessary to be taken in the context of a larger disarmament plan. Canadians will continue to support effective measures for disarmament, but in the meantime we cannot minimize the importance of providing the strongest deterrent to aggression and of protecting the deterrent power against surprise attacks.

Third, there is the consideration of Canada's commitments to support the collective security of the NATO alliance. Whether Canada's effort is made directly in continental defence—the defence of the Canada-United States region of NATO—or whether it is made on the continent of Europe, Canada's contribution will be made in concert with the efforts of our NATO partners. It is our intention to provide Canadian forces with modern and efficient weapons to enable them to fulfil their respective roles.

Believing that the spread of nuclear weapons at the independent disposal of individual nations should be limited, we consider that it is expedient that ownership and custody of the nuclear warheads should remain with the United States. The requirements of Canadian and United States legislation on atomic energy will continue to apply, and there will be no change in Canada's responsibility to regulate all flights of aircraft over Canadian territory.

Our two governments have assumed joint responsibility for the air defence of Canada and the continental United States, including Alaska, and have implemented their responsibilities through the establishment of the North American air defence command. The Canadian government exercises with the United States government joint responsibility for the joint operations of the command, including the use of defensive nuclear weapons if necessary. In the event that these defensive weapons are made available for use by NORAD, they could be used only in accordance with procedures governing NORAD's operations as approved in advance by both governments. Such weapons, therefore, would be used from Canadian territory or in Canadian air space only under conditions previously agreed to by the Canadian government. With respect to decisions as to procedures concerning custody and control of nuclear warheads for use by Canadian forces operating under the supreme allied commander in Europe and the supreme allied commander in the North Atlantic ocean, those decisions will be subject to negotiation with the appropriate NATO partners concerned and with those commanders.

I feel sure, Mr. Speaker, that hon. members will recognize the gravity of the decisions we are called upon to make in these defence matters, by reason of the almost unbelievable nature of the world in which we live. I should like to emphasize the government's desire to ensure the security of Canada by all efficient and reasonable means at our disposal and in concert with our strong and trustworthy allies.

May I say, sir, that I thank the house for giving me this opportunity of making this lengthy statement. In so far as matters such as defence are concerned, I believe that the decisions and discussions will in the future, as in the past, remain above partisan political considerations. It is in that spirit that I place this matter before the house. This is a decision that could not be arrived at without much soul-searching and one which we believe, in the light of the expectations of the future, will be considered right.

APPENDIX IV

U.S. STATE DEPARTMENT PRESS RELEASE ON U.S.
AND CANADIAN NEGOTIATIONS REGARDING
NUCLEAR WEAPONS[1]

The Department has received a number of inquiries concerning the disclosure during a recent debate in the Canadian House of Commons regarding negotiations over the past 2 or 3 months between the United States and Canadian Governments relating to nuclear weapons for Canadian armed forces.

In 1958 the Canadian Government decided to adopt the BOMARC–B weapons systems. Accordingly two BOMARC–B squadrons were deployed to Canada where they would serve the double purpose of protecting Montreal and Toronto as well as the U.S. deterrent force. The BOMARC–B was not designed to carry any conventional warhead. The matter of making available a nuclear warhead for it and for other nuclear-capable weapons systems acquired by Canada has been the subject of inconclusive discussions between the two Governments. The installation of the two BOMARC–B batteries in Canada without nuclear warheads was completed in 1962.

In addition to the BOMARC–B, a similar problem exists with respect to the modern supersonic jet interceptor with which the Royal Canadian Air Force has been provided. Without nuclear air defense warheads, they operate at far less than their full potential effectiveness.

Shortly after the Cuban crisis in October 1962, the Canadian Government proposed confidential discussions concerning circumstances under which there might be provision of nuclear weapons for Canadian armed forces in Canada and Europe. These discussions have been exploratory in nature; the Canadian Government has not as yet proposed any arrangement sufficiently practical to contribute effectively to North American defense.

The discussions between the two Governments have also involved possible arrangements for the provision of nuclear weapons for Canadian NATO forces in Europe, similar to the arrangements which the United States has made with many of our other NATO allies.

During the debate in the House of Commons various references were made to recent discussions at Nassau. The agreements made at Nassau have been fully published.[2] They raise no question of the appropriateness of nuclear weapons for Canadian forces in fulfilling their NATO or NORAD [North American Air Defense Command] obligations.

Reference was also made in the debate to the need of NATO for increased conventional forces. A flexible and balanced defense requires increased conventional forces, but conventional forces are not an alternative to effective NATO or NORAD defense arrangements using nuclear-

1. Source: *U.S. Department of State Bulletin*, XLVIII (February 18, 1963), 243–44.
2. For text, see *Bulletin* of Jan. 14, 1963, p. 43.

capable weapons systems. NORAD is designed to defend the North American Continent against air attack. The Soviet bomber fleet will remain at least throughout this decade a significant element in the Soviet strike force. An effective continental defense against this common threat is necessary.

The provision of nuclear weapons to Canadian forces would not involve an expansion of independent nuclear capability, or an increase in the "nuclear club." As in the case of other allies, custody of U.S. nuclear weapons would remain with the United States. Joint control fully consistent with national sovereignty can be worked out to cover the use of such weapons by Canadian forces.

BIBLIOGRAPHY

Note on Sources

In addition to the obvious difficulties involved in finding suitable materials dealing with recent history—the vast quantities of material and the dearth of reliable documentation—two special problems affected the research for this manuscript. First, many of the events described were and are controversial in Canada, and the polemics to which they gave rise have both increased the amount of information that is available and made it more difficult to interpret accurately. Second, while the events were controversial in Canada, from the point of view of the U.S. they bordered on insignificance (a fact which in itself was an irritant to Canada); thus, there is a singular lack of published material presenting the U.S. side of the disputes involving the two countries. An attempt has been made by the author to remedy these two difficulties by interviewing the politicians, civil servants and military officers of the two countries who were involved in the events. These interviews were, on the whole, quite fruitful, and have materially affected both the representation and interpretation of fact by the author. Instances have therefore been noted in which points of information or interpretation were derived from interviews, although it has not been possible for reasons that are apparent to attribute particular bits of information to particular individuals. Where possible, journalistic accounts the accuracy of which was confirmed by interview have been noted in these instances.

Official Documents

Canada, Department of Defence Production. *Defence Development Sharing* (Ottawa: Queen's Printer, 1962).

Canada, Department of Defence Production. *Canada-United States Defence Production Sharing* (Ottawa: Queen's Printer, 1960).

Canada, Department of Defence Production. *Producing Sharing Handbook* (Ottawa: Queen's Printer, 1964).

Canada, Department of Defence Production. *Thirteenth Report: 1963* (Ottawa: Queen's Printer, 1964).

Canada, Department of Defence Production. *Fourteenth Report: 1964* (Ottawa: Queen's Printer, 1965).

Canada, Department of External Affairs. *Canada and the United Nations, 1960* (Ottawa: Queen's Printer, 1961).

Canada, Department of External Affairs, *Canada and the United Nations, 1961* (Ottawa: Queen's Printer, 1962).

Canada, Department of External Affairs. *Reference Papers.*

Canada, Department of External Affairs. *Statements and Speeches.*

Canada, Department of National Defence. *Defence, 1959* (Ottawa: Queen's Printer, April, 1959).

237

Canada, Department of National Defence. *White Paper on Defence* (Ottawa: Queen's Printer, March, 1964).

Canada, House of Commons. *Debates.*

Canada, House of Commons, Special Committee on Defence, 1963. *Minutes of Proceedings and Evidence.*

Canada, House of Commons, Special Committee on Defence Expenditures, 1960. *Minutes of Proceedings and Evidence.*

Canada, House of Commons, Special Committee on Estimates (Defence Expenditures), 1958. *Minutes of Proceedings and Evidence.*

Canada, House of Commons, Standing Committee on External Affairs. *Minutes of Proceedings and Evidence.*

Canada, House of Commons, *Special Studies Prepared for the Special Committee of the House of Commons on Matters Relating to Defence* (Ottawa: Queen's Printer, 1965).

Canada, The Royal Commission on Government Organization, IV. *Special Areas of Administration* (Ottawa: Queen's Printer, 1963).

Canada, Senate. *Debates.*

Canadian Commercial Corporation. *Annual Report 1963–64.*

U.S. Congress, House, Committee on Appropriations. *Hearings before the Subcommittee on Department of Defense Appropriations,* 86th Cong., 2d Sess., 1960; and 88th Cong., 1st Sess., 1963.

U.S. Congress, House, 85th Cong., 2d Sess., 1959. *House Report No. 1766,* "Report of the Special Study Mission to Canada." (Hays-Coffin Report).

U.S. Congress, Senate, Committee on Appropriations. *Hearings before the Subcommittee on Department of Defense Appropriations,* 85th Cong., 2d Sess., 1959; and 86th Cong., 1st Sess., 1960.

U.S. Congress, Senate, Committee on Foreign Relations. *Review of Foreign Policy, 1958,* 85th Cong., 2d Sess., 1958.

U.S. Congress, Senate, Subcommittee on the Air Force of the Committee on Armed Services. *Study of Airpower Hearings,* 84th Cong., 2d Sess., 1956.

U.S. *Congressional Record.*

U.S. Department of Defense, Office of the Assistant Secretary of Defense (Installations and Logistics), Memorandum on "U.S.-Canada Defense Production and Development Sharing Program," June 4, 1963.

U.S. Department of State Bulletin.

U.S. Department of State. *United States Treaties and Other International Agreements.*

Books

Alexander, Fred. *Canadians and Foreign Policy.* Toronto: University of Toronto Press, 1960.

Atlantic Alliance: NATO's Role in the Free World, Report by a Chatham House study group. London, New York, 1952.

Barber, Joseph. *Good Fences Make Good Neighbors.* Toronto: McClelland and Stewart, 1958.

Beaton, Leonard, and Maddox, John. *The Spread of Nuclear Weapons.* London: Chatto and Windus, 1962.

Bechhoefer, Bernard G. *Postwar Negotiations for Arms Control.* Washington: Brookings Institution, 1961.

Bell, Coral. *The Debatable Alliance.* London: Oxford University Press, 1964.

———. *Negotiation from Strength.* London: Chatto and Windus, 1962.

Brebner, John Bartlet. *North Atlantic Triangle: The Interplay of Canada, the United States and Great Britain.* New Haven: Yale University Press, 1945.

Brown, Neville. *Nuclear War.* New York: Praeger, 1965.

———. *Strategic Mobility,* New York: Praeger, 1964.

Buchan, Alastair. *NATO in the 1960's.* New York: Praeger, 1963.

Buchan, Alastair, and Windsor, Philip. *Arms and Stability in Europe.* London: Chatto and Windus, 1963.

Bull, Hedley. *The Control of the Arms Race.* New York: Praeger, 1965.

Cadieux, Marcel. *The Canadian Diplomat.* Toronto: University of Toronto Press, 1963.

Cohen, Saul B. *Geography and Politics in a World Divided.* New York: Random House, 1963.

Conant, Melvin. *The Long Polar Watch: Canada and the Defense of North America.* New York: Harper for the Council on Foreign Relations, 1962.

Dawson, Robert MacGregor. *The Government of Canada.* 4th ed., Norman Ward, ed. Toronto: University of Toronto Press, 1963.

Deener, David R., ed. *Canada-United States Treaty Relations.* Durham: Duke University Press, 1963.

Dickey, John Sloan, ed. *The United States and Canada.* Englewood Cliffs, N.J.: Prentice-Hall, 1964.

Dziuban, Stanley W. *Military Relations between the United States and Canada, 1939–1945.* Washington: Office of the Chief of Military History, Department of the Army, 1959.

Eayrs, James. *The Art of the Possible: Government and Foreign Policy in Canada.* Toronto: University of Toronto Press, 1961.

———. *Canada in World Affairs: October 1955 to June 1957.* Toronto: Oxford University Press, 1959.

———, ed. *The Commonwealth and Suez: A Documentary Survey.* New York: Oxford University Press, 1964.

———. *In Defence of Canada: I, From the Great War to the Great Depression.* Toronto: University of Toronto Press, 1964; *II, Appeasement and Rearmament.* Toronto: University of Toronto Press, 1965.

———. *Northern Approaches: Canada and the Search for Peace.* Toronto: Macmillan of Canada, 1961.

Forrestal, James. *The Forrestal Diaries,* ed. Walter Millis with the collaboration of E. S. Duffield, New York: Viking Press, 1951.

Garthoff, Raymond L. *Soviet Strategy in the Missile Age.* New York: Praeger, 1958.

Glazebrook, G. de T. *History of Canadian External Relations.* Toronto: Oxford University Press, 1950.

Goodspeed, Captain D. J. *A History of the Defence Research Board of Canada.* Ottawa: Queen's Printer, 1958.

J. King Gordon, ed. *Canada's Role As a Middle Power*. Toronto: Canadian Institute of International Affairs, 1966.

Harrison, W. E. C. *Canada in World Affairs: 1949 to 1950*. Toronto: Oxford University Press, 1957.

Hitch, Charles J., McKean, Roland N., *et al*. *The Economics of Defense in the Nuclear Age*. Cambridge: Harvard University Press, 1960.

Horne, Alistair. *Canada and the Canadians*. Toronto: Macmillan of Canada, 1961.

Huntington, Samuel P. *The Common Defense*. New York: Columbia University Press, 1961.

Hutchison, Bruce. *Mr. Prime Minister, 1867–1964*. New York: Harcourt, Brace and World, 1965.

Institute for Strategic Studies. *The Military Balance*, 1957————. London.

Ismay, Lord. *NATO: The First Five Years, 1949–1954*. Paris, 1954.

Jane's All the World's Aircraft. London: S. Low, Marston & Co., Ltd.

Keenleyside, Hugh L., *et. al*. *The Growth of Canadian Policies in External Affairs*. Durham: Duke University Press, 1960.

Keirstead, B. S. *Canada in World Affairs: September 1951 to October 1953*. Toronto: Oxford University Press, 1956.

Law, Bernard, 1st Viscount Montgomery. *The Memoirs of Field-Marshal the Viscount Montgomery of Alamein*. London: Collins, 1958.

Liska, George. *International Equilibrium*. Cambridge : Harvard University Press, 1957.

Liska, George. *Nations in Alliance*. Baltimore: Johns Hopkins Press, 1962.

Lyon, Peyton V. *The Policy Question*. Toronto: McClelland and Stewart, 1963.

McInnis, Edgar. *The Atlantic Triangle and the Cold War*. Toronto: University of Toronto Press, 1959.

Masters, Donald C. *Canada in World Affairs: 1953 to 1955*. Toronto: Oxford University Press, 1959.

Meisel, John. *The Canadian General Election of 1957*. Toronto: University of Toronto Press, 1962.

Livingston T. Merchant, ed. *Neighbors Taken for Granted: Canada and the United States*. New York: Frederick A. Praeger, 1966.

Minifie, James M. *Open at the Top*. Toronto: McClelland and Stewart, 1964.

————. *Peacemaker or Powder-Monkey*. Toronto: McClelland and Stewart, 1960.

Morton, W. L. *The Canadian Identity*. Madison: University of Wisconsin Press, 1961.

Mulley, F. W., M. P. *The Politics of Western Defence*. London: Thames and Hudson, 1962.

NATO: Facts about the North Atlantic Treaty Organization. Paris, 1962.

Newman, Peter. *Renegade in Power: The Diefenbaker Years*. New York: Bobbs-Merrill, 1963.

Nieburg, Harold L. *Nuclear Secrecy and Foreign Policy*. Washington: Public Affairs Press, 1964.

Osgood, Robrt Endicott. *NATO: The Entangling Alliance.* Chicago: University of Chicago Press, 1962.
Pachter, Henry M. *Collision Course.* New York: Frederick A. Praeger, 1963.
Paul, John, and Laulicht, Jerome. *In Your Opinion: Leaders' and Voters' Attitudes on Defence and Disarmament.* Oakville, Ontario: Esperanto Press, 1963.
Preston, Richard A. *Canada in World Affairs: 1959 to 1961.* Toronto: Oxford University Press, 1965.
Pearson, Lester B. *Democracy in World Politics.* Princeton: Princeton University Press, 1955.
———. *Diplomacy in the Nuclear Age.* Cambridge: Harvard University Press, 1959.
Pickersgill, J. W. *The Mackenzie King Record, I.* Toronto: University of Toronto Press, 1960.
Ritchie, Ronald S. *NATO: The Economics of an Alliance.* Toronto: Ryerson, 1956.
Robertson, Terence. *Crisis: The Inside Story of the Suez Conspiracy.* New York: Atheneum, 1965.
Schlesinger, Arthur M., Jr. *A Thousand Days.* New York: Houghton Mifflin, 1965.
Sévigny, Pierre. *This Game of Politics.* Toronto: McClelland & Stewart, 1965.
Sorensen, Theodore C. *Kennedy.* New York: Harper & Row, 1965.
Spencer, Robert A. *Canada in World Affairs: From UN to NATO, 1946–1949.* Toronto: Oxford University Press, 1959.
Stambuk, George. *American Military Forces Abroad.* Columbus: Ohio State University Press, 1963.
Stanley, George F. G. *Canada's Soldiers: The Military History of an Unmilitary People.* Toronto: Macmillan of Canada, 1960.
Turner, Arthur C. *Bulwark of the West.* Toronto: Ryerson, 1953.
Ulanoff, Stanley. *Illustrated Guide to U.S. Missiles and Rockets.* Garden City, N.Y.: Doubleday, 1959.
Wilson, Edmund. *O Canada: An American's Notes on Canadian Culture* New York: Farrar, Straus and Giroux, 1965.

Articles and Pamphlets

Barkway, Michael. "Canada's Changing Role in NATO Defence," *International Journal,* XIV (Spring, 1959), 99–110.
Baumann, Carol Edler. *Political Co-operation in NATO.* Madison: University of Wisconsin National Security Studies Group, 1960.
Beaton, Leonard. "The Canadian White Paper on Defence," *International Journal,* XIX (Summer, 1964), 364–70.
Brandon, Henry. "Inside Story of the Skybolt," *Sunday Times* (London), December 8, 1963.
Brown, George W. "Canadian Nationalism: An Historical Approach," *International Affairs* (London), XXX (April, 1954), 166–174.
Conant, Melvin. "Canada and Continental Defence: An American View," *International Journal,* XV (Summer, 1960), 219–28.

———. "Canada and Nuclear Weapons: An American View," *International Journal*, XVIII (Spring, 1963), 207–210.

———. "Canada—Time of Trial," *Headline Series*, No. 159 (May–June, 1963).

———. "Canada's Role in Western Defense," *Foreign Affairs*, XL (April, 1962), 431–442.

Cook, Ramsay. "Foreign Policy and the Election: An Uncertain Trumpet," *International Journal*, XVIII (Summer, 1963), 374–380.

Crane, Brian. *An Introduction to Canadian Defence Policy*. Toronto: Canadian Institute of International Affairs, 1964.

Duffy, Robert. "Canada's Foreign Policy in Transition," *International Journal*, XIV (Autumn, 1959), 296–304.

Dulles, John Foster. "Policy for Security and Peace," *Foreign Affairs*, XXXII (April, 1954), 353–364.

"Focus on Canada," *Intercom*, VI (July–August, 1964), 14–80.

Foulkes, General Charles. "Canadian Defence Policy in a Nuclear Age," *Behind the Headlines*, XXI (May, 1961).

Gellner, John. "North America and NATO," *Behind the Headlines*, XXIV (September, 1964—Special Issue on the occasion of the Ottawa meeting of the Atlantic Treaty Association).

———. "Problems of Canadian Defence," *Behind the Headlines*, XVIII (1958).

———, and Jackson, James. "Modern Weapons and the Small Power," *International Journal*, XIII (Spring, 1958), 87–99.

Glazebrook, G. de T. "The Middle Powers in the United Nations System," International Organization, I (June, 1947), 307–315.

Hoag, Malcolm. "On NATO Pooling," *World Politics*, X (April, 1958). 475–483.

Hodgetts, J. E. "Grasping the Nettle: Parliament's Special Committee on Defence," *International Journal*, XIX (Spring, 1964), 213–18.

Holmes, John W. "Canada and the United States in World Politics," *Foreign Affairs*, XL (October, 1961), 105–117.

———. "Canada in Search of its Role," *Foreign Affairs*, XLI (July, 1963), 659–672.

———. "Canadian External Policies since 1945," *International Journal*, XVIII (Spring, 1963), 137–147.

———. "The Political and Philosophical Aspects of U.N. Security Forces," *International Journal*, XIX (Summer, 1964), 292–307.

Ismay, Lord. "Atlantic Alliance," *International Journal*, IX (Spring, 1954), 79–86.

Johnson, Harry G. "Problems of Canadian Nationalism," *International Journal*, XVI (Summer, 1961), 238–249.

Keenleyside, Hugh L. "The Canada-United States Permanent Joint Board on Defence, 1940–45," *International Journal*, XVI (Winter, 1960–61), 50–77.

Knorr, Klaus. "Canada and Western Defence," *International Journal*, XVIII (Winter, 1962–63), 1–16.

Lloyd, Trevor. "Open Skies in the Arctic?", *International Journal*, XIV (Winter, 1958–59), 42–49.

Lower, A. R. M. "Canada in the New, Non-British World," *International Journal*, III (Summer, 1948), 208–221.

Lyon, Peyton V. "Problems of Canadian Independence," *International Journal*, XVI (Summer, 1961), 250–59.

Macdonald, H. Ian. "Canada in Two Hemispheres," *Behind the Headlines*, XXIII (July, 1964).

Martin, Paul. "Peacekeeping and the United Nations: The Broader View," *International Affairs* (London), XL (April, 1964), 191–204.

Meisel, John. "Guns and Butter: Foreign Affairs in Canada's Twenty-Third Parliament," *International Journal*, XIII (Summer, 1958), 184–203.

Pearson, Lester B. "After Geneva: A Greater Task for NATO," *Foreign Affairs*, XXXIV (October, 1955), 14–23.

———. "Canada and the North Atlantic Alliance," *Foreign Affairs*, XXVII (April, 1949), 369–378.

———. "Canada's Northern Horizon," *Foreign Affairs*, XXXI (July, 1953), 581–591.

———. "The Development of Canadian Foreign Policy," *Foreign Affairs*, XXX (October, 1951), 17–30.

———. "NATO: Retrospect and Prospects," *International Journal*, XIV (Spring, 1959), 79–84.

———. "Western European Union: Implications for Canada and NATO," *International Journal*, X (Winter, 1954–55), 1–11.

Redford, Robert, "Making Defence Policy in Canada," *Behind the Headlines*, XXIII (December, 1963).

Ritchie, Ronald S. "Problems of a Defence Policy for Canada," *International Journal*, XIV (Summer, 1959), 202–212.

Smith, Foster Lee. "Canadian-United States Scientific Collaboration for Defense," *Public Policy*, XII (1963), 302–336.

Smith, Sydney, E. "NATO and the Challenge of the Missile Age," *International Journal*, XIII (Summer, 1958), 165–174.

Spencer, Robert A. "Parliament and Foreign Policy, 1960," *International Journal*, XV (Autumn, 1960), 311–331.

———. "Triangle into Treaty: Canada and the Origins of NATO," *International Journal*, XIV (Spring, 1959), 87–98.

Sutherland, R. J. "Canada's Long Term Strategic Situation," *International Journal*, XVII (Summer, 1962), 199–223.

———."The Strategic Significance of the Canadian Arctic," in R. St. J. Macdonald, ed., *The Arctic Frontier*. Toronto: University of Toronto Press, 1966.

Taylor, Alastair M. *For Canada—Both Swords and Plowshares*. Toronto: Canadian Institute of International Affairs, 1963.

von Riekhoff, Harald. "The Changing Function of NATO," *International Journal*, XXI (Spring, 1966), 157–172.

Unpublished Material

Arnett, E. James. "The Canadian Debate on Continental Defence, 1957–1960." Unpublished paper, Harvard Law School, April 1, 1964.

Davy, Grant R. "Canada's Role in the Disarmament Negotiations, 1946–1957," Ph.D. dissertation, Fletcher School of Law and Diplomacy, April 15, 1962.

Jones, D. W. "Canada's Search for a Role in Continental Defence Since 1945," M.A. thesis, Carleton University, Ottawa, March, 1964.

Mueller, John E. "Canada as a Non-Nuclear Power." Unpublished paper, University of California at Los Angeles, June, 1963.

Rivkin, Steven R. "The Quest for Air Defense," Honors thesis, Harvard, 1958.

Periodicals

Armed Forces Management
Canadian Aviation
Canadian Forum
Christian Science Monitor
Le Devoir
Economist
Financial Post
Globe and Mail (Toronto)
Halifax Chronicle Herald
Interavia
Intercom
Maclean's Magazine
Missiles and Rockets
Montreal Daily Star
The Nation
NATO Letter
New York Times
Ottawa Evening Journal
La Presse
Round Table
Saturday Night
The Times (London)
U.S. News and World Report
Vancouver Province
Vancouver Sun
Washington Post
Windsor Star
Winnipeg Free Press

INDEX

Dulles, John F.: on nuclear sharing, 131n; Canada and, 149; 1958 Ottawa visit, 179; mentioned, 24–25, 44, 46

Eden, Anthony, 26
Eisenhower, Dwight D.: appointment as SACEUR, 19; and Diefenbaker, 97; on nuclear sharing, 127; quotation cited by Lester Pearson, 152; 1958 Ottawa visit, 179; mentioned, 180
Elections: of 1957, 40–42; of 1958, 70; of 1963, 164, 166
Ellender, Allen, 88n
Europe: Canadian forces in, 108, 111
European air forces: Canada and, 115
European Defense Community: Canada's position on, 24, 25, 26

F–4 *Phantom*, 200
F–5 *Freedom Fighter*, 191, 200
F–11–1F *Super Tiger*, 118
F–86 *Sabre*, 62, 100, 102, 106, 110, 115
F–101B *Voodoo*: Canadian decision to acquire, 100–05; armament for, 133; and nuclear weapons, 139, 140; mentioned, 63, 162, 167, 191, 201, 202
F–104G *Starfighter*: RCAF and, 104; and Canada, 117; Canadian production of, 172, 182; U.S. order for, 190; mentioned, 43, 118–19, 132, 133, 162
F–105D *Thunderchief*, 117, 118
F–106: competition with the *Arrow*, 72; cancellation of, 78; development of, 101, 102, 103; mentioned, 64
F–108: development of, 74, 101; cancellation of, 78; mentioned, 73, 102
Falcon missile: *Sparrow* followed by, 74; *Voodoo* squadrons' use of, 133; mentioned, 69, 130, 131
Flood, Daniel, 96, 164, 165
Foulkes, Charles: quoted on aircraft purchase, 106; and Air Division, 115, 116; quoted on RCN equipment, 121; delayed retirement of, 138; on nuclear weapons, 144; on Canada's NATO commitment, 160; mentioned, 44, 45, 50, 107, 110, 120, 135
France: and NATO, 115; and Canada, 118, 189, 211, 212; mentioned, 110, 124
Fulton, Davy: on Canada's commitment to NATO, 159

Functional theory, 14
Furnas Committee: *Bomarc* program study by, 92

Gates, Thomas: General Pearkes's consultation with, 94; 1960 Ottawa visit, 139; mentioned, 96, 104, 127
de Gaulle, Charles: proposal for a *directoire*, 15; on foreign bases in France, 205; mentioned, 144, 212
Germany, Federal Republic of: Canadian forces in, 107, 114; F–104 chosen by, 118; NATO and, 205; nuclear proliferation and, 209; mentioned, 111
Goose Bay, Labrador: refueling facilities at, 129; mentioned, 138, 139, 156, 157
Greece: NATO extended to include, 22
Green, Howard: named as Secretary of State for External Affairs, 136; and nuclear issue, 137, 138, 140, 143; on disarmament, 147, 148, 149, 150; in Cuban missile crisis, 158; on Canada's commitment to NATO, 159; mentioned, 104
Grostenquin, France, 205

Harkness, Douglas: named Minister of National Defense, 140; quoted on nuclear arms acquisition, 162; resignation of, 163; mentioned, 156, 157
Harmon Field, Newfoundland: refueling facilities at, 129; mentioned, 138, 139, 156, 157
de Havilland Company, 195
Hawker-Siddeley group, 61
Hees, George: resignation of, 164
Hellyer, Paul: and *Arrow*, 80, 114; on nuclear warheads, 98; on *Bomarc*, 99; quoted on American hardware, 103n; on F–104, 117; on defense policy, 153–54; as defense minister, 194; on military integration, 196, 197; on Canada and NATO, 200, 201, 207, 208; on anti-submarine warfare, 202; mentioned, 58n, 81, 88, 95, 113, 191, 199
Herridge, H. W.: quoted on significance of NORAD, 57
Heuss, Theodor, 109
Hilsman, Roger, 97
"Honest John" system, 113, 132, 133, 141, 160, 167, 204